DATE DUE

NOV 04 1995	
MAY 9 1996	
JAN 0 2 1997	
MAR 17 1996	
DEC - 5 2000	
JUL 19 2002	
MAR 1 3 2008	
NOV 0 1 2003	

Sons and Daughters of God

SONS and DAUGHTERS of GOD

Joseph Fielding McConkie

BOOKCRAFT
Salt Lake City, Utah

Library of Congress Catalog Card Number: 94-72506
ISBN 0-88494-936-2

First Printing, 1994

Printed in the United States of America

This work is dedicated to the memory of my father, Bruce R. McConkie, whose love of truth and whose testimony of Jesus Christ as the Son of God inspired it.

But this I confess unto thee, that after the way which they call heresy, so worship I the God of my fathers, believing all things which are written in the law and in the prophets.

—Acts 24:14

Thou Art My Son

I stood before God's mighty throne;
The time had come to leave my home;
My pilgrimage before me lay;
This was the long-expected day.

For ages past I'd walked by sight;
Now faith must be my guiding light;
To find the Truth, the Light, the Way,
I must be housed in mortal clay.

Before I left, my Father spoke:
"Go now, my son, bear well thy yoke;
I send thee forth to keep my law,
To worship me with reverent awe.

Thy first concern in that new sphere:
Find her whom thou hast chosen here;
These children I shall send to thee;
Choice shall thy chosen family be."

And so I came as Adam's son,
To seek all that may be won,
By those who love and serve their God,
And bow beneath his gospel rod.

To me has come that law divine,
By which I may my name enshrine,
In realms of light and life and love,
In those eternal courts above.

And God be praised, she here is found
Who in celestial garments gowned,
By me shall stand as ages roll,
To comfort, guide, and cheer my soul.

To us have come those spirits dear,
Whom we must lead and guide and rear,
And teach to love and serve the Lord,
And sing as one each gospel chord.

Our home is one where joy abounds,
Where God is served and praise resounds;
Where gospel light in splendor shines,
And each of us its truth enshrines.

—*Bruce R. McConkie*

Contents

Acknowledgments

Help with this project has come from many quarters and spans a number of years. Dwayne Fowles and Rus Rasmussen provided first-rate help with research. Sherilyn Patch and Ann Smith wrestled with the endnotes and bibliography. Dana M. Pike and Robert L. Millet, colleagues at Brigham Young University, have given much good advice, as have my brothers Stanford and Mark McConkie.

Garry Garff handled the thorough and painstaking editorial work for Bookcraft in a very effective manner.

For the work itself I assume full responsibility.

Introduction

Every doctrine and principle of the gospel of Jesus Christ is but the application of the eternal verity that God is our Father. The prime objective of apostate religion in all dispensations has been to rob us as his children of our divine inheritance. That end is accomplished by destroying or distorting the doctrines of the fatherhood of God and the divine sonship of Jesus Christ. Judaism and historical Christianity have joined hands to hide and rewrite our scriptural history for that purpose. Both have freely taken from and added to the canon of scripture they so profusely profess to love. Both have then declared the canon sealed in the hope that their labors in the dark will remain impenetrable to the light of heaven. Like the once wise Solomon, they consummated a marriage outside the temple and outside the faith. They have abandoned the doctrines of salvation, have strayed from the ordinances, and have broken the everlasting covenant; "they seek not the Lord to establish his righteousness, but every man walketh in his own way, and after the image of his own god, whose image is in the likeness of the world, and whose substance is that of an idol, which waxeth old and shall perish in Babylon, even Babylon the great, which shall fall" (D&C 1:15–16).

As to the theologies of Christendom, the bishop of Salisbury put it well when he said, "The total picture does not hang together; and unless we are prepared to believe in a Jesus who was both confused and confusing cannot be correct. This is the reason why all presentations of Jesus edit or gloss the record."[1] That is simply to say that everyone is cheating with the text. The most-often-quoted passage of scripture in the Christian world is John 3:16. In the King James Bible it reads: "For God so loved the world, that he gave his only begotten Son, that whosoever believeth in him should not perish, but have everlasting life." The Bible reader, innocent of both Jewish and Christian tradition, would suppose this statement to say that the God of heaven "loves" mankind and that he actually "begot" a "Son." Such an understanding, however, constitutes what historical Christianity regards to be a shameful anthropomorphism that both Jew and Christian reject as naive, crude, and degrading. The idea that God actually "begot" a Son is sufficiently objectionable that all modern translations of the Bible have removed it. They now tell us that God gave us "his only Son," or "his one and only Son." This change in the text conforms to the labors of centuries in which the churches of the world have sought to distance us from God and remove any notion that we are in reality anything more than God's toys, as one respected commentary puts it.[2]

We have no evidence of serious tampering with scriptural texts for the purpose of changing our perceptions of God before the first verse of the first chapter of Genesis. From that point forward the efforts of those who war against revealed truths have been remarkably consistent. When the physical darkness of night comes, it makes no exceptions as to what it envelops. It makes no concessions to need; it reverences no sanctuaries; it bypasses none, be they old or young, innocent or sincere. All things are engulfed in its ocean of black. So it is with the spirit of apostasy; it knows no bounds in its efforts to despoil all that is sacred and true. As Latter-day Saints, we testify of a universal apostasy, believing it to have been precisely that, universal. Not only did it sweep the whole earth; it robbed all extant scripture, doctrine, and tradition of their purity. Could we possibly be so naive as to suppose that the spirit that sought to depose God in the Grand Council in Heaven, that seeks the blood of his anointed in mortality, and that crucified his Son would not stoop to tampering with Bible texts or the misinterpreting of their plain meaning? Does it not seem obvious that there would be a proliferation of counterfeit gospels and false Christs to deceive even the elect?

The greatest heresies always stand opposite the greatest truths. No truth has been more perverted in the theologies of men than those that deal with the fatherhood of God, the sonship of Christ, and our kinship to the Father as his children and his heirs. That which follows ought to be familiar to every Latter-day Saint and ought to be heralded to the world with the sound of a trumpet.

Prologue

"What has Athens to do with Jerusalem?" Such was the question of Tertullian, father of Latin theology.[1] The question has reverberated down through the centuries. As this work will show, the answer is, plenty! Simply stated, the God of the prophets was supplanted by the god of Plato. From the time that the new God of Christianity was formally sustained in the Council of Nicaea (A.D. 325), those who have chosen to worship the God of Abraham, Isaac, and Jacob, the God of Peter, James, and John, have been classified as non-Christian cultists. In response we feel to echo the words of the Apostle Paul:

> But this I confess unto thee, that after the way which they call heresy, so worship I the God of my fathers, believing all things which are written in the law and in the prophets (Acts 24:14).

Mosheim, in his *Ecclesiastical History* (noted for its unprecedented objectivity and penetration), observed that there would be some who would dispute whether "the interests of Christianity have gained or lost by the writings of the learned, and the speculations of philosophers who have been employed in its defence." He confesses himself incapable of answering the question satisfactorily, and yet concedes that nothing is more evident than "that the noble simplicity and dignity" of Christianity were "sadly corrupted in many places, when the philosophers blended their opinions with its pure doctrines, and were so audacious as to submit that divine system of faith and piety to be scrutinized and modified by the fallible rules of imperfect reason."[2]

No one seems to question the profound role that Greek philosophy played in the formation of what we are told today constitutes traditional and orthodox Christianity. That their traditions and orthodoxy rest on "speculative theology"[3]—or, if you prefer, the "fallible rules of imperfect reason"—seems to increase the enthusiasm and loyalty of Christian theologians rather than to dim it. No longer need they be embarrassed when examined by the wisdom of men, for they have adopted the best of it. The catchall notion of evolutionary or progressive revelation seems sufficient to admit the reasoning of the philosophers into the faith. There have been some voices of concern, but few have heard them over the applause of the many. In the introduction to his work *The Influence of Greek Ideas on Christianity*, Edwin Hatch observed:

> It is impossible for any one, whether he be a student of history or no, to fail to notice a difference of both form and content between the Sermon on the Mount and the Nicene Creed. The Sermon on the Mount is the promulgation of a new law of conduct; it assumes beliefs rather than formulates them; the theological conceptions which underlie it belong to the ethical rather than the speculative side of theology; metaphysics are wholly absent. The Nicene Creed is a statement partly of historical facts and partly of dogmatic inferences; the metaphysical terms which it contains would probably have been unintelligible to the first disciples; ethics have no place in it. The one belongs to a world of Syrian peasants, the other to a world of Greek philosophers.[4]

Irony evidences itself in what professes to be "Bible religion" when it is founded and interpreted through creeds admittedly "unintelligible" to those from whom we obtained the Bible in the first place.

During the lives of the Apostles, those who would pervert the truth were kept in check. Nevertheless they acquired some credit and strength by small degrees. Though it may have been initially imperceptible, they, in the words of Mosheim, "laid the foundations of those sects, whose animosities and disputes produced afterwards such trouble and perplexity in the Christian church." The state of these schismatic divisions, he said, was "more involved in darkness than any other part of ecclesiastical history."[5]

Modern orthodoxy is rooted in what Mosheim called a time of "delusion and folly."[6] His is an understatement; more aptly put, it was a period of conspiracy and assassination, one in which the victors took no survivors. The enemy camp was completely destroyed. No record of what happened exists. As Latter-day Saints, we know that these activities included the taking away "from the gospel of the Lamb many parts which are plain and most precious; and also many covenants of the Lord." This in turn has caused many to stumble and given Satan "great power." (1 Nephi 13:26, 29.)

By the second century, "Christian" writers had begun a restatement of their faith, drawing largely upon Greek thought. This was declared to be orthodoxy. The "church" was clearly following a new road. Where the doctrines of the New Testament disciples centered in the acceptance of Christ and him crucified, the newly born version of Christianity centered in obtaining wisdom. Paul's declaration that "the foolishness of God is wiser than men" was discarded in favor of the notion that the glory of God was the wisdom of men. What was most keenly desired on the part of Christians of that era was respectability in the Graeco-Roman world. It was not peaceful cohabitation with the world that they sought but reconciliation. They sought to defend the faith on philosophical grounds so they could prove it worthy of the attention of pagan intellectuals. Thus philosophy became the disinfectant used to rid Christianity of the anthropomorphic notion that God resembled man and to disallow a literal reading of the many passages of scripture that describe personal encounters with Him. The testimony of God's covenant spokesmen was determined to be metaphor or allegory and thus subject to any distortion imposed upon it.

Thus reason supplanted revelation, scholars replaced prophets, a formless and incomprehensible God deposed the God who created Adam and Eve in his image and likeness, and loyalty to creeds became the measure of faith in preference to holiness. The Bible became an allegory, its most sacred truths became a mystery, and mankind ceased to be heirs of God, becoming instead mere toys created for the amusement of heaven. Such is the story that this volume seeks to tell—as well as that story's sequel, in which darkness gave way to the illuminating light of the restored gospel. This in the hope that those who read these pages will be inspired to lay claim to the divine inheritance that is rightfully theirs.

1

While the Pharisees were gathered together, Jesus asked them,
Saying, What think ye of Christ? whose son is he? They say unto
him, The Son of David.
He saith unto them, How then doth David in spirit call him
Lord, saying,
The Lord said unto my Lord, Sit thou on my right hand, till I
make thine enemies thy footstool?
If David then call him Lord, how is he his son?
And no man was able to answer him a word, neither durst any
man from that day forth ask him any more questions.
—Matthew 22:41–46

What Think Ye of Christ?
Whose Son Is He?

The question "What think ye of Christ? whose son is he?" was directed by the Savior to a group of Pharisees, a sect famed for their knowledge of scripture, their piety, and their loyalty to the religious traditions of their day (see Matthew 22:42). None should have been better prepared to respond to the question. The name *Christ* is a title, and rendering it in the native tongue of those to whom these words of the Savior were initially addressed would make the question read, "What think ye of Messiah? whose son is he?" The great purpose of the law of Moses, of which the Pharisees professed to be the guardians, was to prepare the nation of Israel to receive their Messiah. None should have been more eager or more receptive to the testimony of Jesus of Nazareth that he was indeed God's Son and as such their promised Messiah. Yet, not only did the Pharisees, in concert with the other religious sects of their day, reject Jesus' claim to messiahship; they sought his death and did so with considerable zeal.

Validity Draws the Fire

The rejection of Christ by those who should have been especially prepared to receive him must stand as one of history's great paradoxes. The fact that they did so in the name of loyalty to Moses, who was their schoolmaster in preparing them to accept the Messiah, and in the guise of loyalty to holy writ, which has the same purpose, makes that story even more stunning. Peter assures us that all the holy prophets since the world began knew and testified of Christ (see Acts 3:21–24). An angel told the Apostle John that "the testimony of Jesus is the spirit of prophecy" (Revelation 19:10). Surely none wrote scripture without that testimony of Jesus.

Book of Mormon prophets assure us that those of ancient days knew of Christ. Jacob, brother of Nephi, described the knowledge and conviction of the faithful Saints in the Old World, saying, "Behold, they believed in Christ and worshiped the Father in his name, and also we worship the Father in his name. And for this intent we keep the law of Moses, it pointing our souls to him; and for this cause it is sanctified unto us for righteousness, even as it was accounted unto Abraham in the wilderness to be obedient unto the commands of God in offering up his son Isaac, which is a similitude of God and his Only Begotten Son." (Jacob 4:5.) In like manner, Abinadi assured the wicked priests of King Noah's court that Moses prophesied concerning the coming of the Messiah, and that God would redeem his people. This, he said, had been the testimony of "all the prophets who have prophesied ever since the world began." (Mosiah 13:33.)

We are left to ask, What happened? How is it that the ancients, so favored with the revelations of heaven, lost the knowledge and understanding that their God would send his Son as their Savior and Redeemer? How is it that they were unable to recognize the Messiah when he came among them working all manner of mighty miracles and teaching the gospel of salvation with the voice of an angel? Jacob testifies that had the same miracles been wrought among other nations they would have repented and known him to be their God (see 2 Nephi 10:4).

In seeking an answer to this question it must first be understood that there is no middle ground where the testimony of Christ is concerned. He is actually and literally God's Son or he is not. Articulate and charming voices argue that the Nativity story as found in the scriptures is clumsy and contradictory. Others explain it as myth or metaphor, and yet others see it as a sinister plot, while living prophets testify of its truthfulness. All cannot be right. We must choose what we will believe, and in so doing our situation is no different from that of the Pharisees to whom Christ originally addressed the question as to whose son he was, for like them, we make that choice at the peril of our eternal life. If Christ is God's Son and we reject him, we reject all the blessings associated with having accepted him. If he is simply the creation of a clever and designing myth, then in our devotion we can reap only the fruits of myth and deception. But what we ought not do is to be so shortsighted as to suppose that this is the lone choice that this life affords that has no consequences. We are free to choose what we believe but cannot be free from the consequences of our choices. All actions are rooted in beliefs; our laws are simply the expression of what we have chosen to believe.

Again, there is no middle ground where the testimony of Christ is concerned, and there is no neutrality on the question of divine sonship. Light and darkness will never meet; Christ and Satan will never shake hands. Truth will always stand in opposition to falsehood. The father of lies has an extensive wardrobe designed to hide his wretched ugliness, including duplicity, hypocrisy, perversion, distortion, adulteration, and so on. Whatever form such falsehood takes, truth is its enemy; and the greater the truth, the greater the opposition with which it will be countered. There is nothing sacred in hell, and there are no meaningful truths that are left unopposed. No principle of salvation, no truth that exalts, is without opposition.

The greatest truths in all eternity are those truths that deal with God. Standing opposite them will be found eternity's greatest heresies. We may order them thus: the greatest truths are those that deal with God as our Father and his role as Creator; the second greatest truths are those dealing with his Son and his role as our Savior and Redeemer; the third greatest body of truths are those dealing with the Holy Ghost and his role as a witness or testator.

Now, we know that validity will always draw the fire. The purer the doctrine, the meaner the opposition. History cannot afford us a single example of a truly great or good man who went unopposed. In this sense, we may measure the greatness and goodness of the same not by the list of their friends but by identifying those who opposed them. Rejection and martyrdom have been the common lot of the faithful Saints and prophets in all ages, Christ being the chief illustration. There is something significant in it all. No one was ever martyred for declaring the teachings of Socrates or Plato, yet countless souls have suffered in the name of Christ. In the Vision of the Redemption of the Dead, President Joseph F. Smith saw "an innumerable company of the spirits of the just" gathered to welcome the Savior to their midst. Their numbers included those from the time of Adam to the death of John the Baptist. Of that "vast multitude" it was said that all had "suffered tribulation in their Redeemer's name." (See D&C 138:12–18.) In his Epistle to the Hebrews, Paul describes those living in Old Testament times, saying they experienced "cruel mockings and scourgings, yea, moreover of bonds and imprisonment: they were stoned, they were sawn asunder, were tempted, were slain with the sword: they wandered about in sheepskins and goatskins; being destitute, afflicted, tormented; (of whom the world was not worthy:) they wandered in deserts, and in mountains, and in dens and caves of the earth" (Hebrews 11:36–38).

We are left to wonder what there was about the faith of those ancient Saints that was such an offense to those who chose not to share it. Those principles of the gospel that we have come to call Christian—including love, forbearance, tolerance, honesty, and so on—were all as much a part of their ancient faith as they were a part of the faith of those who lived in the meridian of time or as they ought to be a part of the Christian faith in our day. Such people make good neighbors, and collectively they make good allies. Why, then, the opposition?

We find the same thing in the Americas when Lehi and his family commenced a great gospel dispensation here. Almost immediately his family was divided into two factions, the Nephites and the Lamanites, but in fact we could as well know them (at least in general terms, throughout the course of most of their history) as believers in Christ and nonbelievers. And what was the result? The nonbelievers could not abide the presence of the believers. Peaceful cohabitation was never considered a possibility by the nonbelievers, nor was the idea that somehow the continent might prove big enough for both groups. Nephite-Lamanite history is in large measure the history of a thousand years of war until those opposing a belief in Christ destroyed the others (see Moroni 1:2).

To bring the matter nearer to home, we invite consideration of the experience of Joseph Smith. When the youthful Joseph said that he had seen God, all manner of opposition immediately commenced. He later recalled: "I soon found . . . that my telling the story had excited a great deal of prejudice against me among professors of religion, and was the cause of great persecution, which continued to increase; and though I was an obscure boy, only between fourteen and fifteen years of age, and my circumstances in life such as to make a boy of no consequence in the world, yet men of high standing would take notice sufficient to excite the public mind against me, and create a bitter persecution; and this was common among all the sects—all united to persecute me" (Joseph Smith—History 1:22). It is difficult to imagine people wanting to kill a boy and persecute his family for such a claim. Ridicule, scorn, contempt would be understandable, but not the bitterness that became the common lot of the Smiths. We can offer but one explanation: validity draws the fire. The devil knows both his friends and his enemies.

The Doctrine of Divine Sonship

To those of his generation, Christ was "a stone of stumbling" and "a rock of offence" (see Isaiah 8:14). It was his doctrine that gave offense. While he was faithful in his observance of the law of Moses, Jesus deliberately crossed swords with the uninspired traditions in which the law had been clothed. The Mosaic law forbade work on the Sabbath day. Christ honored that prohibition with exactness. To do his Father's work on that day, the labors of the Spirit, was another matter. For him it was a day for preaching and blessing. It was a day to heal both body and spirit. Here lay possible conflict with those who reverenced tradition more than goodness and truth. The rabbinical traditions with which the day had been surrounded included a taboo against healing the sick. To administer to the sick, it was reasoned, caused the body to work in the healing effort. Such was regarded as sin. To spit was sin, for if the spittle fell on bare ground rather than on a stone it could be construed as irrigation. To mold clay was to make bricks, a sin. To carry a burden, a sin; to walk more than a given number of paces, a sin; and on and on it went.[1]

Christ knew these traditions and deliberately sought conflict with them. In Jerusalem, of all places, he chose to heal a man and did so on the Sabbath. He commanded the man: "Rise, take up thy bed, and walk" (John 5:8). He so offended the Jewish leaders that they sought his life (see John 5:16). Later in his ministry he returned to Jerusalem and once again chose to heal a man on the Sabbath. The man in this instance had been born blind. In order to heal him the Lord spat on the ground, then took the moistened clay and placed it in the man's eyes. Then he directed him to go to the pool of Siloam and wash it away. (See John 9.) We have every reason to suppose that in this sequence of events the Savior was dramatizing his contempt for rabbinical tradition while illustrating the powers of heaven to restore sight. For the Savior to spit upon bare ground could have been considered irrigating; to mold clay was to be guilty of making bricks. Undoubtedly the distance the man had to traverse to the pool of Siloam constituted a violation of the Sabbath, as would the act of washing his eyes.[2] The message was clear to all who could see—they could accept Jesus as the Messiah, the living law, and worship the Father through him, or they could sustain the religious traditions of the day and remain blind.

Of those traditions and those who originated them, the Savior said: "Ye [have] made the commandment of God of none effect by your tradition. Ye hypocrites, well did Esaias prophesy of you, saying, This people draweth nigh unto me with their mouth, and honoureth me with their lips; but their heart is far from me. But in vain they do worship me, teaching for doctrines the commandments of men." (Matthew 15:6–9.)

There were many points of offense between the doctrines that Christ taught and the religious system of his day. The orthodoxy of man-made theology is always threatened by the presence of a living prophet and offended by the doctrine of continuous revelation. Christ, as a living prophet, had no qualms about adding to extant scripture. That he would be opposed by those professing to represent orthodoxy was a certainty, for that orthodoxy had long since sealed the heavens. "Every plant, which my heavenly Father hath not planted, shall be rooted up," was the doctrine he espoused (Matthew 15:13). He had no reverence for tradition posing as gospel truth. He clearly testified that he was the promised Messiah, the Son of God, and that salvation was in him and in none else (Matthew 26:63–65; John 5:25; 9:35; 10:36; 11:4). By so doing he assured himself a martyr's crown.

Why Another Book

This book is written to testify of those same truths for which the Savior chose to die. It is written to espouse the reality of the most basic and fundamental principles of the gospel of Jesus Christ—doctrines wholly lost in the long night of apostate darkness, doctrines fundamental to the restoration of the gospel and thus doctrines that are the exclusive province of the Latter-day Saints. They are doctrines of salvation—that is, there is no salvation independent of the knowledge and testimony of them. Those doctrines are the divine sonship of Christ, our heirship as the spirit children of God, and thus the doctrine of the fatherhood of God.

The doctrine of divine sonship holds that Jesus of Nazareth is actually and literally the Son of the Eternal Father. President Ezra Taft Benson stated the doctrine thus: "The Church of Jesus Christ of Latter-day Saints proclaims that Jesus Christ is the Son of God in the most literal sense. The body in which He performed His mission in the flesh was sired by that same Holy Being we worship as God, our Eternal Father. Jesus was not the son of Joseph, nor was He begotten by the Holy Ghost. He is the Son of the Eternal Father!"[3]

The doctrine of heirship holds that our spirits were begotten of God in a pre-earth estate, that we came to the earth, our second estate, to obtain a physical body and to see if we would do the things that God commanded. In this, our earthly estate, we are subject to all the effects of Adam's fall. This includes our separation from the presence of God, our Eternal Father. The prophets have referred to this separation as spiritual death. We are also subject to physical death, which is the separation of the body and the spirit. Through the atoning sacrifice of Christ all mankind are to be resurrected, that is, to enjoy the inseparable union of body and spirit in a physically perfected state. Also through the atonement of Christ we can, by obedience to the laws and ordinances of the gospel, overcome the effects of spiritual death and return to the presence of our creator. Thus as his children we are his heirs and, as his heirs, may become the rightful inheritors of all that he has. This is tantamount to saying that we can become as he is.

Both the doctrine of Christ's divine sonship and the doctrine of heirship are manifestations of the doctrine of the fatherhood of God. Thus Latter-day Saints speak of our Father in Heaven, not in a metaphorical sense but in a literal sense, for we know him to be the Father of our spirits.

What Think Ye of Christ?

In responding to the Savior's question, "What think ye of Christ?" we as Latter-day Saints answer that Jesus of Nazareth was and is the Messiah of the Jews and the Savior of all who chose to accept and obey the law of his gospel. We further testify that he is actually and literally the Son of the Eternal Father. In that testimony we stand alone. We may share some language and scriptural heritage in common with traditional Christianity, but the meaning that stands behind these is entirely different. We believe that words mean what they say and say what they mean. Our testimony is that the word *Father* as applied to God actually and literally means that he is a father. When we so testify we are not speaking metaphorically. We believe that the word *Son* as it refers to Christ actually and literally means that he is God's Son. We are not speaking metaphorically. We believe that the word *begotten* as it is used to describe the manner of Christ's conception actually and literally means begotten. We are not speaking metaphorically. Thus when the scriptures speak of us as the *children of God* we believe them to mean what they say. In making such a claim we are not speaking metaphorically. In each instance our expression of belief sets us apart from the rest of the so-called Bible-believing world.

Two illustrations of what is involved here will help the reader appreciate why I am at such pains to be emphatic in the previous paragraph. The first represents a very conservative point of view, the second a more liberal viewpoint. We will note, however, that the conclusion of both writers is the same. The first comes from a book titled *Blasphemy and the Battle for Faith*. The book defends the historical thesis that to oppose the dogma of the Holy Trinity is to commit blasphemy. It also considers some of the problems associated with promulgating that doctrine. One problem faced by trinitarians, the author points out, is the misimpression that is given to Muslims when Christians speak of Jesus as God's Son. "They believe that we are talking about 'son' in the sense of a *physical* offspring," he laments. He points out how shocking this idea is to the Muslim mind. Allah's purity is at stake here. The Koran accepts Jesus as a prophet while declaring that to suppose he is God's Son is a sin of such enormity that the earth itself is close to splitting in two at the promulgation of such a heresy.[4] The concern of our author is that some uninformed Muslim is going to interpret the Christian's belief in Jesus' sonship literally, when in fact he is the Son of God, according to traditional Christianity, only "in a spiritual sense." He concludes, "We must somehow convince them [believers of the Koran] that the idea is of the One God becoming Jesus."[5]

The second illustration comes from one of the Christian world's liberal spokespersons, an Episcopal bishop by the name of John Shelby Spong. The thesis of his book *Born of a Woman* is that the scriptural story of Christ's birth is a myth concocted by men to oppress women. He calls the Nativity story the "scandal of the crib." Spong argues that the biblical story is neither good history nor good theology. His primary concern centers in the doctrine of the virgin birth, which he rejects, and the attendant myth of Mary's perpetual virginity. He correctly sees that this latter myth demeans womanhood by suggesting that virginity is the greater good while there is something sinful or degrading in becoming a mother. To establish his thesis, Spong weaves an intricate philosophical web, the purpose of which is to reinterpret the role of the Bible as the rule of faith. The problem that Spong faces is an ancient one. It is to find an intellectually acceptable way to get past the plain meaning of the Bible story while still professing faith in it. To do so, he reasons that to give form to anything distorts it. True reality, he holds, is found only in our personal perceptions. Since two people looking at the same object or reporting on the same event do not see exactly the same thing, the truth or reality of the experience is different for both of them. Thus, to give it form would distort its meaning. It follows that not only must God be formless and thus be perceived differently by everyone, but the same holds true of the stories and messages in holy writ.

Spong explains: "The experience is always primary, the reflective understanding of the experience is always secondary, and the tales that illumine or explain the understanding are always tertiary. We probe the mythology and folktales to illumine the conclusions people drew that enabled them to talk about their experience. An intense experience ultimately has no form. As soon as it achieves form it is distorted."[6]

It is not difficult to anticipate where all this is to lead—nothing in the Bible really means what it says. Bible stories are like the crayons

we give children to color with. Each is expected to make his own picture. It is not a matter of coloring within the lines, because lines con-
note form, and form distorts. "Even the word *God*," Spong states,
"was, and is, a culturally conditioned construct."[7] (Note how quickly
and easily we can color over the Rembrandt of holy writ to give it all a
new meaning.) He makes his point by explaining how people come to
perceive God. The first-century people thought of God as a super-
human person. The person of the highest rank in their society was a
king. Thus God was described as a king. The king was male, so they
thought of their God as male. Because God was so powerful, the
people groveled in fear and sought to win his favor. This was done
with sacrifices, offerings, and with words of flattery and praise. Their
own shortcomings caused them great anguish. They responded by
throwing themselves on the mercy of their God in a plea for acceptance. Having no way to climb to heaven, they prayed that God would
come down to earth to overcome their alienation and to embrace them
with his divine love and affirm their eternal worth.[8]

Again, one can easily anticipate what is to follow—no one is to seriously suppose that God is a king, a man, and so on. If the ancients
had lived in a society that was a democracy or a dictatorship, God
would have been represented that way. If their government had been
matriarchal, "He" would have been "She," and so forth. As to the story
of Christ's birth, we are told that "no recognized New Testament
scholar, Catholic or Protestant, would today seriously defend the his-
toricity of these [the scriptural] narratives. This does not mean that
the birth stories of our Lord are not loved, valued, or even seen as
valid proclamations of the gospel. It does mean, however, that they are
not taken literally, nor are they used any longer to undergird such a
well-known doctrine as the virgin birth, which is in fact a popular
misnomer for what would more accurately be called the doctrine of
the virginal conception."[9]

Whose Son Is He?

In this work we will ask anew the question with which Jesus of
Nazareth challenged those of his day: "What think ye of Christ? whose
son is he?" Is he God's Son, or is he a mysterious metaphor? When the
Father opened the meridian dispensation at the baptism of Christ with

the announcement, "This is my beloved Son, in whom I am well pleased" (Matthew 3:17), was he speaking literally or figuratively? When Jesus implored the heavens, praying, "Abba [literally, "Daddy"], Father" (Mark 14:36), did he mean to convey the idea that he was actually God's Son or that he was a symbolic representation of the mind of God, a grand and glorious mystery?[10]

This question is of the greatest importance. Latter-day Saints are commonly denounced as non-Christian cultists because of their belief that Jesus of Nazareth is literally the Son of God.[11] The issue is of the greatest theological importance. If Jesus is actually the offspring of God, then God is a personal being, and the declaration that he created man in his image and likeness is also to be understood literally, thus making each of us his heirs. We would be, as the Psalmist said, "gods; . . . children of the Most High" (Psalm 82:6). If on the other hand the answer to such a question is that Jesus is God's Son only in a metaphorical sense, then we must surrender as foolishness the notion that God is the Father of our spirits, that we lived with him in a pre-mortal existence, that we have been foreordained to special purposes here in mortality, that a fulness of joy is obtained in the eternal union of body and spirit, and that marriage and family were intended to be eternal. Indeed, every fruit of the gospel that is sweet to the taste of a Latter-day Saint is appended to the doctrine of divine sonship.

The Course We Will Follow

In the chapters that follow we will consider the manner in which simple and direct biblical texts that describe the nature of God have been subject to both interpretive and textual tampering. We will trace the activities of our so-called Bible-believing friends to see how it was that they were able to rob God of his body, parts, passions, gender, and even his speech. We will see how the God of the prophets became indistinguishable from the god of the Greek philosophers for Jew and Christian alike. Against this dark skyline we will announce the doctrines of the Restoration and will thus be able to see and appreciate their beauty and power as never before. We will see that the God of Joseph Smith is the God of the ancient Saints, and that through the restoration of the doctrine of divine sonship we obtain a faith in all that is sweet and precious in the gospel of Jesus Christ.

2

*And God said, Let us make man in our image, after our likeness:
and let them have dominion over the fish of the sea, and over the
fowl of the air, and over the cattle, and over all the earth, and over
every creeping thing that creepeth upon the earth.*

*So God created man in his own image, in the image of God
created he him; male and female created he them.*

—Genesis 1:26–27

In the Image of God

While serving as the president of the Scotland Edinburgh Mission, I received a postcard in the mail one morning notifying me that sometime in the next few days I would receive a special book about God. I was encouraged to give very thoughtful attention to its important message. There is something of a feeling of isolation in the mission field, and I often hungered for something more than missionary reports to read, so my thought was one of appreciation for my anonymous benefactor. I looked forward to receiving and reading the book.

Of Mountains, Melons, and Mice

A few days later an unmarked envelope arrived. It would take a little imagination to call it a book.[1] It was sixteen pages in length, though it only used eight page numbers. The title, *God—the Power Who Rules*, sent cold chills down my spine. How can a loving Father be spoken of as a power? I thought. Despite the warm colors on the cover, it seemed cold and impersonal. The preface affirmed the title: God, by definition, I was told, is "the power who rules."

Page 1 explained that before coming to the world Jesus was known as "The WORD." His coming to earth made the invisible word visible.

The Bible, it explained, is the living word written down. (I was left to wonder if this meant that the Bible is Jesus and thus worshipped as such. Much that I have read since sustains that suspicion.[2])

Continuing, the booklet quoted from a modern Bible translation, in part as follows: "The Word became a human being and, full of grace and truth, lived among us. We saw his glory, the glory which he received as the Father's only Son." Again I was stunned by what I read. As a student of the King James Bible I was familiar with the phrase "only begotten of the Father." I was immediately aware that to drop the word *begotten,* leaving the text to read "only Son," meant that I had been disinherited. No longer could I claim to be a son of God in anything more than a vague and metaphorical sense. Was this a major theological scam in which the whole Christian world was being cheated out of their birthright? I had a very unsettled feeling, but kept reading.

Page 2 discussed God's role as Creator. He was defined as "invisible and all powerful." He created all things out of nothing, I was told. As to Christ, it was explained that he "is the visible likeness of the invisible God. He is the firstborn Son, superior to all created things." No explanation was afforded as to how Christ can be the visible likeness of his invisible Father. Nor was it explained how Jesus could be both the "firstborn" (meaning, according to any dictionary, "first in order of nativity"—that is, there were others who followed) and the "only Son" of the Father.

Page 3 introduced me to God as a spirit. "No one has ever seen all of God at any one time," the booklet explained, "because God is not made of flesh and blood but is that invisible power and person who rules. God is SPIRIT." What parts of the invisible God have been seen was left unexplained, as were the many appearances of God to his prophets throughout the scriptures. The Son, however, "who is the same as God" (to use the words of the Bible translation quoted in the booklet) has made him known. Again, explanation was not given as to how it is that we can see the Son, "who is the same" as the invisible God, who cannot be seen.

Page 4 assured me that God is love. "At the moment of everyone's conception, when the egg and the seed become one, God gives that human being a breath of His own life which is spiritual. From then on that breath of life from God is known as our spirit." Thus any good feelings that we have are an expression of God's nature within us. Feelings that we might have that are not right and proper were left unexplained.

Page 5 dealt with the matter of sin. It told the story of the war in heaven, wherein God was compelled to cast Lucifer and other angels out because of their rebellion. (The booklet's illustrations depicted these angels as men.) Lucifer (Satan) tempted Adam and Eve, and thus sin was brought into the world.

Page 6 explained how God, in human form, came into the world to rectify the effects of Adam's fall. The writer no longer made distinction between the Father and the Son. From this point on in the pamphlet, they were the same.

Page 7 explained that we have been created in God's image. An explanation was finally in order. Lest we be confused and suppose that we are actually in God's image and that God is a personal being who could be seen and known, the booklet asked: "Does this mean that God looks more like a man than a mountain, or a melon, or a mouse?" The answer? A resounding "No." The image of God as found in man is the breath of life given at the time of conception, it was explained.

Page 8 was titled "So What!" It consisted of a brief discussion as to whether we can pass such things off by simply muttering "So what," or were we going to be provoked to ask "SO—WHAT should I do about it?" The booklet then invited readers to believe in Christ and to read a brief prayer with which the publication concluded.

A few days after the receipt of this booklet, I received a follow-up card. It asked if I had read the book *God—the Power Who Rules* and if I had believed it. If I had believed, I was asked to "tick" (check) the box so indicated on the card and return it. I did not do so. Nevertheless a few days later I received a letter from my new "Christian fellowshiper," who "witnessed" to me and invited me to join him at their meetings. I made no response. This was followed by still another letter. Again I was encouraged to accept Christ and be saved. This letter, however, contained a special warning. My fellowshiper, Peter, aware of my address, had driven past my home. In doing so he had noticed that it was immediately adjacent to a Mormon chapel. He was greatly alarmed. This letter included a vigorous warning against the Mormons, of whom he had nothing nicer to say than that they were a wicked, non-Christian cult.

His letter evoked a response. I noted in a letter back to Peter that the booklet he had sent to me spoke repeatedly of an invisible God, one who had never been seen. I asked, What became of the God who walked and talked with Adam and Eve in Eden? the God who sealed them together as husband and wife? the God who taught them the law of sacrifice and clothed them in a garment of protection? (See Genesis 2 and 3.) Was he invisible? What of the God who walked with Enoch (see Genesis 5:24), appeared to Abram (see Genesis 17:1), appeared to Isaac (see Genesis 26:2), evoked Jacob to say, "I have seen God face to face" (Genesis 32:30), and also conversed with Moses face to face, speaking with him as one man speaks with another? (See Exodus 33:9, 11.) Were we to disregard the plain meaning of words? And what of Moses, Aaron, Nadab, and Abihu, and the seventy elders of Israel who "saw the God of Israel" and the paved work of sapphire under his feet? (Exodus 24:9–10.) Again, does not the Bible attest that "they saw God, and did eat and drink" with him? (Exodus 24:11.) What of the God whom Isaiah saw seated upon a throne? (See Isaiah 6:1–8.) Did not Ezekiel testify to having seen God and describe him as being in the likeness of a man? (See Ezekiel 1:26–28.) What about the account of Joshua the priest, who was caught up into a heavenly council? (See Zechariah 3.) Did not John the Revelator bear witness of a similar experience in a heavenly assembly? (See Revelation 4.) Did not Stephen see the heavens open, and did he not testify that he saw the glory of God, and Jesus standing on the Father's right hand? (See Acts 7:55–56.)

Continuing, I wrote: "The Bible, your pamphlet tells me, is the announcement of God's plan 'to save mankind and restore them to His image.' How are you going to be restored to God's image if God is invisible? And to what is man to be restored if your purpose is simply to rob him of his image also? Never have I read anything so confusing. This strange work quotes the Bible as saying, 'And God said, let us make man in our image after our likeness . . . male and female He created them.' I am then told that men and women are no more in the image of God than is 'a mountain, or a melon, or a mouse.' Should this not cause you to blush a little? Where does innocent error end and heresy begin? 'And God said, Let us make man in our image, and so in the image of a melon created he him.' Or 'God said, Let us make man in our own image, and so in the image of a mouse created he him.' Has all spiritual sensitivity been lost? Does that not strike something of a discordant note in your ears?

"As a matter of curiosity, when did the personal pronoun 'He' in reference to Deity cease to be used in preference to the 'Power Who Rules'?"

Further, I noted "that the scriptural text in question says, 'Let us make man. . . .' Does not the reference to 'us' demand explanation? With whom is this Supreme Power, of whom the writer of your booklet speaks, conversing? Who is Supreme Power's companion in the act of creation, and why does he need one?

"I find little or nothing in this pamphlet which is true to the Bible, true to the Spirit, or even true to the English language. Under the heading 'Image,' I am told that the 'Dictionary says: A likeness of a person or object; a person or thing that is the double or copy of another.' Now, what is God? A 'person' or a 'thing'? My dictionary, *The Shorter Oxford English Dictionary on Historical Principles,* under the main entry 'God,' has the following subentry: '**God's image**, the human body (Gen. 1:27).'[3]

"Could it be that the Bible means what it says and says what it means when again and again it says that God appeared to holy men in both the Old and New Testaments? Could it possibly mean it when it says that we are created in God's image?"

I had a few other observations to make in that letter, and then concluded thus: "You warn me against the Mormons and tell me they are not Christians. Who, pray tell, ordained you to be their judge? Is salvation in your hands to dispense or withhold? If so, what kind of a salvation is it that cannot distinguish between that which is Godlike and mice and melons? Perhaps it is just as well that all things in such a kingdom be in the likeness of their invisible God."

Peter did not take occasion to respond to my letter.

The Nature of God

My exchange with Peter is but one of many experiences that have dramatized for me how different the conceptions of Deity are among people who profess a common faith in and a loyalty to the Bible. If I had asked him if he believed in and was true to the God of the Bible, I have no doubt that he would have responded in the affirmative and have done so vigorously. Were he to address the same question to me, I would respond in the same manner. How, then, is it that on this matter (and virtually all others that appertain to the salvation of men) he and I have such a pronounced difference? Given that we are reading the same words, the difference obviously rests in the interpretation that we are placing on them. When I read that "the Lord spake unto Moses face to face, as a man speaketh unto his friend" (Exodus 33:11), I take the story at face value. I believe that God has physical form, that he can be seen, that Moses actually saw him, that he in reality spoke to Moses. When I read that we are created in the image and likeness of God, I am led to believe that God is a personal being. When I read that Christ has declared himself to be the Son of God, I believe him to mean precisely so. To my correspondent Peter, such interpretations are a combination of childish naiveté (a God with form, a God who can be seen, and a God who speaks), heresy (that we are literally in God's image), and blasphemy (that God would actually father a Son).

Peter's understanding represents traditional Christian doctrine. My understanding grows out of faith in the reality of events that took place in a grove in upstate New York in the spring of 1820. Both stories deserve telling. One is simple and easy to tell; the other is not. We will begin with the more difficult of the two stories. Indeed, we will begin our story with the issue of interpreting the first verse of the first book of the Bible.

Interpretive Tampering

The first verse in our English Bible reads: "In the beginning God created the heaven and the earth." Latter-day Saint theology challenges this rendering of the Hebrew text. Indeed, we hold that this traditional translation has been forced on the text to sustain a predetermined theological mind-set. The reference to "God" in this text is a translation of the Hebrew word *Elohim*. *El* is the Hebrew word for "God," while the addition of *im* makes it plural. Thus our text properly reads: "In the beginning, Gods created the heaven and the earth."

The making of *El* plural (*Elohim*) denotes either masculine plural or a combined masculine and feminine plural (a different ending is required to make it feminine only). Scholars admit that the biblical translation of *Elohim* in the singular is not justified by the etymology of the word,[4] but are unperturbed by that because the contexts in which it is used throughout the Old Testament seem to justify the manner in which it has been translated in the Creation story. This tradition went unchallenged until the ministry of the Prophet Joseph Smith, who had the audacity to trust the text and suggest that it ought to have been rendered: "In the beginning the head of the Gods brought forth the Gods," and they created the heavens and the earth. "I defy all the world to refute me," he challenged.

Continuing, the Prophet said: "In the beginning the heads of the Gods organized the heavens and the earth. Now the learned priests and the people rage, and the heathen imagine a vain thing. If we pursue the Hebrew text further, it reads, 'The head one of the Gods said, Let us make a man in our own image.' I once asked a learned Jew, 'If the Hebrew language compels us to render all words ending in *heim* in the plural, why not render the first *Eloheim* plural?' He replied, 'That is the rule with few exceptions; but in this case it would ruin the Bible.' He acknowledged I was right."[5]

It appears that Joseph Smith learned the doctrine of the plurality of Gods while translating Abraham's account of the Creation (see Abraham 4–5). He did not indicate, however, that the word *Elohim* should be rendered as a plural in its many other usages in the Old Testament. Following that lead, Latter-day Saints have developed the tradition of using *Elohim* in the singular sense to refer to God the Father unless they are telling the story of Creation, in which case it is understood to be referring to the heavenly council of the Gods.

How the word *Elohim* is to be translated or interpreted is at best a difficult issue. While we disagree with the conclusions of the scholarly world relative to the manner in which it is used in the account of the Creation, we do so on the basis of modern revelation, not with the accusation that they are deliberately seeking to distort the meaning of the Bible. Nevertheless if we are to act on the assumption that the Bible is holy writ, then we are obligated to conclude that the only truly acceptable method of translation would be by the same power and authority through which it was originally written. The carnal—howbeit scholarly—mind cannot do it. It is seership, not scholarship, that is needed here. Joseph Smith is the first man in nearly two thousand years to dare profess seership in translating and interpreting the Bible. He spoke as one having authority, not the authority of classrooms, textbooks, or public acceptance. His was the authority of heaven, and with it came the boldness of a heavenly messenger. In translating the Bible he was willing to defy the world and to stand alone. But as we shall see, this is but the beginning of our troubles in untangling the God of the ancients, the God of the prophets, from the traditions and philosophies of men.

Man in God's Image:
Theological Explanations

In our attempt to find the God of the prophets, we appropriately begin the search in Genesis. The first chapter makes it abundantly plain that God was not alone in the labor of creation. The text reads, "And God [Elohim] said, Let us make man in our image, after our likeness" (Genesis 1:26). To whom, we ask, are the Gods speaking? Whose help do they require in the act of creation? What are the implications of the declaration that man has been created in the image of the Gods? Further, how are we to understand the declaration that both male and female are in the image and likeness of the Gods?

Another of these troublesome "Elohim" texts in Genesis is the passage in which the serpent tells Eve that if she will partake of the fruit of the tree of knowledge she "shall be as gods, knowing good and evil" (Genesis 3:5). Two standard explanations are given for this text. One is that it could not possibly mean what it says, because Adam and Eve knew that there was only one God (a classic circular argument). The other, which is common to anti-Mormon books and tracts, is that the notion that men could become as God, is a great heresy that originated with the serpent. The use of this argument evidences a failure to have read the entire chapter. In verse 22 we read: "And the LORD God [Jehovah Elohim] said, Behold, the man is become as one of us, to know good and evil."

Another writer notes that what may be of special interest here is that only the man and the woman were told that they were in the image of God. The argument that they would become as God "would not have worked on a beast or a bird or a fish"—or a mountain, or a melon, or a mouse—"because they do not participate in the divine. Only humans are created in God's image, and so only humans would aspire to the divine."[6]

The Tower of Babel story contains still another instance in which God is portrayed as conversing with heavenly companions. "Let us go down," he says, and "confound their language" (Genesis 11:7). We find the same pattern in the book of Isaiah. The prophet is invited to attend a heavenly council, where he hears the Lord asking, "Whom shall I send, and who will go for us?" Realizing that this is the reason he has been invited to join the council, Isaiah responds, "Here am I; send me." (Isaiah 6:8.)

Now, what do we do with it all? Jewish sources suggest that the name Elohim has an "ancient pre-Israelitish and polytheistic origin" and that it was a "true plural both in form and in meaning."[7] Traditional Christian commentary on these verses runs like this: "As the Divine Being is infinite, he is neither limited by parts, nor definable by passions; therefore he can have no *corporeal image* after which he made the body of man. The image and likeness must necessarily be intellectual; his mind, his soul, must have been formed after the nature and perfections of his God."[8]

Christian commentaries suggest one of three possible explanations for the plural "us" in the Genesis text. It is argued that the Apostolic Fathers and the earlier theologians saw it as indicative of the Trinity. Modern commentators, however, favor the explanation that it is a matter of *pluralis majestatis* (plural majesty), meaning God is so great he can only be described in plural terms, which of course they assiduously avoid doing. The third explanation is that God is speaking to himself; and if not to himself, to the animals and the elements; and if not to them, then to the spirits or angels who constitute his heavenly council.[9]

The attempt to associate the "let us" text in Genesis with the doctrine of the Trinity is generally regarded as bad history and as being "too ingenious to have occurred to the early Hebrew mind." The explanation is offered that such expressions are "survivals" in language of a polytheistic stage of thought."[10] Developing this thought, *The Abingdon Bible Commentary* states: "We have here a relic of the old polytheistic phraseology which has escaped the careful expurgation of the writer. A further hint of a lower theological position has been seen by some in the repeated phrase *in our image, in his image, in the image of God,* which is thought to point to a time when men believed that God had a material frame like that which man possesses."[11]

Given that *Elohim* appears 2,555 times in the Old Testament, decisions as to how it ought to be translated are significant. In 2,310 instances it is used as a name for the God of Israel, and thus Jew and Christian alike have chosen to translate it as "God" rather than "Gods." The other instances are references to the god of the pagans, which makes translating it as "gods" acceptable. Joseph Smith observed that it was an awesome thing to speak in the name of the Lord.[12] The question here is, by what authority did the translators, both Jewish and Christian, make the decision that the references to the Gods ought to be rendered in the singular?

Man in God's Image:
Scholarly Explanations

The contention of most scholars is that the five books of Moses represent the weaving together of manuscripts from four different sources. The theory has evolved over the course of many years. It began with the observation that the books of Moses contain what have been called doublets—that is, stories that are told twice, often with differing details. For instance, it is held that there are two differing stories of the creation of the world. There are, we are told, two stories of the covenant between God and Abraham; two stories of the naming of Abraham's son, Isaac; of Abraham's claiming to a foreign king that his wife, Sarah, is his sister; of Isaac's son Jacob making a journey to Mesopotamia; of a revelation to Jacob at Beth-el; two stories of God's changing Jacob's name to Israel; two stories of Moses' getting water from a rock at Meribah; and so on.

Further, it was found that there was a distinctively different way that Deity was referred to in the stories that were doublets. In most cases, one of the two versions of a doublet story would refer to Deity by the divine name Jehovah, while the other version of the story would refer to Deity as Elohim. For instance, in the Creation account, Elohim is used 33 times in the first 34 verses and is followed by Jehovah Elohim 20 times in the next 45 verses, and then by Jehovah 10 times in the 25 verses which follow.[13] Thus was born the idea that someone had found different source documents and woven them together.

As source criticism became more intensive and more sophisticated, triplets of some stories were found. Apparent contradictions were magnified, and differing language characteristics identified. Eventually the conclusion was drawn that the books of Moses represented the combining of four different strands, or sources. For working purposes the four documents are identified by alphabetic symbols. The document associated with the divine name Yahweh/Jehovah is called J. The document representing the Elohim tradition is designated as E. The third document, which is by far the largest and includes the legal sections and the duties of the priests, is called P. The source that is believed to be found almost exclusively in the book of Deuteronomy is called D.

As this idea was evolving, so was the idea that the religion of ancient Israel evolved. So the next great step in the development of the documentary hypothesis theory was to attempt to date the various manuscripts and determine the bias of their originators. Since no original documents exist, this had to be done by examining the content of the texts in the context of the scholars' views about the evolution of Israel's religion. It is held that the J and E documents contain the oldest versions of the stories told in the Pentateuch. This was reasoned on the basis that they showed no awareness of what was treated in the other supposed documents. D is generally believed to have been written next, and P, the priestly version, the latest of all because it referred to a variety of matters apparently unknown in the earlier sources.

Thus it is held that J and E represent a very early stage in the development of Israelite religion (tenth to ninth century B.C.), when it was essentially a nature-fertility cult. D, it is felt, represents the middle period (seventh to sixth century B.C.), when it became spiritual and ethical, this being the period of the prophets. And finally, P represents the latest stage (fifth to fourth century B.C.), when Israel's religion centered in sacrifices, ritual, and obeisance to the Mosaic law.[14] The scholarly explanation of the plurality of gods in the Creation account and also of the idea that we are in God's image is that these notions represent the most primitive period of Israel's understanding, one in which they were strongly influenced by Canaanite religious practices—an understanding which the later writer or writers (the D document) sought to erase from their history.

In his book *God and the Gods: Myths of the Bible,* Walter Beltz writes: "Some notion of the erstwhile multiplicity of the gods has survived in Jewish tradition and may be seen in the person of Yahweh. For the Jews never pronounced the name of God. Every time the word appears, they read 'Adonai,' which literally means 'my lords.' So, like the tip of an iceberg breaking the surface of the ocean, the full variety of ancient religious beliefs about the gods breaks through the monolatry of a later period. We have here living proof that the efforts to impose monotheism failed."[15]

Elsewhere in his book, Beltz observes: "The hand of the biblical writer then gradually shapes the abstract plural into an absolute singular, which is both a name and a programme. But in Elohim's statement, 'Let *us* make man,' the plural refers to the community of the gods that Elohim belongs to. The earliest narrators took it for granted that this community existed before creation."[16]

Among other illustrations cited by Beltz is the story of Abraham. Scholars identify it as coming from a ninth century B.C. Elohist source (E document).[17] Beltz writes:

> The original narrator has learned from the Canaanite elders in his country that there once were many gods involved in the life of man. With characteristic straightforwardness the narrator has Abraham (invoked by others as a star witness for the true and strictly monotheistic faith) acting at the behest of the gods. It was clear to the narrator that there were as many gods as there were cities (Jeremiah 11:13). . . .
>
> The story shows that the idea of monotheism was foreign to the unsophisticated popular piety of the ninth century B.C. Abraham lives with many gods. To be sure, in this passage as in many others the translators have erased the presence of poly-theism. Thus the pious reader is obliged to view the "living Elohim" (plural, i.e. the living gods, as in, say, Deuteronomy 5:26; 1 Samuel 17:26; Jeremiah 10:10; 23:36), and to take the "holy Elohim" (the holy gods, as, for example, in Joshua 24:19; 1 Samuel 2:25; 2 Samuel 7:23; Genesis 35:7; 1 Samuel 4:8) for none other than 'the one holy God of Israel,' as the dogmatic teaching of the Jerusalem Yahweh priests prescribes. But stories like this one demonstrate that old Canaanite religious beliefs survived in places remote from Jerusalem.[18]

A common biblical motif is that of the heavenly council, wherein the hosts of heaven consider the needs of those on earth, make plans, and call prophets and other leaders to implement them. One variation of this theme is found in the book of Job, of which Beltz writes: "The author of this poetic work was not scandalized, any more than his listeners and readers, by the idea that Yahweh had active dealings with the gods, the Elohim. 'Sons of the gods' means, in general, 'belonging to the race of the gods,' and this includes Satan too. Like the other gods, Satan performs a positive function, i.e. he keeps an eye on the earth and reports to Yahweh (that being the mythological background to this tale). Yahweh is the lord of heaven and president of the council of the gods. Satan plays his negative role, as the spirit who plagues Job, on orders from Yahweh."[19]

Sorting It Out

The idea that Israel's understanding of God evolved through the ages from the polytheistic god of her neighbors to the monotheistic God of later years is described as a necessary part of progressive revelation. We will see this same kind of reasoning used again when theological justification is sought for the dogma of the Trinity. Such a concept of revelation is wholly foreign to scriptural writ. It is hard to imagine the same God who said, "Ask, and ye shall receive," now responding to the earnest appeal of his prophet by saying, "Ask, and I will lead your people through hundreds of years of error, argument, debate, and contention, but eventually a superior doctrine will emerge."

As to the documentary hypothesis, a critical examination of it would far exceed the scope of this book and the interest of most of its readers. Let it suffice, therefore, to say that the 1992 book *The Pentateuch* by Joseph Blenkinsopp states, "It is true that the documentary hypothesis has increasingly been shown to be flawed, and will survive, if at all, only in a greatly modified form."[20] The hypothesis assumes that all of the documents, J, E, P, and D, were written long after the days of Moses. The revelations of the Restoration announce otherwise. We are clearly told that Moses is the author of the Creation account in Genesis (see JST, Genesis 1:1, or Moses 2:1), and Book of Mormon prophets consistently credit him with the authorship of the Pentateuch (see 1 Nephi 5:10–11).

Joseph Smith has been credited with an uncanny genius in finding his way back to the understanding of God that was had by those from whom the ancient texts originally came.[21] What would have to be obvious to even the casual reader of the Good Book is that the God of modern Christianity has no resemblance to the God spoken of in holy writ. The profiles of the two are no more alike than a holy man is like an invisible essence or a loving Father is like the law of gravity. Spiritual charlatans posing as men of great spiritual wisdom have done much to obscure the truths of heaven and have so confused their well-intended and naive followers that they cannot tell the difference between the image of God and a mountain, a melon, or a mouse.

Wise and honest truth seekers will not rest their hope of salvation on the theories of men, nor will they be naive enough to suppose that scoundrels down through the ages have not tampered with and counterfeited sacred things. The greatest single need in the world today is to obtain a true knowledge of the God of heaven and our kinship with him. It is that key of knowledge that we must now seek.

3

And this greater priesthood administereth the gospel and holdeth the key of the mysteries of the kingdom, even the key of the knowledge of God.

—D&C 84:19

Key of the Knowledge of God

During our experience in Scotland, I was contacted by a minister from the Church of Scotland who indicated that he was quite disaffected with his own church and its teachings. The man had been a professor of theology at a church school for twenty years. We arranged to meet. In the course of a long conversation, in my efforts to get across to him the essence of our faith I told him that as Latter-day Saints we had a greater faith in the Bible than any people on earth and that it was important for him to understand why.

The reason for our faith in the Bible, I explained, was that the doctrines it taught in its pristine purity had been revealed anew in our day to us and that we had experienced the kind of things that were the common lot of the faithful Saints of ages past. When we read of miracles we were inclined to believe them because we too had experienced them. When we read of prophets in the Old and New Testaments we had no difficulty believing in them because our experience included living prophets. In like manner we had no difficulty with the idea of Apostles and the kind of things they were doing in the meridian of time because we had Apostles in our church who were doing the same things. I told him we had no difficulty believing in angels because we had experienced the administration of angels. I even told him who some of those angels were. The list included Adam, Enoch, an Elias from Abraham's dispensation, Moses, Elijah, John the Baptist, Peter,

James, and John. I told him that these men had come to the Prophet
Joseph Smith, instructed him, and laid their hands on his head and
given him the same keys, powers, authority, and priesthood that they
held anciently.

Now, since we had had personal contact with many of the great
characters of the Bible, and had gotten the message firsthand from
them along with the authority to continue the same good works, we
had better reason than anyone on earth to believe the Bible, its stories
and doctrines.

He said that he could not accept what I was saying as true.
"Why?" I asked. Because, he explained, there were no such persons as
Adam or Enoch or Noah. And if there were no such persons, they certainly could not have appeared to Joseph Smith. He explained that the
stories of the Creation and of the Flood, the stories of Adam and of
Noah, were ancient myths used to explain the otherwise unexplain-
able. His response reflected views common to the scholastic circles in
which he taught. They are views that are shared by many Christian
and Jewish ministers.

Our conversation took place about a week before Easter Sunday. I
told my minister friend that I thought he was going to have a tough
time preparing his Easter talk. He seemed puzzled at my remark. I responded that if Adam was a myth, then the story of the Fall was myth
also, which in turn meant that the need for an atonement for that fall
was myth as would be the idea that Christ was our Redeemer. We
hardly need redemption from a mythical fall. He was not pleased with
that chain of thought, and changed the subject.

Can God Be Known?

"All our thoughts about God are conjectures." Such is the conclusion of John Austin Baker,[1] writing as the bishop of Salisbury, after
more than four hundred pages of thoughtful and scholarly consideration of the nature of God and Christ. "Once the primitive stage, at
which the environment itself was regarded as imbued with personal
life, was left behind," Baker explains earlier in the same work, "and the
supernatural, the invisible world interlocked with the visible realm of
Man and Nature, had become the frame of reference within which
men's thinking about God was done, *'God' could never again be a cer-*

tainty. It was no longer possible to say, 'Behold the god!' The divine must henceforth be the object of faith, *upheld or attacked by rational conjecture.*"[2]

God Stands Revealed or Remains Unknown

How a God, who Christian theologians tells us is beyond our comprehension, can be "upheld" by "rational conjecture" must itself rank as a religious mystery. Nevertheless the traditional Christian faith is based on what they have chosen to call "speculative theology."[3] According to such a doctrine, our salvation rests on unprovable theory. It is the best bet of men who have no relevant qualifications to make it.

We can talk endlessly of spiritual things, and we can speculate to our hearts' content, but sooner or later we are reduced to the plain fact that the only sure knowledge of God that anyone can profess must of necessity be revealed knowledge. God stands revealed or remains forever unknown; therefore, all true religion is revealed religion.[4] Either God turns on the light or we remain in the dark.

To deny revelation, either ancient or modern, is to choose darkness. The ancient Saints knew God to the extent that he was revealed to them—no more, no less. Some small portion of what they knew has been preserved for us in holy writ, but it is not a revelation to us until we have learned it by the same Spirit by which it was originally given to them. The experience must always be firsthand. You can't borrow another man's revelation any more than you can borrow his feelings or his goodness. We can share them, but in doing so we must make them ours. The point is that if a revealed truth is to be handed from generation to generation, it will take the spirit of revelation to keep it alive. We can know what the ancients knew, but only if we know it by the same Spirit by which they knew it. To deny the spirit of revelation in our day is to close the door to an understanding of that Spirit as it was enjoyed by those of the household of faith in earlier dispensations.

To say that the Bible is God's final revelation is to consign oneself to a secondary citizenship in the realm of spiritual understanding. It is to say the ancients had a living faith and we have a record of it. They partook of the feast and we are to satisfy our hunger by reading an account of what they ate. The idea that their revelation was to be the final revelation never occurred to a soul mentioned within the covers of the Bible. No such notion is found there.[5] The idea of a sealed canon never occurred to them. The declaration of their God was, "There is no end to my works, neither to my words" (Moses 1:38). When the miracle of God's creation ends, when man and all other species cease to exist, then will God cease to speak, but not until.

The Bible is not a book of conjecture or of speculative theology. It is a book of revelation. Its writings span thousands of years and come from divers cultures and circumstances. The common bond that binds them together is a God who speaks; there is no hint that at some point he would lose his voice and that they must carefully gather whatever memorabilia they could find of him. True religion never did consist of the worship of relics, and there is little difference between a book as a relic and a supposed tunic or a bone.

To Whom Does God Speak and When?

In response to the question, To whom does God speak? the answer must be, To all who will listen. In fact, however, the greater effort seems to be directed at those who refuse to do so. In any event, the invitation to "ask of God" is extended to all. None have been excluded from the privilege of personal communication with him. True religion will always be found extending that invitation, even teaching it as an obligation. All must ask of God. Again, another man's revelation will not save you any more than the revelations of the ancients can save us. Salvation is not a matter of stolen promises or borrowed faith. Institutional revelations constitute the framework, the foundation of the house of our faith. The Spirit will confirm them to us. But from that point we become the builders and the decorators. We must learn to ask questions and get answers for ourselves. Much could be said about improving our abilities to do so, but that is not the purpose of this work. For our purpose here, let it suffice to say that the message of heaven is pure, and a pure message cannot remain so in an impure vessel. Paul describes both the community of the Saints and the individual members as temples of God. He warns us not to defile those temples, for then the Holy Spirit—that is, the spirit of revelation—cannot dwell in them. (See 1 Corinthians 3:16–17; 6:19.) If the idea seems lost upon the modern world, it was not upon those of the ancient world. They knew that no unclean thing could enter the divine presence and that those who bore the vessels of the Lord must be clean. Such obligations are universal.

This is not to say that those laden with guilt cannot importune the heavens. Were that the case, none of us could do so, "for all have sinned, and come short of the glory of God" (Romans 3:23). This would place us in a situation where we would only be quibbling about the degree of our culpability, which none of us is capable of judging anyway. The real issue is one of purity of intent. There are those who seek to counsel God, and there are those who seek counsel from him. There are those who glory in transgression and those who feel shame and despair in their weaknesses. There are those who search the pages of the Bible only for proof texts to justify a religion of their own making, and there are those who search honestly in its pages to find the mind and will of their Maker. As our spirits differ, so does our susceptibility to the voice of heaven. God has given his promise that he will speak to those who still listen, to those sufficiently clean and pure to associate with his Spirit, and to those who sincerely deserve to hear his voice.

True Theology

True theology will represent what God has said—not what we have to say about what he said. Much that purports to be theology is idle (and idol) talk spoken in the absence of his Spirit. Theology was the pious cloak used by Philo and other Alexandrian Jews to explain away all within the scriptures that placed them at odds with the Greek philosophical world in which they sought citizenship. It was in the clerical robes of a theologian that Origen and others of the ante-Nicene Fathers wrote as they betrayed the New Testament faith in a marriage with Greek sophistry.

Elder James E. Talmage tells us that "the word 'Theology' is of Greek origin; it comes to us from *Theos*, meaning God, and *logos*—a treatise, or discourse, signifying by derivation, therefore, collated knowledge of Deity, or the science that teaches us of God, implying also the relation existing between Him and His creatures. The term is of ancient usage, and may be traced to pagan sources. Plato and Aristotle speak of theology as the doctrine of Deity and divine things."[6] Theology played no part in the Hebrew Bible. That is, truths were declared; they were not explained.

All true theology will be rooted in the spirit of revelation. God, and all truths associated with him or that profess to have come from him, can be, as already noted, known only by revelation. One cannot tamper with the revelations and not at the same time tamper with one's relationship with God. Whenever a passage of scripture is interpreted, the interpretation is a reflection of the spiritual maturity and integrity of the interpreter. To get the same interpretation that the writer of the text intended we must have the same Spirit by which he wrote. Thus it takes a prophet to interpret a prophet, and the Spirit to interpret the Spirit.

Scholarly interpretations may have the advantage of being free from the need to screen through the fine mesh of theological bias what scriptural texts are saying. This affords them objectivity (and honesty) to see and acknowledge what the theologian in some instances cannot. Nevertheless it would be naive not to recognize that scholasticism is also a religion, one that in some ways is more demanding of its adherents than that which bears a denominational tag. Among many scholars orthodoxy embraces a refusal to accept the possibility of either revelation or miracles.

Angels visit prophets. They do not visit scholars. Scholars may claim objectivity, but they cannot claim theophany. As for me and my house, I have no sympathy for the theology of the churches of the world, simply because that is where their theology came from—the world. I respect good scholarship while recognizing its limitation. My premise (or bias, if you will) is one of faith—that is, faith in the divine mission of the Prophet Joseph Smith and the revelations of the Restoration. Defining the spirit of revelation, the Lord told Oliver Cowdery, through Joseph Smith, that He would speak to Oliver in his mind and in his heart (see D&C 8:2). I like the feel of that; pure truth is neither mindless nor heartless but satisfies both.

Revealed Explanation

Shortly after Joseph Smith completed the work of translation and publication of the Book of Mormon, the Lord directed the Prophet to commence a translation of the Old and New Testaments. This labor, known to us today as the Joseph Smith Translation (JST), was not a "translation" in the traditional sense of transmitting a text from one language to another, but rather was one in which the text was transmitted from a state of imperfection to one more perfectly representing the original. Under the direction of the spirit of revelation, the same Spirit by which the original texts were written, missing verses were restored and others corrected.

The early chapters of the JST have been included in the Pearl of Great Price under the title of the book of Moses. The verse equivalent to Genesis 1:1 reads: "And it came to pass that the Lord spake unto Moses, saying: Behold, I reveal unto you concerning this heaven, and this earth; write the words which I speak. I am the Beginning and the End, the Almighty God; by mine Only Begotten I created these things; yea, in the beginning I created the heaven, and the earth upon which thou standest." (Moses 2:1.) Thus two Gods are identified as being involved in the work of creation, that is, the Father and his Only Begotten Son.

In the JST, the other two verses in the Creation account that have proven so problematic to the scholars read, in part: "And I, God, said unto mine Only Begotten, which was with me from the beginning: Let us make man in our image, after our likeness; and it was so. . . . And I, God, created man in mine own image, in the image of mine Only Begotten created I him; male and female created I them." (Moses 2:26–27.) Thus a harmony begins to form between the Genesis text with its use of *Elohim* and the other biblical texts that identify Christ as the Creator under the direction of his Father (see Ephesians 3:9; Colossians 1:15–16; Hebrews 1:1–4).

The Abraham papyrus that was subsequently translated by Joseph Smith and became the book of Abraham also contains an account of the Creation. In this instance what is being described is the plan of the Gods as they sat in council prior to the actual labor of creation. It is a blueprint, or plan, for the Creation. The first verse of Abraham 4 reads: "And then the Lord said: Let us go down. And they went down at the beginning, and they, that is the Gods, organized and formed the heavens and the earth." Thereafter the account consistently reads "they (the Gods)" or just "the Gods" did thus and thus. Verse 26 of the same chapter reads: "And the Gods took counsel among themselves and said: Let us go down and form man in our image, after our likeness; and we will give them dominion over the fish of the sea, and over the fowl of the air, and over the cattle, and over all the earth, and over every creeping thing that creepeth upon the earth."

Walter Beltz holds that "in Elohim's statement, 'Let us make man,' the plural refers to the community of the gods that Elohim belongs to. The earliest narrators took it for granted that this community existed before creation."[7] What we are learning from the book of Abraham, however, is that this is not a myth that the Israelites adopted from some pagan source but rather is a part of the Creation account from the earliest of times, an account which was appropriated in various forms by all the religions of the ancient Near East.

Who, then, constituted the council of the Gods? Besides the Father and the Son, it appears that it also included those who labored in the Creation as companions in the ministry with the Only Begotten. Abraham's account seems to suggest that the "noble and great ones" of our first, or pre-earth, estate were part of that council. Abraham was one of the "noble and great," as were the prophets of our dispensation. (See Abraham 3:22–28; D&C 138:53–56.)[8] The Only Begotten obviously presided over that significant heavenly council.

Thus for Latter-day Saints the "Let us" in the Creation account is resolved by revelation. God was not alone. The creative work was planned in heavenly councils, with divisions of labor being assigned accordingly. Presumably tasks were delegated to the noble and great ones, who, by virtue of their commission to participate in the work, were designated, even in the pre-earth estate, as Gods. (See Abraham 3:22–28; 4; 5.)

The Creation of Adam and Eve

Scripturally we know more about the creation of man and how he became what he is than we do with reference to any other form of life. To understand the nature of the creation of earth's first man and first woman, we need simply combine the revealed accounts of their creation with what else has been revealed to us about the plan of salvation.

Our basic sources are the books of Abraham and Moses, and because of their importance we shall quote virtually all that they have to say on this matter. Abraham's account deals with the decisions and plans of the Gods when they counseled among themselves to create man in their image, and Moses' writings record the creative acts themselves. The accounts are in Abraham 4:26–31; 5:1–3, and Moses 2:26–31; 3:1.

Abraham: "And the Gods took counsel among themselves and said: Let us go down and form man in our image, after our likeness" (4:26).

Moses: "And I, God, said unto mine Only Begotten, which was with me from the beginning: Let us make man in our image, after our likeness; and it was so" (2:26).

An image is an incarnation; it is a reproduction or imitation of the form of another person; it is an exact likeness. It is a tangible and visible representation of another person; it is one person who is strikingly like another person. Paul says Christ is in "the express image of his [Father's] person" (Hebrews 1:3). Likeness is the quality or state of being like another; it is resemblance; it is the same appearance; it is having the same semblance. Man is made in the likeness of God physically and has power to become like him in respect to all the attributes of godliness.

Thus God made man in his own image physically and spiritually, and God is a holy Man. "In the language of Adam, Man of Holiness is his name" (Moses 6:57). The name-title *Ahman,* or *Ah Man,* is a translation or transliteration of God's name that has come down to us from the ancient tongues. And thus when "the book of the generations of Adam" was written, it said, "In the day that God created man, *in the likeness of God made he him; in the image of his own body, male and female, created he them,* and blessed them, and called *their* name Adam, in the day when they were created and became living souls in the land upon the footstool of God" (Moses 6:8–9, emphasis added). The creation of Adam on this earth, with a tangible body of flesh and bones, was the creation of a human soul in the image and likeness of the tangible body of his eternal parents.

Abraham: "And we will give *them* dominion over the fish of the sea, and over the fowl of the air, and over the cattle, and over all the earth, and over every creeping thing that creepeth upon the earth" (4:26, emphasis added). Such was the plan.

Moses: "And I, God, said: Let *them* have dominion over the fishes of the sea, and over the fowl of the air, and over the cattle, and over all the earth, and over every creeping thing that creepeth upon the earth" (2:26, emphasis added). Such was the eventuality. And thus man—

meaning *them* (the man and the woman, or mankind in general)—was given dominion over all things. He was and is the governor of the earth and all that inhabits it.

Abraham: "So the Gods went down to organize man in their own image, in the image of the Gods to form they him, male and female to form they them" (4:27).

Moses: "And I, God, created man in mine own image, in the image of mine Only Begotten created I him; male and female created I them" (2:27).

Commenting on these matters, Elder Bruce R. McConkie wrote:

> In the ultimate and final sense of the word, the Father is the Creator of all things. That he used the Son and others to perform many of the creative acts, delegating to them his creative powers, does not make these others creators in their own right, independent of him. He is the source of all creative power, and he simply chooses others to act for him in many of his creative enterprises. But there are two creative events that are his and his alone. First, he is the Father of all spirits, Christ's included; none were fathered or created by anyone else. Second, he is the Creator of the physical body of man. Though Jehovah and Michael and many of the noble and great ones played their assigned roles in the various creative events, yet when it came time to place men on earth, the Lord God himself performed the creative acts. "I, God, created man in mine own image, in the image of mine Only Begotten created I him; male and female created I them." (Moses 2:27.)[9]

An Official Doctrinal Declaration

In a 1909 official doctrinal declaration by the First Presidency of the Church, the matter of the origin of man is addressed, in part, as follows:

"God created man in his own image, in the image of God created he him; male and female created he them." In these plain and pointed words the inspired author of the book of Genesis made known to the world the truth concerning the origin of the human family. Moses, the prophet-historian, "learned," as we are told, "in all the wisdom of the Egyptians," when making this important announcement, was not voicing a mere opinion, a theory derived from his researches into the occult lore of that ancient people. He was speaking as the mouthpiece of God, and his solemn declaration was for all time and for all people. No subsequent revelator of the truth has contradicted the great leader and lawgiver of Israel. All who have since spoken by divine authority upon this theme have confirmed his simple and sublime proclamation. Nor could it be otherwise. Truth has but one source, and all revelations from heaven are harmonious with each other. The omnipotent Creator, the maker of heaven and earth—had shown unto Moses everything pertaining to this planet, including the facts relating to man's origin, and the authoritative pronouncement of that mighty prophet and seer to the house of Israel, and through Israel to the whole world, is couched in the simple clause: "God created man in his own image" (Genesis 1:27; Pearl of Great Price—Book of Moses, 1:27–41).

The creation was two-fold—firstly spiritual, secondly temporal. This truth, also, Moses plainly taught—much more plainly than it has come down to us in the imperfect translations of the Bible that are now in use. Therein the fact of a spiritual creation, antedating the temporal creation, is strongly implied, but the proof of it is not so clear and conclusive as in other records held by the Latter-day Saints to be of equal authority with the Jewish scriptures. The partial obscurity of the latter upon the point in question is owing, no doubt, to the loss of those "plain and precious" parts of sacred writ, which, as the Book of Mormon informs us, have been taken away from the Bible during its passage down the centuries (1 Nephi 13:24–29). Some of these missing parts the Prophet Joseph Smith undertook to restore when he revised those scriptures by the spirit of revelation, the result being that more complete account of the creation which is found in the book of Moses, previously cited. . . .

These two points being established, namely, the creation of man in the image of God, and the two-fold character of the creation, let us now inquire: What was the form of man, in the spirit and in the body, as originally created? In a general way the answer is given in the words chosen as the text of his treatise. "God created man in his own image." It is more explicitly rendered in the Book of Mormon thus: "All men were created in the beginning after mine own image" (Ether 3:15). It is the Father who is speaking. If, therefore, we can ascertain the form of the "Father of spirits," "The God of the spirits of all flesh," we shall be able to discover the form of the original man.

Jesus Christ, the Son of God, is "the express image" of His Father's person (Hebrews 1:3). He walked the earth as a human being, as a perfect man, and said, in answer to a question put to Him: "He that hath seen me hath seen the Father" (John 14:9). This alone ought to solve the problem to the satisfaction of every thoughtful, reverent mind. The conclusion is irresistible, that if the Son of God be the express image (that is, likeness) of His Father's person, then His Father is in the form of man; for that was the form of the Son of God, not only during His mortal life, but before His mortal birth, and after His resurrection. It was in this form that the Father and the Son, as two personages, appeared to Joseph Smith, when, as a boy of fourteen years, he received his first vision. Then if God made man—the first man—in His own image and likeness, he must have made him like unto Christ, and consequently like unto men of Christ's time and of the present day. That man was made in the image of Christ, is positively stated in the book of Moses: "And I, God, said unto mine Only Begotten, which was with me from the beginning, Let us make man in our image, after our likeness; and it was so. . . . And I, God, created man in mine own image, in the image of mine Only Begotten created I him, male and female created I them" (2:26, 27).

The Father of Jesus is our Father also. Jesus Himself taught this truth, when He instructed His disciples how to pray: "Our Father which art in heaven," etc. Jesus, however, is the firstborn among all the sons of God—the first begotten in the spirit, and the only begotten in the flesh. He is our elder brother, and we, like Him, are in the image of God. All men and women are in the similitude of the universal Father and Mother, and are literally the sons and daughters of Deity.

"God created man in His own image." This is just as true of the spirit as it is of the body, which is only the clothing of the spirit, its complement; the two together constituting the soul. The spirit of man is in the form of man, and the spirits of all creatures are in the likeness of their bodies. This was plainly taught by the Prophet Joseph Smith (Doctrine and Covenants 77:2). . . .

Adam, our progenitor, "the first man," was, like Christ, a pre-existent spirit, and like Christ he took upon him an appropriate body, the body of a man, and so became a "living soul." The doctrine of the pre-existence,—revealed so plainly, particularly in latter days, pours a wonderful flood of light upon the otherwise mysterious problem of man's origin. It shows that man, as a spirit, was begotten and born of heavenly parents, and reared to maturity in the eternal mansions of the Father, prior to coming upon the earth in a temporal body to undergo an experience in mortality. It teaches that all men existed in the spirit before any man existed in the flesh, and that all who have inhabited the earth since Adam have taken bodies and become souls in like manner.[10]

We Are All Children of God

Implicit in the doctrine of an Only Begotten Son is the eternal verity that all peoples of the earth are also sons and daughters of God. We rightfully and properly address our Creator as our Father in Heaven. We presume the familiarity of addressing him in such a manner because in reality we are his children; he fathered our spirits. Spirits, we know by modern revelation, have form and are the prototype of the physical body and the resurrected body which will follow. Christ is the pattern. When he appeared as a spirit personage to the brother of Jared, he appeared as he would in the flesh; and when he appeared in the flesh during his mortal ministry, he appeared as he would in the resurrection. True enough, the resurrection will bring its corrections, giving us each a perfect body to house our spirits in the worlds to come; nevertheless, the likeness of the spirit forms the appearance of the body, and both body and spirit are eternal. People have no problem or difficulty recognizing each other in the world of the spirits, nor will we have any such difficulty in the resurrection.

By revelation we are also told the Only Begotten of the Father is the creator of worlds without number and that in and through him the inhabitants thereof "are begotten sons and daughters unto God" (see Moses 1:27–33; D&C 76:22–24). Thus the doctrine of an Only Begotten Son extends to the countless creations of Christ under the direction of our Heavenly Father. Those of other worlds were also created in the image and likeness of their eternal parents; all children are.

They too pray to their Creator as their Father in Heaven. Having penned scripture to this effect, Joseph Smith also declared it in poetic form as follows:

> And I heard a great voice, bearing record from heav'n,
>   He's the Saviour, and only begotten of God—
> By him, of him, and through him, the worlds were all made,
>   Even all that career in the heavens so broad,
>
> Whose inhabitants, too, from the first to the last,
>   Are sav'd by the very same Saviour of ours;
> And, of course, are begotten God's daughters and sons,
>   By the very same truths, and the very same pow'rs.[11]

We refer to the system of salvation as one eternal round. In doing so we do not mean an endless evolutionary system but rather the extension of the family unit. This is the grand key that unlocks an understanding of the eternities. Thus it is that we read in the book of Moses that "a genealogy was kept of the children of God. And this was the book of the generations of Adam, saying: In the day that God created man, in the likeness of God made he him; in the image of his own body, male and female, created he them, and blessed them [in their marriage union], and called their name Adam. . . . And Adam lived one hundred and thirty years, and begat a son in his own likeness, after his own image, and called his name Seth." (Moses 6:8–10.)

Salvation in a Name

There is power in the name of Deity. Indeed, salvation is found in taking upon ourselves the name of our God. Only those doing so can be saved. (See Mosiah 5:8–10; Alma 5:38–39; D&C 18:21–25.) A name implies possession. There are a lot of lovely women in the world, one of whom is my wife. She can be identified by the fact that she bears my name. Together we are the parents of children. They too are identifiable by the fact that they bear our name. So it is with Christ. He has invited us to take his name upon us as a means of declaring allegiance. To bear that name means we belong to him, that we are his children and as such are rightful heirs to all that he has. Such is the system of salvation.

Shortly after their expulsion from the Garden of Eden, an angel of the Lord visited Adam and Eve and instructed them in the doctrine of names. "Wherefore," the angel said, "thou shalt do all that thou doest in the name of the Son, and thou shalt repent and call upon God in the name of the Son forevermore" (Moses 5:8).

We are redeemed, or freed, from the effects of the Fall only in and through the grace of Christ, the Only Begotten Son of God. There is no good work that we can perform that will enable us to resurrect ourselves. We cannot remit our own sins. His name, properly invoked, brings forth all the blessings of heaven. We take that name upon us in a sacred covenant. To improperly use that name is to violate the terms of that covenant. It is to take the name of the Lord in vain. To change the name is to belong to another. It is to violate the terms of salvation.

A dramatic illustration of this is found in the way the word *Elohim* has been interpreted. When left untampered with and thus in a plural form it embraces various levels of understanding—including the role of Christ and others who participated in the labor of creation. It also includes the role of our Mother in Heaven, who is one with the Father in the creation of all of his children, as husband and wife are one in that creation which is the earthly counterpart of the eternal system. This in turn means that we are their heirs, and that as such it is our destiny as we grow to maturity to become as they are. It means that salvation is a family affair and that both marriage and the family unit were intended to endure throughout the endless expanses of eternity.

In contrast, if the word *Elohim* as used in the Creation account is thought of as singular, when we are told that we are in the image and likeness of God it can be argued that this is only a metaphor, for God, the argument goes, is not a personal being and we have no rightful claim to our physical bodies throughout the eternities. This in turn means the body is not godlike and thus has no place in heaven. Motherhood and marriage, in like manner, would no longer be a part of our heavenly state; they and the family would simply be temporary accommodations to a fallen world. And thus the entire plan of salvation has been derailed. This view of God holds in contempt such things as the physical body, love, and the companionship of family and spouse. Those gifts of God that make this life most meaningful, according to this system of theology, are but evidences of the Fall. The body, the love shared between husband and wife and between parents and children—these things are viewed as a part of the bondage of sin, from which we will be freed in the world to come. God, according to such reasoning, is the great abstraction, and our destiny is to be equally abstract.

Such interpretive tampering with holy writ has the effect of robbing all the children of God of their divine inheritance as his sons and daughters. It strips the tree of life of all its fruits, while making God and heaven a great mystery. Surely the greatest truths are opposed by the greatest heresies. No one understood this better than Moses, the author of the texts we have been considering. Singularly, he confronted the prince of darkness face-to-face over this very issue. The scriptural account of this confrontation, once a part of holy writ, was numbered among the plain and precious things expunged from the Old Testament by designing men. Properly it became one of the first to be restored in this, the dispensation of the fulness of times.

Satan came, saying: "Moses, son of man, worship me."

"Who art thou?" Moses responded. "For behold, I am a son of God, in the similitude of his Only Begotten; and where is thy glory, that I should worship thee?" Moses was able to discern the efforts of the great counterfeiter of all spiritual truths because Satan was without glory, while Moses had to be transfigured to stand in the presence of the true and living God. "Get thee hence, Satan; deceive me not; for God said unto me: Thou art after the similitude of mine Only Begotten. And he also gave me commandments when he called unto me out of the burning bush, saying"—and here Moses had been given the key words that unlock all the blessings of heaven—"Call upon God in the name of mine Only Begotten, and worship me."

Again Satan was told to depart. He refused to do so and commanded Moses, saying: "I am the Only Begotten, worship me." Satan ranted, and Moses feared exceedingly as the bitterness of hell opened before him. Nevertheless, using the formula given him on Sinai, Moses called upon God, and again commanded Satan to leave.

Satan trembled, the earth shook, and Moses, calling upon God once more, said, "In the name of the Only Begotten, depart hence, Satan." Wailing, and gnashing his teeth, Satan reluctantly departed. (Moses 1:12–23.) That he has repeatedly returned in his attempts to be worshipped as God will come as no surprise.

The Knowledge of God

In the spring of 1820 when Joseph Smith came out of that grove that we have since regarded as sacred, he knew more about God than any man on earth. His knowledge was born of experience. He was earth's most competent witness of both the reality and the nature of God. In the ensuing years, that knowledge would continue to grow and deepen, yet at that time the young prophet knew that the Father and the Son were personal beings and that the Son exactly resembled his Father in features and likeness.[12] He also knew that the faith of a humble boy could rend the heavens, that God spoke, and that all of the various sects were wrong: "The Personage who addressed me said that all their creeds were an abomination in his sight; that those professors were all corrupt" (see Joseph Smith—History 1:17–19). The language is harsh, but it is God's and it is true. One cannot drink the dregs of corruption without being corrupted. When Adam and the doctrine of the Fall become myth and when God becomes an unknowable mystery, all else that one professes in the name of Deity has been corrupted. Beliefs shape actions. If we believe that God is unknowable, will we not also suppose that we can participate in some actions that will remain unknown, that somehow we can escape the consequences of improper behavior?

Joseph Smith's parting of the heavens was to be followed by a series of events, each of which would bring men closer to God and God closer to men. In May of 1829 both the Aaronic and Melchizedek Priesthoods were restored.[13] By revelation, Joseph Smith was told that the Melchizedek Priesthood was to govern the teaching of the gospel and that it also held "the key of the mysteries of the kingdom, even the key of the knowledge of God" (D&C 84:19).

As used in this context, a "mystery" is any knowledge that can be known only by revelation. Thus all knowledge of God and the principles of his gospel are mysteries. That is, they are and will be unknown to the citizenry of the world until each individually chooses to approach God in the same spirit as did the youthful Joseph Smith. All must ask. All must have knowledge and experience that is firsthand. With the restoration of the higher priesthood came the keys whereby men, as they grow in the realm of spiritual things, can come to know God in the perfect sense of the word. "The power and authority of the higher, or Melchizedek Priesthood, is to hold the keys of all the spiritual blessings of the church—to have the privilege of receiving the mysteries of the kingdom of heaven, to have the heavens opened unto them, to commune with the general assembly and church of the Firstborn, and to enjoy the communion and presence of God the Father, and Jesus the mediator of the new covenant" (D&C 107:18–19).

4

How can you say, "We are wise, we have the law of the Lord,"
when scribes with their lying pens have falsified it?
                                    —New English Bible, Jeremiah 8:8

And after they go forth by the hand of the twelve apostles of the
Lamb, from the Jews unto the Gentiles, thou seest the formation of
that great and abominable church, which is most abominable above
all other churches; for behold, they have taken away from the
gospel of the Lamb many parts which are plain and most precious;
and also many covenants of the Lord have they taken away.
    And all this have they done that they might pervert the right
ways of the Lord, that they might blind the eyes and harden the
hearts of the children of men.
                                    —1 Nephi 13:26–27

Textual Tampering

M y secretary came into my office to see if I would be able to talk
to a Ms. Marshall who had stopped at the mission home to ask
a few questions about the Church. I said I would be pleased to do so.
In a few moments I was introduced to a woman about forty years of
age. She said that she was a Sunday school teacher in one of the local
churches, that their course of study was comparative religions, and
that she was giving a lesson on the Mormons that Sunday and thought
that it would be helpful if she could ask someone some questions.

How Do Latter-day Saints Differ from
the Churches of the World?

The moment she was seated she asked: "How do you differ from
the major Christian faiths?"

51

"Entirely," I said, though I couldn't suppress the smile that accompanied the answer. Nor was I quick to add anything to it; I wanted it distinctively silhouetted in her mind. After a moment or two I commenced to explain. We are not Catholic, nor are we Protestant; we are a restored church. I gave her a brief account of the First Vision. I told her that from that vision we learned that the Father and the Son are separate and distinct, just as they are consistently depicted in the New Testament.

"Didn't Jesus say that if they had seen him they had seen the Father?" she queried.

"Yes," I responded. "In fact, Joseph Smith told us that they exactly resembled each other in features and likeness."[1] I also explained that in the First Vision, Christ told Joseph Smith that the creeds of Christendom, which attempt to combine the Father, the Son, and the Holy Ghost into one essence, were an abomination in his sight (see Joseph Smith—History 1:19).

"Do you mean that you do not embrace the doctrine of the Holy Trinity?" she asked.

"We most assuredly do not. Our religion takes us back to the pure intention of the Bible. If you can find a thing in either the Old Testament or the New Testament that justifies the doctrine of the Trinity I will give you the deed to this house." (The mission office was attached to the mission home, a 130-year-old mansion.)

She raised her eyebrows and pulled back in her chair. The motion bespoke the fact that she was standing at the edge of her understanding and wanted to get back on more secure ground. It was obvious that she, like most Christians, was very uncomfortable about the doctrine of the Trinity. She said that she didn't feel that the church necessarily had to be right about everything. Its purpose, she explained, was to be a shelter where people of faith could come to worship.

I wondered why people were willing to be so tolerant with what they knew to be wrong in their own churches while being so intolerant of Mormonism, but I said nothing. She admitted that she had struggled with the mystery of the Trinity, that she could not resolve it and had concluded that the Father and the Son were separate, as the scriptures indicated, and of one essence, as the creeds held. Somehow both were right.

I refrained from telling her that such a view would have labeled her a heretic a few centuries earlier.

"Let me show you something," I said. I handed her a book that contained eight parallel translations of the New Testament. I had turned it to John 3:16, and I now called her attention to that verse. The King James reads: "For God so loved the world, that he gave his only begotten Son, that whosoever believeth in him should not perish, but have everlasting life." I asked if she saw any significant differences in the seven more recent translations.

She looked at them thoughtfully and then responded, "Yes, the King James uses the word *begotten,* the others do not."

"Why was it dropped?" I asked.

"I suppose it is just a difference of semantics," she said.

"Can you see any way in which it could make a difference in our understanding of the nature of God?" I asked.

She was quiet for a moment, and then said, "Yes."

"What would it be?" I asked.

"To say that Jesus is the Only Begotten suggests that the rest of us could also be sons and daughters of God, though not in a physical sense like Jesus."

The clarity of her perception surprised me, nor did it stop there. She quickly added, "But I wouldn't want that to be so, because if it was it would mean that we could become gods."

"Why are you in such a hurry to shut the door on that possibility?" I asked. "Aren't you selling yourself short?"

"No." And there was a sense of crispness in her voice, betraying the feeling that she had been trapped. "We have only one Father in Heaven. He is God and will always be the only God that we have."

"I have only one father," I responded. "He will always be my father. Gratefully nothing in all the eternities can change that. That does not mean, however, that I cannot become like him, that I am not his heir, or that I cannot be a father myself." I kept my eyes locked on hers as we spoke so that she could not slip away from the importance of what I was saying. A sweet spirit attended it. "That message is all over the pages of the Bible," I added. I then quoted Psalm 82:6: "I have said, Ye are gods; and all of you are children of the most High."

"I would like to find a way out of that one," she said.

"Don't," I responded. I told her that Jesus himself quoted this text, affirming his belief in it (see John 10:34). I quoted a number of other texts, including Paul's statement, "The Spirit itself beareth witness with our spirit, that we are the children of God: and if children, then heirs; heirs of God, and joint-heirs with Christ" (Romans 8:16–17).

She was thoughtfully silent for a while, and then said, "I still have trouble with the idea of our being perfect."

I read to her from Ephesians 4:11–13: "And he gave some, apostles; and some, prophets; and some, evangelists; and some, pastors and teachers: for the perfecting of the saints, for the work of the ministry, for the edifying of the body of Christ: till we all come in the unity of the faith, and of the knowledge of the Son of God, unto a perfect man, unto the measure of the stature of the fulness of Christ."

I told her that I was a member of a church that believes in those same things, that in our church she would find Apostles and prophets along with the other offices that were a part of the ancient Church. I told her that they labored, as did their ancient counterparts, for the "perfecting of the saints" and that their labors were not in vain. I told her that our purpose in mortality was to obtain a true knowledge of the Son of God so that we might become "perfect," as the text declared, and thus obtain the "stature of the fulness of Christ." Ours, I told her, was the same faith embraced by those about whom she studied in the Bible. I also told her that on one occasion someone approached the Prophet Joseph Smith with the same question that she had asked me, "How does Mormonism differ from the other religious denominations?" He responded by saying, "We believe the Bible, and all other sects profess to believe their interpretations of the Bible, and their creeds."[2]

"Can you see what he meant?" I asked. "We have chosen to accept the plain meaning of the Bible rather than read it through a glass darkly, that is, through the traditions and creeds of Christendom. We stand independent of that tradition. It was our faith that we are, as scripture attests, the sons and daughters of God."

Truth has its own spirit, and she seemed very drawn to it. It was as if she sensed that were she to stay so much as a moment longer she would not want to leave. She pulled away from my desk and almost darted to the door, throwing an expression of appreciation over her shoulder. The scene had the appearance of a little girl running away from home.

Spiritual Blindness

As this woman virtually ran from the mission home, so also she was running from the fact that she could not harmonize the tenets of her faith with the feelings of her heart or the searchings of her mind. Like so many others, she approached her faith with a blind eye, supposing that if she refused to see certain things they would not be there. This matter of selective cognizance is a practiced art among many in the religious world. Classic illustrations include the refusal of the old rabbis to acknowledge the existence of the scriptural texts that announced that the Messiah would also be a light to the hated Gentiles (see Isaiah 42:6; 49:6) and the Protestant refusal to acknowledge the nearly countless scriptural texts which sustain the fact that we will be judged by our works (see Matthew 5:16; 7:20; Revelation 20:12).

Like teenagers embarrassed of their parents, Old Testament theologians are both defensive and apologetic when speaking of the God of ancient Israel. The image of God as portrayed in the Old Testament is typically spoken of as being "naive," "unsophisticated," "crude," "degrading,"[3] "simple," or "primitive."[4] It is a little surprising to find that even the fundamentalist Protestant who argues for the infallibility and the inerrancy of the Bible is quick to disavow the language it uses to describe Deity. At issue here is whether the language of the prophets was intended to be understood literally or figuratively.

Theologically the issue divides itself into two parts—*anthropomorphism,* that is, ascribing human form to God, and *anthropopathism,* that is, ascribing human feelings, attitudes, or passions to God. The God of the scriptures is both anthropomorphic and anthropopathic, while the God of traditional Christianity is neither. Thus the question becomes, Do you adjust your belief to the scriptures or the scriptures to your belief? The Catholic and Protestant worlds have chosen to adjust the scriptures to their belief. This is where the grand key of mischief proves so helpful. All that they need do to accomplish this is to designate the literal as figurative and where necessary the figurative as literal. In so doing, traditional Christianity follows a well-marked path, a path blazed by Jewish scholars who replaced the prophets they rejected when they denied their faith and were scattered because of their wickedness and disbelief.

It will be remembered that approximately six hundred years before the birth of Christ, Lehi was commanded to take his family and leave Jerusalem. They did so to avoid the destruction and captivity that was about to come upon the Jewish nation as the Lord chastened the Jews at the hands of the Babylonians. Only repentance and a return to the worship of the God of their fathers could stay the calamity. Many prophets, Lehi among their number, sought to warn the people of the impending disaster. Summarizing his father's experiences, Nephi wrote: "And when the Jews heard these things they were angry with him; yea, even as with the prophets of old, whom they had cast out, and stoned, and slain; and they also sought his life, that they might take it away" (1 Nephi 1:20). Apostasy, which always embraces a rejection of the true and living God and of responsibility for sin, was not new to this people.

Translating the Old Testament into Greek

After they were taken from the Holy Land, generation after generation of Jews grew up in captivity. To provide for themselves required fluency in the language of their new homelands. In the natural course of time and events, the knowledge of Hebrew, the language of the scriptures, was lost to them. In the great cities of the day it was replaced by Greek, then the universal language of learning and trade. At first, in their worship services the law was read in Hebrew, with someone giving an oral translation. As time went on, a written Greek version was provided so that it could be read directly.

As with virtually everything else, a legend attached itself to this Greek version of the law. The tradition maintained that the work of translation was done by seventy-two elders of Israel, six from each tribe, who were brought for that purpose to Alexandria in Egypt from Jerusalem. The labor is said to have been miraculously accomplished in seventy-two days; thus it is known to us as the Septuagint (LXX), the term coming from the Latin *septuaginta* (seventy), representing the miracle of its translation. According to later accounts, each translator labored in isolation from the others, and when compared, all seventy-two translations matched perfectly.[5] It is the five books of Moses, then, to which the name "Septuagint" chiefly applies; in the third century the name came to be applied to the entire Old Testament in Greek. In any case, the above tradition served to give an aura of authority to the translation of the Hebrew scriptures into Greek.[6]

Perhaps the most distinguishing characteristic of this, the first historically significant Bible translation, was its scrupulous avoidance of anthropomorphisms and phrases that did not seem to sustain the idea of a transcendent God. Like their neighbors, the Jews of the third century B.C. wanted a God who transcended human understanding, one who was above and beyond the comprehension of the mortal mind. The god of their captivity, unlike the God of the prophets whose words they were translating, was a mysterious power that ruled the universe. Lehi's son Jacob, in a prophetic description of what had happened, described this process, saying that the Jews "were a stiff-necked people" who "despised the words of plainness, and killed the prophets" while seeking in their stead "for things that they could not understand. Wherefore, because of their blindness, which blindness came by looking beyond the mark, they must needs fall; for God hath taken away his plainness from them, and delivered unto them many things which they cannot understand, because they desired it. And because they desired it God hath done it, that they may stumble." (Jacob 4:14.)

The LXX is famed for its effort to change the language of scripture so that its readers might be in the image and likeness of the god of the Greek philosophers rather than the God of their fathers. The passage in Exodus 4:16 where Moses is told that he will be "instead of God" (one modern translation renders this "as God") to Aaron was changed in the LXX to read: "Thou shalt be for him in things pertaining to God." Such a change does not accord well with the promise recorded in the book of Moses: "I, the Almighty, have chosen thee, and thou shalt be made stronger than many waters; for they shall obey thy command as if thou wert God" (Moses 1:25). The passage in verse 24 of Exodus 4 which states that Moses met "the Lord" was changed in the LXX to say that he met "the angel of the Lord." Similarly, Exodus 5:3, where it states that God "hath met with us," was changed to read, "has called us." Exodus 15:3, which reads, in part, "The Lord is a man of war," was changed to, "The Lord bringing wars to nought." In the LXX, Moses no longer goes "up unto God in the mount, but goes "up to the mount of God" (see Exodus 19:3). Exodus 24:10, where the text states that Moses, Aaron, Aaron's two sons, and seventy elders of Israel "saw the God of Israel" and the "paved work of a sapphire stone" under his feet, was changed to read, "They saw the place where the

God of Israel stood." In the following verse where the text affirms that the seventy elders saw God and he "laid not his hand" upon them, the LXX translators had it read, "They appeared in the place of God." Similarly, "the sons of God" (Genesis 6:2) became "the angels of God." In Numbers 12:8, where God says he will speak to Moses "mouth to mouth," the LXX reads, "mouth to mouth apparently." In Joshua where the Hebrew Bible referred to the "hand" of the Lord, the LXX changed it to the "power" (see Joshua 4:24).[7]

Thus expressions concerning God, which were regarded as crude or offensive, were softened, and anthropomorphisms were frequently removed. In many cases the translator accomplished this by playing with the Hebrew roots.[8] That the translators were deliberately influencing the content of the book is beyond question. As one source explains, the "LXX had numerous words, phrases, or even whole paragraphs with no counterpart in the Hebrew. On the other hand, the reverse was also often the case."[9]

Commenting on this, Elder Bruce R. McConkie observed:

> The translation of the Septuagint from Hebrew to Greek illustrates the problems that have attended translations ever since. Aside from the sorry state of the text due to scholastic incompetence, there was a far more serious problem, namely, the theological bias of the translators. This caused them to change the meaning or paraphrase texts that were either unclear or embarrassing to them. Concrete terms in Hebrew came out as abstract terms in Greek. Expressions about God—deemed by the Greek translators to be crude or offensive because they described Deity as the Holy Man that he is, rather than the immanent spirit they supposed him to be—were changed or toned down or deleted entirely. Passages setting forth the so-called anthropomorphic nature of Deity were simply assumed by the translators to be false and were translated, paraphrased, and changed accordingly.[10]

This textual tampering would be followed in later Hellenism (that is, Greek tradition) by interpretive tampering, namely, the allegorizing of the Old Testament. Philosophical concepts were substituted for the Bible's anthropomorphism. The rabbis described anthropomorphisms as divine accommodations to human frailty, though they themselves could not avoid them as they prayed to God as Father, spoke of his ears, hands, and other body parts, and referred to his weeping over Jerusalem.[11] It was hoped that the LXX would make the religion of the Jews, if not attractive, at least respectable in the new world in which the Jews were now living. Yet, if it did nothing to convert or enlighten the Gentiles, "it must," as F. E. Peters observes in his *Harvest of Hellenism*, "have had considerable effect in Hellenizing the Jews."[12] By the Middle Ages the great Jewish writer Maimonides was prepared to declare, as the *Encyclopaedia Judaica* states, "that every anthropomorphism was outright heresy."[13]

Significantly, virtually every manuscript of the LXX that has survived, with the exception of what was found in the Dead Sea caves, comes from Christian rather than Jewish sources. There are two primary reasons the Jews lost interest in the LXX. First, the Christians from the first century A.D. onwards adopted it as their version of the Old Testament and used it with some effect in their missionary efforts. Those efforts were obviously directed against the Jews, the only other .people with a scriptural heritage. Second, during the same time period a revised standardized text was established for the Hebrew Bible by Jewish scholars. When this text was fixed, versions in other languages fit for Jewish use were expected to conform to it. This translation is known as the Masoretic text. Thereafter the LXX was represented as the work of Satan, and the accursed day upon which the seventy-two elders wrote the law in Greek was compared to the day on which Israel had made the golden calf. The Jews then sustained their indignation with an annual day of fasting and humiliation to atone for that profanation.[14]

The Scribal Transformation of God

In a classic work edited by James Hastings, we read that the Jewish concept of God was based on tradition, "not on the spiritual teaching of the Prophets. God was put further and further away; the conception of Him became increasingly abstract and transcendental."[15] The idea was to remove God as far as possible from direct contact with man and the world. He is pictured in the Jerusalem Talmud, our source tells us, "as a great Rabbi. He studies the Law three hours each day, and observes all its ordinances. He keeps the Sabbath. He makes vows, and on their accomplishment He is released

by the heavenly Sanhedrin. . . . Thus the external, ceremonial conception of religion at last took complete possession of the future world,
and threw the mesh of its enslavement to the letter even around God
Himself. The prophet's spiritual conception of Jehovah was lost; the
glow of lovingkindness which they held in His face faded out utterly,
and there remained a Being who was called 'the Holy One,' interesting
perhaps to the scribe, but whom no one could really love."

The observation is then made: "To this conception of God the revelation of His Fatherhood by Jesus formed an absolute contrast. The
scribes put God in the seventh heaven; Jesus taught that He is near.
The scribes held that He is intensely concerned with outward ordinances; Jesus taught that He is full of love, and cares only for the heart
of man. To the scribal mind God was the God of scribes; to Jesus He
was the Father of all men."[16]

These traditions reflect the changes that were being made, not just
in the way Israel was interpreting the scriptures but also in the way
they were being copied and passed from generation to generation.
Thus we have the Savior lamenting and sounding a warning to the
scribes of his day, "Woe unto you, lawyers! for ye have taken away the
key of knowledge: ye entered not in yourselves, and them that were
entering in ye hindered" (Luke 11:52). In his translation of this verse,
Joseph Smith makes a significant clarification that bespeaks the whole
story. It reads, "Ye have taken away the key of knowledge, *the fulness of
the scriptures;* ye enter not in yourselves *into the kingdom; and those who*
were entering in ye hindered" (JST, Luke 11:52, emphasis added).[17]
Nor are we to suppose that there was anything new in these scribes'
craft. Some six hundred years earlier, Jeremiah also lamented, saying:
"How do ye say, We are wise, and the law of the Lord is with us? Lo,
certainly in vain made he it; the pen of the scribes is in vain."
(Jeremiah 8:8.) The New English Bible gives us a plainer rendering of
the text: "How can you say, 'We are wise, we have the law of the Lord,'
when scribes with their lying pens have falsified it?"

Interestingly, Justin Martyr, writing in the second century A.D.,
preserves for us two examples of the kinds of things that were taken
from the writings of Jeremiah himself. From the sayings of Jeremiah,
he said,

> they have cut out the following: "I [was] like a lamb that is
> brought to the slaughter: they devised a device against me, saying,

Come, let us lay on wood on His bread, and let us blot Him out from the land of the living; and His name shall no more be remembered." And since this passage from the sayings of Jeremiah is still written in some copies [of the Scriptures] in the synagogues of the Jews (for it is only a short time since they were cut out), and since from these words it is demonstrated that the Jews deliberated about the Christ Himself, to crucify and put Him to death, He Himself is both declared to be led as a sheep to the slaughter, as was predicted by Isaiah, and is here represented as a harmless lamb; but being in a difficulty about them, they give themselves over to blasphemy. And again, from the sayings of the same Jeremiah these have been cut out: "The Lord God remembered His dead people of Israel who lay in the graves; and He descended to preach to them His own salvation."[18]

As to New Testament manuscripts, we have an old text in which Peter is reported as writing to James, saying: "They think they are able to interpret my own words better than I can, telling their hearers that they are conveying my very thoughts to them, while the fact is that such things never entered my mind. If they take such outrageous liberties while I am alive, what will they do after I am gone!"[19]

The Transformation of God in the Masoretic Text

Tampering with the text was seen as the antidote to the impiety of the ancient prophets. "As a result," Michael Fishbane observes in his scholarly work *Biblical Interpretation in Ancient Israel,* "words, letters, and syntax were variously manipulated. Traditions regarding such intentional scribal corrections go back to antiquity. It is a phenomenon attested both among the Alexandrian grammarians and copyists, and in contemporary rabbinic sources."[20] One scholarly source suggests, "The many differences between synoptic portions of the [Old Testament] strongly suggest that the priests entrusted with the responsibility of teaching the Bible felt free to revise the text."[21] Indeed, we are told that "some liberal-minded scribes altered the text for both philological and theological reasons. . . . They supplemented and clarified the text by the insertion of additions and the interpolation of glosses [glosses being marginal notes written by earlier scribes that were then added to the text] from parallel passages. In addition, they substituted euphemisms for vulgarities, altered the names of false gods, removed the harsh phrase 'curse God,' and safe-guarded the sacred divine name by failing to pronounce the tetragrammaton (*YHWH* [*Yahweh*]) and occasionally by substituting other forms in the consonantal text."[22]

The justification for such changes was the honor of God. It was the pagan element that was being removed. Then, as now, that which was adjudged pagan was that which did not conform to accepted traditions or popular notions. Fishbane writes: "Those persons most responsible for maintaining the orthography [correct writing] of the texts tampered with their wording so as to preserve the religious dignity of these documents according to contemporary theological tastes. However, the rabbis did not have to look to the neighbouring Alexandrian scribes for motivation. They were themselves heir to an older, native tradition. Thus, not only do the old rabbinic lists preserve considerable older biblical traditions of scribal corrections, but there are also examples of theological corrections in the MT [Masoretic text] unattested in rabbinic literature."[23] As noted earlier, the Masoretic (*Masora*, meaning traditional) text is the traditional Hebrew text of the Old Testament.

Further on, Fishbane states: "Thus, an analysis of several old liturgical settings shows how references to the pagan 'gods' and their assemblies have been transformed"—that is to say, references to Elohim and heavenly councils have been tampered with. "In a related vein, one can still detect a theological sensitivity to the fact that the divine name Elohim is a collective plural, originally meaning 'gods.' As in later rabbinic times, when there was recurrent concern to emphasize the unity of the creator, and to leave no room for any biblical support to heretical speculations of divine multiplicity ('that they . . . do not say: "there are many powers in heaven"'—*M. Sanh.* iv.5), ancient Israelite scribes were attentive to ambiguous formulations and 'corrected' such potential trouble-spots."[24] Illustrations include the instance in Exodus where the children of Israel asked Aaron to make them "gods" to worship (see Exodus 32;4, 23). In these passages, plural verbs are used with the plural "gods." We find that a later reference to the same event is rendered with the singular "God" and with a corresponding singular verb (see Nehemiah 9:18). The Masoretic text changes the Exodus passages so that they read singular.[25] In Exodus 22:20, where we read, "He that sacrificeth unto any god, save unto the

Lord only, he shall be utterly destroyed," the phrase "save unto the Lord only" is apparently a scribal addition designed to clarify any ambiguity caused by the word *Elohim*.[26] In Exodus 34:24, where we read that men were to "appear before the Lord," the text originally read that they were "to see" God, implying God had form. The text was altered, according to the *Encyclopaedia Judaica*, "to avoid an objectionable anthropomorphism."[27]

Perhaps the classic illustration for Latter-day Saints of this business of textual tampering is found in Psalm 8:4–5, which reads: "What is man, that thou art mindful of him? and the son of man, that thou visitest him? For thou hast made him a little lower than the angels, and hast crowned him with glory and honour." A footnote in the LDS edition of the Bible indicates that the word translated as "angels" (*Elohim* in the original) should have been translated "gods." Thus the text ought to read, "Thou hast made him a little lower than the gods," an idea that would scandalize those whose theology is rooted in Hellenism.

Referring to the examples of textual changes that he gives in his book, Fishbane concludes: "The striking fact about such theological changes as the foregoing is their non-systematic nature. Indeed, in many instances a word was left intact in one place though changed elsewhere. This inconsistency suggests that many of these changes were the product of isolated scribes or scribal schools. It is thus rare to find even fairly systematic revisions of these theological trouble-spots, such as one can regularly find even in such so-called 'vulgar' or popular textual traditions as the Samaritan."[28]

Textual Tampering in the New Testament

As far as we know, Jesus wrote nothing. Those called to be his special witnesses were not, at least as far as the story tells us, called because they had any special qualifications for literary composition. This was not the sort of thing to which we would expect them to be naturally inclined, but then neither was preaching. Their writings, Paul's included, were supplementary to their oral teachings. Such writings were generally called out by emergencies, like the squabbling within the church at Corinth or the constant efforts of the Judaizers to undo Paul's missionary efforts with the Gentiles. These epistles were generally sent by messengers who were expected to amplify them. Church leaders did not write with the idea that what they wrote would be compiled into a volume of scripture. For the New Testament Church, the scriptures were the writings of the Old Testament prophets, which had not as yet been compiled into book form. It was not a book of scripture that directed the Church. Nor, for that matter, was it a statement of creed or traditions of any sort. Apostles and prophets, men directed by the Holy Ghost, constituted the constitution of the Church.

We know that John was ordained in the councils of heaven long before his birth to pen the words that he did (see 1 Nephi 14:24–27). It seems reasonable to suppose that the others who contributed to what we know today as the New Testament were prepared in a like manner. We also know that the things these men wrote would be tampered with and that the tampering would take place in large measure *before* their records would go forth to the nations of the earth (see 1 Nephi 13:29).

The safety of the early Church rested in the living voices of those whom the Lord had called. Eusebius (ca. A.D. 260–339), the earliest writer of church history, records: "But when the sacred band of the apostles had in various ways reached the end of their life, and the generation of those privileged to listen with their own ears to the divine wisdom had passed on, then godless error began to take shape, through the deceit of false teachers, who now that none of the apostles was left threw off the mask and attempted to counter the preaching of the truth by preaching the knowledge falsely so called."[29]

A book on early church history by Edward Backhouse, published in the nineteenth century, observes: "One of the hindrances with which Christianity had to contend from within, was the publication of Spurious Gospels and pretended apostolic canons. Many of these writings are believed to have been fabricated by heretical sects and parties in the Church, for the purpose of supporting their views of doctrine and practice."[30] Most apocryphal works, whether they were written in Old or New Testament times, fall into the category of pious frauds or lying for God. Their purpose was to give credibility to doctrines not taught by the Apostles and prophets and to make it appear that these men were their authors. In this connection author John Romer states:

> Like Paul, who wrote the oldest known Christian texts of the New Testament, many other Christians were also writing mystical narrations, poems, stories, abstract speculations; there were people

who saw their faith as Paul did, in terms of the culture from which they had come. By the second century, there were more than a dozen gospels circulating, along with a whole library of other texts. These included letters of Jesus to foreign kings, letters of Paul to Aristotle, histories of the disciples and of many other characters in Jesus' life and times. And despite the fact that they were all outlawed by the later church, many of these writings quietly survived in Christendom to become a source, a secret source, of mystic Christian knowledge. Indeed, their influence upon Christian art and literature is much greater than is generally realized. In a religion where faith is usually held in the written word, much of the gesture and symbolism of Christian ritual can be traced to these forgotten and once-forbidden sects.[31]

In the work by Backhouse, cited above, we read: "The falsification of the gospels, and even of his own letters, is complained of by Dionysius, Bishop of Corinth (A.D. 168–177). 'As the brethren,' he says, 'desired me to write epistles, I wrote them; and these the apostles of the devil have filled with tares, exchanging some things and adding others, for whom there is a woe reserved. It is not [a] matter of wonder if some have attempted to adulterate the sacred writings of the Lord, since they have done so with those which are not to be compared with them.'"[32]

Paul's Second Epistle to the Thessalonians was written to counter false notions that may have arisen, in part, from what some have thought to be a forged letter (see 2 Thessalonians 2:2). In his work *The Original New Testament,* Hugh J. Schonfield observes: "The practice [of forgery] was common and not considered so immoral in those days. The Nazarene 'Zealots for the Law' were no doubt responsible. These did all they could to turn Paul's converts against him, with considerable success, and did not scruple to pervert his teaching. See Romans 3:8."[33]

A writer quoted by Eusebius indicated that corrupted manuscripts were so prevalent that agreement between copies was hopeless. Those who had thus "adulterate[d] the simplicity of that faith contained in the holy Scriptures," as the writer states, and "mutilate[d] the Scriptures" claimed to have corrected them.[34] Authorities tell us that "the worst corruptions to which the New Testament has ever been subjected, originated within a hundred years after it was composed,"[35] which accords perfectly with the prophecy of Nephi wherein he tells us that the writings of the Apostles would be altered before they went forth to the nations of the earth (see 1 Nephi 13:24–29).

Celsus, the sharp-tongued anti-Christian writer of the second century, observed: "It is clear to me that the writings of the Christians are a lie, and that your fables have not been well enough constructed to conceal this monstrous fiction. I have even heard that some of your interpreters, as if they had just come out of a tavern, are onto the inconsistencies and, pen in hand, alter the original writings three, four, and several more times over in order to be able to deny the contradictions in the face of criticism."[36]

It was the forging of apostolic writings that awakened the interest in collecting and preserving those things thought to be genuine.[37] The difficulty was that there was no uniform agreement on what was apostolic and what was spurious. Eusebius becomes our source here. He tells us that the books vying for inclusion in the New Testament canon were categorized as "recognized," "disputed," and "spurious." The recognized books were the Gospels, Acts, the epistles of Paul, 1 John, and 1 Peter. Disputed books were James, Jude, 2 Peter, and 2 and 3 John. The spurious writings included the Acts of Paul, the Shepherd, the Apocalypse of Peter, Barnabas, the Teachings of the Apostles, and the book of Revelation.[38] Somehow the book of Revelation gained respectability while others of the "spurious" books were included in various Bibles for only short periods of time.

The Ongoing Tradition of Textual Tampering

There are those apologists for the Bible who argue that despite the difficulties the book has seen, the hand of the Lord has been over it in such a manner as to guarantee that it has come to us in the manner that the Lord desired. Should integrity replace emotion, it must be admitted, as the King James translators did, that there are "too many" discrepancies to claim them all good. Nephi told us that because of the "plain and precious things" that were taken from the texts, "an exceedingly great many do stumble, yea, insomuch that Satan hath great power over them" (1 Nephi 13:29).

Joseph Smith's study of the Bible confirmed for him the prophecy of Nephi. The Prophet said, "From sundry revelations which had been received, it was apparent that many important points touching the salvation of men, had been taken from the Bible, or lost before it was compiled."[39] He also said: "I believe the Bible as it read when it came from the pen of the original writers. Ignorant translators, careless transcribers, or designing and corrupt priests have committed many errors."[40]

As to our own day and age, scriptural tampering continues at perhaps even a quickened pace. Reference was made at the beginning of this chapter to how modern Bible translations have dropped the doctrine of Christ's being the "Only Begotten Son of God." Some radical feminist movements provide a current example as they rewrite scripture and redefine the nature of God to conform to their political agenda. Their efforts reach far beyond granting priesthood and its offices to women. They include a thorough purging of traditional, or historical, Christian theology and a rewriting of the Bible. References to God as male are either eliminated or neutralized by making them both feminine and masculine. For instance, where we once read that "he" (Christ) was the Word, and that the world was made by "him," and that "he" came unto his own and they received "him" not, we now are invited to read the doctrine thus: "The Word was in the world, and the world was made through the Word, yet the world did not know the Word. The Word came to the Word's own home, but those to whom the Word came did not receive the Word." (See John 1:10–11.)[41] And where we once read the command of the Lord that his disciples go to all nations and people, "baptizing them in the name of the Father, and of the Son, and of the Holy Ghost," the new feminist revelation reads, "Go therefore and make disciples of all nations, baptizing them in the name of God the Father and Mother and of Jesus Christ the beloved Child and of the Holy Spirit" (see Matthew 28:19).[42]

For the radical feminist the issue is clear. If God is thought of as male, then people will equate power with maleness. The doctrine must be that God does not have gender and that he must not be addressed as Father, or our Savior as God's Son. Nor is the idea that Deity may be addressed as both Father and Mother wholly acceptable to some, because this suggests the dreadful dualism or paganism that all the twisting and contorting of language in the creeds have sought to avoid. Somehow the new God must embrace both masculinity and femininity without having sexual gender.

In keeping with such trends, the student of the Bible now has available to him a work titled *The Five Gospels,* which reevaluates everything in the Gospels attributed to Jesus.[43] It uses a color-coding process: red print for those words a scholarly seminar felt definitely were those of Jesus, pink print for those words that were likely his, gray print for those things that it was doubtful were his and black for those things that were judged to be not authentic sayings of Jesus. The seminar concluded that 82 percent of Jesus' words fell into the last category. Also, all references to his being the Messiah, or being divine, are in black print. From a scholarly point of view, Jesus is simply not God's Son.

As we will repeatedly see, the element common to all of these rewritings of scripture is that God gets moved farther and farther from us while our right of heirship as his sons and daughters is lost. According to such theology, nothing in this world represents the reality of the world to come.

The Guardians of Scripture

Elder Bruce R. McConkie wrote: "As long as inspired men are the keepers of holy writ; as long as prophets and apostles are present to identify and perfect the scriptures by revelation; as long as scriptural translations . . . are made by the gift and power of God—all will be well with the written word. But when the gospel sun sets and apostate darkness shrouds the minds of men, the scriptural word is in jeopardy."[44]

The labors of darkness have always included scriptural tampering—declaring the literal to be figurative, replacing scripture with tradition, ignoring the existence of certain texts, and hiding obvious contradictions under the cloak of religious mysteries. Any period of earth's history that is without the authority to pen scripture is also without the authority to interpret scripture, and it is also without the authority to either condemn or canonize that which professes to be scripture. The truths of heaven can be properly taught only by those conversant with the language of heaven. The things of the Spirit are known only to those who have the Spirit. The author and interpreter of all scripture must be God, not man.

5

O Lord, my strength, and my fortress, and my refuge in the day of affliction, the Gentiles shall come unto thee from the ends of the earth, and shall say, Surely our fathers have inherited lies, vanity, and things wherein there is no profit.

Shall a man make gods unto himself, and they are no gods?

Therefore, behold, I will this once cause them to know, I will cause them to know mine hand and my might; and they shall know that my name is The Lord.

—Jeremiah 16:19–21

Traditions of the Fathers

As a young man I was commissioned as a chaplain in the United States Army and given orders to attend a chaplains' training school at Fort Hamilton in New York. There were one hundred chaplains in my class—mostly Catholic and Protestant, a few Jewish chaplains, and I, the lone Mormon boy. We sat at long tables in our classroom. To my right sat a man of some sincerity, a Methodist chaplain by the name of Martin. It was his habit to slip me notes during the course of the day with questions challenging my faith. It was my habit to respond.

"You Can't Say That!"

At one of our morning devotionals I presented a thought from the Doctrine and Covenants; it was not well received, but it did give me the excuse to have my triple combination with me in school that day. When class began I placed it on the table at which I sat, near the imaginary dividing line between Chaplain Martin's table space and mine. For most of the first hour of class he was disdainfully blind to the presence of the book. Then curiosity gained victory over arrogance and he cautiously reached out and took it. He was thumbing through it when his eyes were attracted to a passage in Doctrine and Covenants 130 that I had underlined in red. This passage reads: "The Father has a body of flesh and bones as tangible as man's; the Son also; but the Holy Ghost has not a body of flesh and bones, but is a personage of Spirit. Were it not so, the Holy Ghost could not dwell in us." (D&C 130:22.)

Chaplain Martin understood what he read and it made him angry. His face flushed and his jaw tightened; then, as the bell that ended class rang, he slammed his fist on the table, saying to me: "You can't say that! That's contrary to all the traditions of the fathers!" His words reminded me of something I had memorized as a missionary. I handed him the Bible and invited him to read these words from Jeremiah:

> O LORD, my strength, and my fortress, and my refuge in the day of affliction, the Gentiles shall come unto thee from the ends of the earth, and shall say, Surely our fathers have inherited lies, vanity, and things wherein there is no profit.
>
> Shall a man make gods unto himself, and they are no gods?
>
> Therefore, behold, I will this once cause them to know, I will cause them to know mine hand and my might; and they shall know that my name is The LORD. (Jeremiah 16:19–21.)

My friend's face was now pale and his voice subdued. He simply said, "Well, I must admit you have a scripture for everything."

That, of course, was not the issue. The issue was whether true religion was to be founded on revelation or tradition. On that matter Jeremiah had prophesied of a day when the true and living God would be known by revelation. These revelations, Jeremiah held, would be instrumental in gathering Israel, and with them would come the knowledge that their fathers had "inherited lies, vanity, and things wherein there is no profit" relative to their traditions about God. Let us now retrace the story as to how tradition came to replace revelation.

How the Traditions of Men Replaced Revelation

As the Jews of the Diaspora became imbued with the elements of their new Hellenic culture, they sought a mean between what was fashionable and the religion of their fathers. To this end they availed themselves of the system most in vogue with those who busied themselves with religious matters, that of the Platonic philosophy, which had already become a significant influence in their intellectual life. In order to do so they found it necessary to give the scriptures, as Neander tells us, "a sense foreign to these records themselves, supposing all the while, that they were thus really exalting their dignity as the source of all wisdom."[1] They built the bridge between their love of the scriptures and their headiness with the supposed knowledge of learned men out of that ever flexible essence known as allegory.

The architect of that bridge was a Jewish philosopher-theologian by the name of Philo (ca. 13 B.C.–A.D. 45 to 50). His labors would ultimately have a greater influence in shaping the doctrines of traditional Christianity than even Christ himself. The scion of an ancient priestly family, Philo was a product of the Diaspora. Born in Alexandria, Egypt, at about the same time Christ was born in Bethlehem, Philo's greatest aspiration in life was to reconcile the Jewish scriptures and customs with Greek ideas, and above all else to see that the former were in harmony with the teachings of "the most holy" Plato.[2] To accomplish this end he simply made use of the grand key of mischief—that is, the declaring of the literal to be figurative and, as necessary, the figurative to be literal. Philo's theology was to become very familiar to future generations—God is incorporeal and indescribable; he can be known by reason, though no quality can be ascribed to him, since every quality constitutes a limitation. To perceive God as having human form would be a concession to a sensuous imagination. The labor of the Creation was accomplished with the help of a host of intermediary beings known to the Jews as angels but understood in the language of Plato to simply be ideas. These, said Philo, may popularly be conceived as persons, though in reality they are the thoughts of God and thus exist only in the Divine Mind. Together these powers constitute what the Stoics called the Logos, or Divine Reason, which Reason is responsible for the creation of the world and has been guiding it ever since. Thus the Logos can be thought of as a person, though of course it is not. Philo, in his poetic moments, called the Logos "the first-begotten of God," conceived by the virgin Wisdom. Thus God, who is beyond man's comprehension, could be revealed through the "person" of the Logos, or, more literally, through reason, meaning the reasoning of the philosopher, which is the true Divine Wisdom.[3]

No less a historian than Will Durant concluded that "Philo's Logos was one of the most influential ideas in the history of thought." Thus Philo shared unknowingly in forming Christian theology. Singularly the rabbis had little use for Philo's allegorical interpretations, viewing them as a threat to the literal observance of the laws of Moses and the horde of oral traditions they had heaped on them. Nor was Philo's passion for Greek looked upon by them with any favor. It was seen as leading to cultural assimilation and racial dilution, which in turn they believed would bring the end of their people. The ante-Nicene Fathers, on the other hand, admired Philo's contemplative devotion and made abundant use of his allegorical principles to answer the critics of the Hebrew scriptures, thus finding refuge in his mystical view of God. So the Jewish man who set out to mediate between Hellenism and Judaism found himself, in one of history's ironic twists, as the matchmaker in the union between Christianity and Greek philosophy.[4]

The Greek Fathers of the Christian church identified what they felt to be elements of truth in the Hellenic literature, especially, as Philip Schaff notes in his *History of the Christian Church,* "in the Platonic and Stoic philosophy, and saw in them, as in the law and the prophecies of Judaism, a preparation of the way for Christianity. Justin attributes all the good in heathenism to the divine Logos, who, even before his incarnation, scattered the seeds of truth (hence the name 'Logos spermaticos'), and incited susceptible spirits to a holy walk. Thus there were Christians before Christianity; and among these he expressly reckons Socrates and Heraclitus." This notion of the common origin of Greek philosophy and Christianity was also adopted by the Alexandrian Fathers, Clement and Origen.[5]

The Christians, like the Jews before them, could not resist the seductive reasonableness of the union of two divergent beliefs. And like the Jews before them, they too were embarrassed by the implications of an anthropomorphic God. It was simply not acceptable in the intellectual climate of the Hellenized world to suppose that God could love and hate, that he could get angry or jealous. Further, to suppose that he involved himself immediately in the affairs of the world brought the attendant difficulty of his responsibility for the existence of evil. All such difficulties were resolved by reinterpreting the scriptures metaphorically.[6] Mosheim described this as the loss of the simplicity and beauty of true Christianity. These, he said, were "gradually effaced by the laborious efforts of human learning, and the dark subtilties of imaginary science. Acute researches were employed upon several religious subjects, concerning which ingenious decisions were pronounced; and, what was worst of all, several tenets of a chimerical philosophy were imprudently incorporated into the Christian system." And what brought it all about? Mosheim responds, "The eagerness of certain learned men to bring about a union between the doctrines of Christianity and the opinions of the philosophers; for they thought it a very fine accomplishment, to be able to express the precepts of Christ in the language of *philosophers, civilians, and rabbis.*" In it all, "genuine Christianity almost disappeared," he concluded.[7]

In his work *The Influence of Greek Ideas on Christianity*, Edwin Hatch observes that "it was impossible for Greeks, educated as they were with an education which penetrated their whole nature, to receive or to retain Christianity in its primitive simplicity."[8] As Hatch describes it, Christianity was profoundly modified, though in fact all that was retained of New Testament Christianity was the name. At the conclusion of his work, Hatch suggests that a large part of what are "called Christian doctrines, and many usages which have prevailed and continue to prevail in the Christian Church, are in reality Greek theories and Greek usages changed in form and colour by the influence of primitive Christianity, but in their essence Greek still. Greece lives; not only its dying life in the lecture-rooms of Universities, but also with a more vigorous growth in the Christian Churches."[9] The question that needs answering here is, If a church changes gods but retains the old name, is it still the same religion?

The theology of historical Christianity was not shaped by prophets, nor was it rooted in scripture. During the second century it borrowed from the Jews the concept of God that they adopted after they had replaced prophets with scholars. "The conception, for example, of the one God whose kingdom was a universal kingdom and endured throughout all ages, blended with, and passed into, the philosophical conception of a Being who was beyond time and space," Hatch writes. "The conception that 'clouds and darkness were round about Him,' blended with, and passed into, the philosophical conception of a Being who was beyond not only human sight but human thought. The conception of His transcendence obtained the stronger hold because it confirmed the prior conception of His unity; and that of His incommunicability, and of the consequent need of a mediator, gave a philosophical explanation of the truth that Jesus Christ was His Son."[10]

All of traditional Christianity's speculative theology was forged in the fires of conflict. In each instance some school of Greek thought played a decisive part. The conflict, Hatch holds, had three leading stages—speculations as to (1) the transcendence of God, (2) the manner in which he reveals himself, and (3) his nature. We will briefly consider each.

1. *The Transcendence of God.* A transcendent God is a God who is above and beyond the understanding of man. Seven hundred years before Christian missionaries first knocked on Gentile doors, philosophers had concluded that God constituted the Absolute Being. Unlike the God of the prophets, he was the ultimate generalization of all things, unlimited by body, parts, or form; all of him was sight, all of him was understanding, all of him was hearing. He was the perfect sphere that filled all space, undying and immovable. He was the grand supremacy. God was, according to the Platonic conception, "Mind, a form separate from all matter, that is to say, out of contact with it, and not involved with anything that is capable of being acted on."[11]

To describe a transcendent God is to enumerate what he is not. For instance, he is unborn, undying, uncontained, unheard, unseen, immovable, and incomprehensible. Philo described him thus:

> He is not in space, but beyond it; for He contains it. He is not in time, for He is the Father of the universe, which is itself the father of time, since from its movement time proceeds. He is "without body, parts or passions": without feet, for whither should He walk who fills all things: without hands, for from whom should He receive anything who possesses all things: without eyes, for how should He need eyes who made the light. He is invisible, for how can eyes that are too weak to gaze upon the sun be strong enough to gaze upon its Maker. He is incomprehensible: not even the whole universe, much less the human mind, can contain the conception of Him: we know *that* He is, we cannot know *what* He is: we may see the manifestations of Him in His works, but it were monstrous folly to go behind His works and inquire into His essence. He is hence unnamed: for names are the symbols of created things, whereas His only attribute is to *be*.[12]

2. *The Manner in Which He Reveals Himself.* Since a transcendent God is by definition incommunicable, some kind of intermediate link between him and man was necessary. *Logos* constituted the answer—for the Greeks this could be demons or spirits; any being that was inferior to God but superior to man could provide that link. For second-century Christianity, as it refined Greek philosophy to fit itself, Logos became Jesus the Message, or Word, of God.[13]

3. *His Nature.* God, who is above and beyond having a nature, manifests himself to man through the Logos. This is possible because the human intelligence is an offshoot of the Divine. Standing between God and men, the Logos can reflect God downward and man upward.[14]

The Union of Paganism and Christianity

In the marriage between paganism and Christianity, paganism agreed to take her husband's name and be known as Christian. Solace could be found in the fact that she would be the dominant partner in the marriage. Her hope chest included her transcendent god, which Christianity eventually adopted without modification. In the early Christian teaching the concept of a transcendent God is absent. Initially God was near to men, he spoke to them, he could be angry with them, as appropriate and necessary he would chasten them, he extended his mercy to them, and so forth. When scholars replaced prophets, all of this changed. The philosophical conceptions of God were adopted by the Apologists (the scholars who wrote after the spirit of revelation ceased) and through such adoption found acceptance in Christian communities.

For instance, Justin (ca. 100–165) protested against a literal interpretation of the anthropomorphic expressions in the Old Testament, saying: "You are not to think that the unbegotten God 'came down' from anywhere or 'went up.' For the unutterable Father and Lord of all things neither comes to any place nor walks nor sleeps nor rises, but abides in His own place wherever that place may be, seeing keenly and hearing keenly, not with eyes or ears, but with His unspeakable power, so that He sees all things and knows all things, nor is any one of us hid from Him: nor does He move, He who is uncontained by space and by the whole world, seeing that He was before the world was born."[15]

Athenagoras, a second-century Apologist, defended Christianity against the charge of atheism, stating: "I have sufficiently demonstrated that they are not atheists who believe in One who is unbegotten, eternal, unseen, impassible, incomprehensible and uncontained: comprehended by mind and reason only, invested with ineffable light and beauty and spirit and power, by whom the universe is brought into being and set in order and held firm, through the agency of his own *Logos*."[16]

Theophilus, second-century bishop of Antioch, responded to the challenge to describe the form of the Christian God by stating that he is "incomprehensible," "inconceivable," and "incomparable." He went on to say: "If I speak of Him as light, I mention His handiwork: if I speak of Him as reason, I mention His government: if I speak of Him as spirit, I mention His breath: if I speak of Him as wisdom, I mention His offspring: if I speak of Him as strength, I mention His might: if I speak of Him as providence, I mention His goodness: if I speak of His kingdom, I mention His glory."[17]

As to how this transcendent Christian God manifests himself to man, the answer became—any way he chooses; having all power he can manifest himself in any way that he deems appropriate for the moment. Thus Jesus Christ became the temporary mode of the one God. His manifesting himself as a corporeal being is not to be taken as evidence that he has form or substance. He is also Fire, Wind, and Mind.

The Logos

The God of the Greek philosopher was, as we have seen, unknowable. He (if I can be excused the heresy of a designation which suggests both personhood and masculinity for a God who has neither) was in all things beyond mortal comprehension. He had no body, because he was beyond form; he was neither father nor mother, because he was beyond gender. He had no virtue, because he was beyond virtue; no compassion, because he was beyond compassion. He did not speak or communicate with his creations, because he was beyond speech or communication. Because his greatness defied description, it was reasoned by early Christian writers that we can know only *that* he is but we cannot know *what* he is. Thus anything we say in an affirmative way about him can be true only in a figurative sense. Summarizing the views (clearly Hellenistic in nature) of two influential theologians, one from the sixth century and one from the ninth, a work entitled *The Doctrine of God* states: "Affirmative theology is figurative, metaphorical. It is excelled by negative theology. 'For it is more correct to say that God is not that which is predicated concerning him than to say that he is.'" This line of reasoning leads to the announcement: "'He [God] is known better by him who does not know him, whose true ignorance is wisdom.'" God having now been removed from the understanding of any who would desire it, the crowning conclusion is: "Indeed, so highly is he exalted above all creatures that the name 'nothing' may justly be ascribed to him."[18]

Such was the God to whom Jew and Christian alike became the adopted sons and daughters. The need for communication between them and their newly acquired God was resolved in the further adoption of Philo's notion of Logos. The concept of Logos was to the theologian as clay to the potter. It could be molded and fashioned according to his needs. As already noted, Logos is the source of communication between God and mortals, though angels, archangels, or demons could be logoi (the plural form of Logos). Logos is known by many names, including the Son of God. Justin Martyr, who like Philo argued that the Greek philosophers borrowed their wisdom from Moses,[19] explains it thus: "God begat from Himself a kind of rational Force, which is called by the Holy Spirit (i.e. the Old Testament) sometimes 'the Glory of the Lord,' sometimes 'Son,' sometimes 'Wisdom,' sometimes 'Angel,' sometimes 'God,' sometimes 'Lord and *Logos*,' sometimes he speaks of himself as 'Captain of the Lord's host:' for he has all these appellations, both from his ministering to the Father's purpose and from his having been begotten by the Father's pleasure."[20] Any communication from God is described as Logos. According to one scholarly work, for Philo Logos connoted "God's mental activity during the act of creating. The *Logos*, one of the powers of the intelligible world, reaches into our world, mainly through the mediators Moses and Aaron, both called *Logos*." Philo also used Logos to include the scripture, biblical figures, heavenly beings, the laws of Moses, and wisdom.[21]

Logos reveals the nature of God by reflecting that nature. God is Mind, and Logos is the only begotten Son of Mind and thus reveals

Eternal Reason to man. As far as scripture is concerned, this conception of Christ as Logos, or the Word, is peculiar to the Gospel of John. The classic work *A Dictionary of Christ and the Gospels,* edited by James Hastings, observes: "There can be no doubt in regard to the main source from which his [John's] Logos doctrine was derived. It had come to him through Philo after its final elaboration in Greek philosophy."[22] Adolph Harnack, author of a seven-volume work on the history of Christian dogma, would disagree, arguing that Philo's philosophy exercised no appreciable influence on the first generation of believers in Christ. He does concur, however, that it "became operative among Christian teachers from the beginning of the second century" and then became "a standard of Christian theology."[23]

Harnack describes a "gradual incorporation of the Logos doctrine in the rule of faith. *The formula of the Logos, as it was almost universally understood, legitimised speculation, i.e., Neoplatonic philosophy, within the creed of the Church.* When Christ was designated the incarnate Logos of God, and when this was set up as His supreme characterisation, men were directed to think of the divine in Christ as the reason of God realised in the structure of the world and the history of mankind. This implied a definite philosophical view of God, of creation, and of the world, and the baptismal confession became a compendium of scientific dogmatics, *i.e.,* of a system of doctrine entwined with the Metaphysics of Plato and the Stoics."[24] Harnack further observes that because the Logos-speculation could be understood only by those trained in philosophy, its adoption as a tenet of faith created for the great mass of Christians a theology of mystery. Its appeal, he asserts, was found in its "high-pitched formulas and the glamour of the incomprehensible." This in turn created the need for a trained ministry. Thus gospel understanding was taken from the common people and given to guardians to whom the masses would be dependent for their salvation.[25]

It is difficult to imagine those who profess a belief in the Bible and the God of Israel, whether their orientation be the Old Testament or the New, pursuing a course more divergent than the one we have just traced. It ought be observed that the Gospel of John, which is used to sustain the Logos-speculation, in point of fact knows nothing of the absolute transcendence of God. The Gospel of John makes man the direct object of God's love and providence (see John 3:16). It maintains that God acts immediately on the human soul and so makes possible the redeeming work of Christ (John 6:44; 17:6). To suppose that the Gospel of John seeks to subordinate Christ to a philosophical speculation is to suppose that John sought to undo his own testimony.[26] Significantly, no scriptural text can match the Gospel of John for its emphasis on the personal nature of both the Father and the Son. Whenever the personal relationship between him and the Father is involved—and there are approximately 120 textual instances of this— Jesus uses no name to address Deity but "Father." In no instance in this work does the Father address Christ by any other appellation than "Son."

Also of great significance is the fact that in his Bible translation Joseph Smith made changes in the Logos text of John that give appreciably stronger emphasis to the doctrine of divine sonship. Examples include the following (italics indicate changes made by the JST):

> In the beginning was the Word, and the Word was with God, and the Word was God (King James Version, John 1:1).

> In the beginning was the *gospel preached through the Son. And the gospel was the word, and the word was with the Son, and the Son was with God, and the Son was of God.* (JST, John 1:1.)

In the Prophet's inspired translation the doctrine of divine sonship was consistently inserted into subsequent verses in John 1. For example, verse 16 of the Joseph Smith Translation reads:

> *For in the beginning was the Word, even the Son, who is made flesh, and sent unto us by the will of the Father. And as many as believe on his name shall receive of his fulness.* And of his fulness have all we received, *even immortality and eternal life, through his grace.*

Perhaps the passage most often quoted by those who oppose the story of the First Vision is John 1:18. The King James Version reads:

> No man hath seen God at any time; the only begotten Son, which is in the bosom of the Father, he hath declared him.

The Joseph Smith Translation rendering reads:

> *For the law was after a carnal commandment, to the administra-*
> *tion of death; but the gospel was after the power of an endless life,*
> *through Jesus Christ,* the Only Begotten Son, who is in the bosom
> of the Father. *And* no man hath seen God at any time, *except he*
> *hath borne record of the Son; for except it is through him no man can*
> *be saved.* (JST, John 1:18–19.)

What Joseph Smith restored to the ancient text is a very clear emphasis on the doctrine of divine sonship. It could be argued that this is
no more than Logos appearing in the form of the Son, but such an interpretation of the doctrine of divine sonship is unnecessary when the
reality that God is a personal being who appears to the true witnesses
of the Son is also restored, as it is in this text. It might also be noted
that Joseph Smith made other textual restorations sustaining the idea
that God appears to men in the flesh and that the purpose of the
priesthood is to prepare men to stand in his presence (see JST, Psalm
14:1–4; JST, Genesis 14:30–31).

Relative to the transcendence of God, which in turn gave birth to
the Logos concept, Hatch observes, "from the earliest Christian
teaching, indeed, the conception of the transcendence of God is absent. God is near to men and speaks to them: He is angry with them
and punishes them: He is merciful to them and pardons them."[27] We
would also note that their faith was a simple one which did not require a trained clergy to expound. Words carried their common
meaning. God walked with the righteous and spoke to them face-to-
face. When he was spoken of as their "Father in Heaven," the assumption was that he had literally been their Father in a pre-earth estate.
When Christ was spoken of as his "Son," it was assumed that he was
literally God's Son as we are all the sons and daughters of our own
parents. And, of course, the word *begotten* was assumed to mean precisely what it says also. The language of the scriptures was accepted at
face value with its countless anthropomorphisms—God had body,
parts, and passions.

The Ante-Nicene Fathers and the New Gospel

As we have seen, it was not long after the death of the Apostles
that a dramatic change took place in both the spirit and the doctrine

of the Christian faith. That God who had been known to the meridian Saints as a loving Father became Eternal Reason, while Christ became his altar ego, the reflection of God's mind. Those who laid the foundation for this reinterpretation are known as the ante-Nicene Fathers, men who wrote between A.D. 90 and 150. In his history of Christianity, Neander describes this as a singular phenomenon, a "striking difference," as the Spirit known to the unlearned Apostles was not to be found among the learned and erudite Apostolic Fathers.[28] The pattern, of course, was obvious: whatever the mischief one sought to work, the secret was to seek refuge in the name of the Apostles. Thus it is said that the ante-Nicene Fathers either knew some member of the Twelve or at least knew someone who did.

Describing a related matter, Mosheim observes that "not long after the Savior's ascension, various histories of his life and doctrines, full of impositions and fables, were composed by persons of no bad intentions, perhaps, but who were superstitious, simple, and piously fraudulent; and afterwards various other spurious writings were palmed upon the world, falsely inscribed with the names of the holy apostles."[29] In actual fact it is a little hard to argue that forgeries carry with them a spirit of innocence. The testimony of Hegesippus, a second-century Jew who was converted to Christianity in Palestine, illustrates the point. Eusebius says that Hegesippus spoke of the Church as being "a pure and uncorrupt virgin; whilst if there were any at all, that attempted to pervert the sound doctrine of the saving gospel, they were yet skulking in dark retreats; but when the sacred choir of apostles became extinct, and the generation of those that had been privileged to hear their inspired wisdom, had passed away, then also the combinations of impious error arose by the fraud and delusions of false teachers. These also, as there was none of the apostles left, henceforth attempted, without shame, to preach their false doctrine against the gospel of truth."[30]

At first Christianity was preached by Jews to Jews. It centered in the testimony that Jesus of Nazareth was their long-promised Messiah. Following his ascension, that testimony embraced his suffering, his atoning sacrifice, wherein he became the Savior or Redeemer of mankind. Salvation, they declared, was to be found in his name and none other. These missionaries could take for granted a belief in God's existence along with a faith in the Jewish scriptures among those they taught. When the Church began to expand into non-Jewish societies, it met with inquirers who challenged such beliefs, and thus arose those who sought to defend Christianity with rational and philosophical arguments. That is, they chose to meet the adversary on his own ground. By the second century, Christian writers had begun to restate their faith, drawing, as all sources agree, upon Greek thought, which was easily the most important intellectual influence in the Roman Empire.

So it was that when Christians tried to explain their God to pagans they felt that it would be advantageous to associate him with principles familiar to pagans. Philosophers had long defined Perfection, meaning God, in a unitary way. Perfection, to the philosophers, could be found only in monotheism. Thus the first tenet of their faith was that there could be only one God, though he bore various names throughout the Empire. H. A. Drake writes: "Pagans, moreover, became increasingly willing to leave the name of this deity vague, referring to him as the 'Supreme God' or 'Greatest Sovereign.' Following Plato's example, and that of the new cults of Mithras and Sol Invictus, they were inclined to associate Him with the most universal of religious symbols, light and the sun." As we have already seen, there was a scriptural precedent for explaining Christ as the Logos; in like manner, it could be argued from scripture that he was like the sun.[31]

Thus the ante-Nicene Fathers, men like Clement and Origen, followed the example of Philo in seeking to reconcile their faith with Platonism. The key was simply to declare all offending texts to be allegories, for, as Origen said, "the Scriptures are of little use to those who understand them as they are written."[32] This, of course, embraced all affirmative statements about God. Perhaps no source has said it more directly or better than *The Cambridge History of the Bible*: "Eusebius is a faithful enough disciple of Origen to agree with Plato that it is sometimes necessary for the lawgiver to lie in order to persuade people rather than coerce them, and to suggest that this is an explanation of the anthropomorphism of the Old Testament."[33] So now we have the matter plain. God, prophets, and scripture lie when they say anything that contradicts the wisdom of the Greeks and their great high priest, Plato. So it was that, as we are told in another scholarly source, "philosophy could help, and did in fact help, to purify the notion of God, especially the God of the Jewish religion, from the anthropomorphic idea that He resembled man, to denationalize it and to acknowledge God as the Father [allegorically speaking, no doubt] of all mankind and the universe."[34]

Such were the revisions made to the Christian faith by the early Catholic Fathers. As we have already seen, they were sustained in their efforts by those who "alter[ed] the words of Scripture in order to make them more serviceable for the polemical task. Scribes modified their manuscripts to make them more patently 'orthodox' and less susceptible to 'abuse' by the opponents of orthodoxy."[35] Writing in 1845, Cardinal John Henry Newman stated that the doctrine of the old mother church in all ages has been that the faith is "not to be found on the surface" of the scriptures, nor may it be "gained from Scripture without the aid of Tradition." Newman claimed that this "is shown by the disinclination of her teachers to confine themselves to the mere literal interpretation of Scripture. Her most subtle and powerful method of proof, whether in ancient or modern times, is the mystical sense [symbolic or allegorical], which is so frequently used in doctrinal controversy as on many occasions to supersede any other." This method, he said, is the "very basis of the proof of the Catholic doctrine of the Holy Trinity." Whether it be the ante-Nicene writers or the Nicene, texts "which do not obviously refer to that doctrine" are put forward as proof of it, he explains. Indeed, he said, "it may be almost laid down as an historical fact, that the mystical interpretation and orthodoxy will stand or fall together."[36]

6

For no man has seen God at any time in the flesh, except quickened by the Spirit of God.
Neither can any natural man abide the presence of God, neither after the carnal mind.

—D&C 67:11–12

How God Became Invisible

No principle became more evident to me in the context of missionary work than the simple verity that there was a special spirit and power that always attended a missionary in telling the story of the First Vision. Ours is a God who speaks, and he is a God who is visible.

In the early years of my teaching career I taught with a man who had been a sectarian minister for twenty-five years before he met some Mormon missionaries and heard, for the first time, the story of the First Vision. As a man of integrity he was duty bound to pray about their message. He did so, and its truthfulness was affirmed for him in a sacred and powerful way. After having resigned his pastorate and readied himself and his family to come west, not knowing what would become of them, he felt obligated to gather his former colleagues in the ministry together and tell them why he had chosen to do what he was doing. He told them the same simple story about the prayer of a young boy that had changed his life. He also told them of attendant events that included the restoration of keys and authority by prophets of old. When he was through, the informal spokesman for the group said, "Oh, John, we could never believe a story like that," to which he responded, "Yes, but don't you wish you could!"

Israel's Invisible God

Surely it must be puzzling to the reader of the Bible as to how the good book, which is replete with stories of prophets entertaining angels or even seeing God "face to face," can be squared with the traditional teaching of both Judaism and Christianity that God has neither face nor form. As a case study, let us take Genesis 3:8. Here we read that Adam and Eve "heard the voice of the Lord God walking in the garden in the cool of the day: and Adam and his wife hid themselves from the presence of the Lord God amongst the trees of the garden."[1] It seems apparent that the God known to Adam and Eve was a personal being, one with whom they had shared company on many occasions. Had they known him as an ephemeral spirit they hardly would have hid themselves from him, nor would they have supposed that it was he whom they heard walking in the garden.

Let us begin by sampling Bible commentaries to see how they explain a bodiless and formless God walking in a garden and conversing with Adam and Eve. The commentary edited by Dummelow finds it sufficient to acknowledge that "anthropomorphism runs through the whole of the Paradise story." This source cites Genesis 2:7, 8, 19, and 21 as examples and observes that God in this instance has chosen to be intimate rather than transcendental.[2] The reasoning here is that God, who has the power to do all things, can choose to be or not to be as it fits his purposes, but his appearing with a body is not intended to imply that he has a body. *Clarke's Commentary,* referring to the phrase "the voice of the Lord" in Genesis 3:8, argues that "the *voice* is properly used here, for as God is an infinite Spirit, and cannot be confined to any *form,* so he can have no *personal* appearance."[3] Thus it was actually God's voice that was walking in the garden and not God. This, of course, would have to mean that where the Bible says that Adam and Eve were created in the image and likeness of God, what it really means is that they were created in the image and likeness of his voice. Another commentator suggests that "Yahweh, whose abode the garden is, manifests himself in the rustling of the trees as the cool wind springs up at sunset."[4] The thought here is essentially the same as that of the previous commentary. Adam and Eve have been created in the image and likeness of a cool wind in the trees. *The Interpreter's Bible* suggests that the idea that God would walk in a garden like a man was derived from an earlier myth that influenced the writer. The whole thing is considered "childlike."[5] Yet another source suggests that "Jehovah delights to walk in the garden when the morning or evening breeze is blowing cool, and to enjoy the company and conversation of his living toys." In this instance he cannot find them, and calls till they answer him. The fact that he cannot find them suggests that he is not omniscient, but even with that limitation he is still "far wiser than the man or the snake."[6]

The one thing that is evident in all of this is that whatever the reader of the divine text concludes, he or she is not to be so naive as to suppose that words mean what they say. The text is to be understood either as another of the ancient and childlike myths borrowed from pagan neighbors or as a metaphor. The real danger in such a text is if someone should pick up the book on his or her own and read it without the aid and guidance of religious traditions and dogmas. For this reason some religious denominations discourage or even forbid untutored or unsupervised Bible study. To accept the scriptural story at face value would undermine the theological foundations of both Judaism and traditional Christianity.

If we start our reading of the scriptures with the fixed determination that God has no form or body, then somehow we can find a way to make the scriptures conform to that determination; but no one reading them without that predetermination would ever conclude it from the text itself. Any predetermined conclusion can be sustained while professing loyalty to the Bible simply by declaring whatever the Bible says to be a metaphor. When the scriptural text says, "And the Lord spake unto Moses face to face, as a man speaketh unto his friend" (Exodus 33:11), we simply turn to another text (one obviously tampered with) wherein the Lord says to Moses, "Thou canst not see my face: for there shall no man see me, and live" (Exodus 33:20). We then declare that the second negates a literal reading of the first. The fact that the context of the second statement is that the unworthy or unclean cannot see God must be ignored to sustain such an interpretation. (For confirmation that this is indeed the context of the second statement, see JST, Exodus 33:20.)

The book *Alleged Discrepancies of the Bible* addresses the issue of God's invisibility. Acknowledging a few of the many texts that testify of various prophets' seeing God, the book uses the following chain of thought: First, the basic premise is stated, "It is beyond question that God—as a spirit—as he is in himself,—is never visible to men." (As already noted, the premise must stand independent of the reading of the Bible and is not to be questioned.) Two possible explanations are then given for those instances in the Bible where God is said to have been seen "1. He [God] might assume temporarily, and for wise purposes, some visible form in which to manifest himself to his creatures. Cases of this kind are termed 'theophanies,' in which, as Hengstenberg says, God appears 'under a light vesture of corporeity, in a transiently-assumed human form.' This seems in some instances the best solution."[7]

Now, consider the strength of the argument. Appearances of God, we are told, are really *theophanies*. And what, by definition, is a theophany? According to the dictionary it is simply "a physical presentation or personal manifestation of a deity to an individual: a brief appearance of Deity."[8] Then we are told that God appeared in the image and likeness of man but that he was only temporarily assuming a body to do so. Thus we have the "unchangeable" God of the prophets constantly changing from his formless state to one of form and back again. How does our authority know this? And if it is the understanding that all Bible readers are to have, why don't the scriptures tell us, or why didn't one of the prophets who testified that he saw God ever think to mention it?

A second explanation to the problem is given as follows: "2. He [God] might be seen, as we may say, by proxy,—in his accredited representative. This explanation is a very ancient one. In the Samaritan Pentateuch in the narratives of divine appearances, it is not God himself—Jehovah—who is mentioned as the Person appearing, even where this is the case in the Jewish text, but always an Angel. So, in the Chaldee Targum, Jacob's language stands, 'I have seen the Angel of God face to face.'"[9]

The suggestion here is that the Bible really ought to tell us that Moses saw a proxy of God with which he spoke "face to essence." To give credibility to this explanation, the writer tells us that it is ancient. This is an especially interesting twist, given that we were told not to trust Moses' account of Adam and Eve walking and talking with God because it was so old. So we are referred to the Samaritan Pentateuch, which may well be the most tampered with of all extant scriptural texts.[10]

In summary we are then told that on either of "these hypotheses [tentative assumptions], there is no difficulty, *for God was seen, and yet not seen*." Though it would be difficult to add to that crowning statement, our source continues: "The Lord spake with his servant Moses 'face to face,' that is, familiarly. Two men may speak face to face, in darkness, neither seeing the other."[11] That someone was standing in the darkness here seems evident. I suggest that it wasn't Moses.

Refusing to See God

It would certainly be true that God remains unseen to those who refuse to see him. The refusal of the children of Israel to do so at Sinai is the classic scriptural example of a people rejecting the fulness of the gospel. It was for this very reason that the privilege of holding the Melchizedek Priesthood was taken from the people generally and that they were given the Aaronic, or lesser, Priesthood in its place. In modern revelation we learn that Moses not only stood in the presence of God but also sought diligently to sanctify his people so that they might enjoy the same privilege that had been his. "But they hardened their hearts and could not endure his [God's] presence; therefore, the Lord in his wrath, for his anger was kindled against them, swore that they should not enter into his rest while in the wilderness, which rest is the fulness of his glory. Therefore, he took Moses out of their midst, and the Holy Priesthood also; and the lesser priesthood continued, which priesthood holdeth the key of the ministering of angels and the preparatory gospel." (D&C 84:24–26.)

It is interesting to see how others have refashioned the Sinai story. In his *Legends of the Jews*, Louis Ginzberg shares a pathetic remaking of it. The issue, as he recounts it, is not seeing God but receiving the Torah. Thus the great thing is not coming into the divine presence but being in possession of God's word. This is everlastingly the pattern followed by apostate religion. Its prophets remove God and place his word in his stead, but in reality what they are placing in his stead is their interpretation of his word. It was this theological posture that caused the nation of Israel to reject Christ. His coming in the flesh forced a choice between their loyalty to the traditions and interpretations with which they had surrounded his word and their acceptance of the Word himself. Having exalted their traditions above the living voice, they rejected Christ. They saw him as a threat to the law (see Matthew 5:17). This same scenario repeats itself today as the voice of living prophets is rejected in the name of loyalty to the Bible.

Ginzberg tells us that in order to receive the Torah the Israelites had to be sanctified, which required the same three ceremonies as those required upon conversion to Judaism. These are given as circumcision, baptism, and sacrifice. They had been circumcised in Egypt but not baptized. Two days before the revelation was imposed upon them, all were baptized. The day before the revelation was given, sacrifices were offered. Moses was said to have erected an altar on the mount, as well as twelve memorial pillars, one for each of the twelve tribes. The blood of the animals sacrificed was sprinkled, one-half on the people as a token that they would not worship false gods, and one-half on the altar as a token that the Lord would not reject them in favor of another nation.

Before this covenant was made, Moses was said to have read all of the Torah to the people so that they would know its terms. To ensure that no one would suppose that God could be seen, and yet to comply with the promise that he was to be seen by all the children of the Lord, we are told that his voice sounded differently to each ear and, in like manner, "the Divine vision appear[ed] differently to each, wherefore God warned them not to ascribe the various forms to various beings, saying: 'Do not believe that because you have seen Me in various forms, there are various gods, I am the same that appeared to you at the Red Sea as a God of war, and at Sinai as a teacher.'"[12]

Such traditions reflect the changes that were being made not just in the way Israel was interpreting the scriptures but in the way they were being copied and passed from generation to generation.

How the Scribes Dethroned God

Israel's temple was the embodiment of the Sinai experience. As all were to be brought into the presence of God at Sinai, so they were to stand in his presence in the temple. But the meaning of the temple as the house of God, the place of the divine presence, underwent a dramatic change, one in which God was dethroned in Jewish theology. One source tells us that in later scriptural texts the temple "is no longer the place in which God dwells, enthroned like a king, since he is held to reign from heaven. Instead, the Temple becomes a 'house of prayer,' in the sense that God hears the prayers offered by men 'toward this place' (1 Kings 8:29, 30, 38, 42, 44, 48)."

The temple simply "ceased to function" according to its original intent. It ceased to be the place of his presence, becoming instead the place of his name. The scholarly source continues: "This radical theological re-orientation may be held to form the background which enables us to understand the Name theology of the D-Work. If one honours the requirement to examine these issues in their proper context, and thus evaluates this Name concept in a greater theological perspective, then one soon recognizes a grandiose attempt by the Deuteronomistic theologians to expel the pre-exilic doctrine of the Presence. Not heaven, nor even the heaven of heavens can contain God; how much less, then, any earthly Temple? We no longer encounter the immanent God in the Temple, the Lord Sabaoth who thrones above the cherubim, but God's *šēm*, his 'Name.'"[13]

Repeatedly these scribes hammer in the insight that it is only the name of Deity which is in the temple and the idea that the temple was constructed "for the name of the Lord" rather than as a dwelling place for God (see 1 Kings 8:16, 17, 18, 20, 29, 44, 48). This, our author tells us, represents "a thorough-going transformation of the understanding of God. The Name theology undeniably represents a 'strategic retreat' in relation to the front lines of the old Zion-Sabaoth theology"—the doctrine in which God and the premortal spirits, i.e., the heavenly council, labor in behalf of those in mortality—"yet at the same time it represents a theological advance!" Hold your breath! "It is namely impossible to doubt that this theology accomplished an important mission in a changed situation, in that the Name theology presents us with a transcendent God"—just what we have been waiting for—"who is invulnerable to any catastrophe which might conceivably affect his Temple." So, finally, with the help of the scribes and some serious scriptural tampering, we are able to get a "transcendent God" after all, and this despite all the efforts of the prophets. Now we can lay claim to a God who transcends man's ability to comprehend; a God far too great to mean it when he says that he created man in his image, or that others in the divine council aided in the labor of creation. This is a God far too great to be serious when he says that he appears to men "face to face" and that the temple would be his house. How correctly our scholar friend concludes that this represents "a profound change of theological ideas."[14]

No consideration is given in the work just cited to the simple but obvious fact that when a people pollute their temple, when they break their covenants, the God of heaven withdraws. Keep in mind that these are the very events that caused the Lord to direct Lehi and his family to leave Jerusalem, but only after repeated efforts to warn the people as to precisely what was going to happen if they would not repent. Then, elsewhere in our scholarly source we get this summary statement: "The concept of God advocated by the Deuteronomistic theology is strikingly abstract. The throne conception has vanished [God sitting upon his throne in his temple], and the anthropomorphic characteristics of God are on their way to oblivion. Thus the *form* of God plays no part in the depiction in the D-Work of the Sinai theophany: 'Then the Lord spoke to you out of the midst of the fire; you heard the sound of words, but saw no form; there was only a voice.' (Deuteronomy 4:12)."[15]

And thus the deed was done. Israel no longer had prophets; she no longer had a God who could speak, let alone manifest himself to his chosen servants or his people. In his stead they had a new god, one well known to the Greek world. Now Israel too could boast a god the equal of anyone else's, an abstract, transcendent, invisible, impersonal, incomprehensible, genderless, speechless god. What more could she want, unless it was the Spirit, power, and knowledge of an earlier day?

How God Lost His Name

"Somewhere between the fifth and second centuries B.C. a tragic accident befell God: he lost his name," writes David Clines. "More exactly, Jews gave up using God's personal name Yahweh [Jehovah], and began to refer to Yahweh by various periphrases: God, the Lord, the Name, the Holy One, the Presence, even the Place. Even where Yahweh was written in the Biblical text, readers pronounced the name as Adonai. With the final fall of the temple, even the rare liturgical occasions when the name was used ceased, and even the knowledge of the pronunciation of the name was forgotten."[16]

In truth it was not just the name of God that was lost; "the key of the knowledge of God" (D&C 84:19) also had been taken from them. It is natural that a people in a state of transgression would seek a less attentive and more impersonal God. Such was the desire of apostate Israel. By ceasing to speak and think of Deity as the personal being known to the prophets, they sought to distance themselves and their conduct from his attention. Consistently their efforts in preserving, translating, and interpreting scriptural texts were directed to that end. By the time Bible manuscripts are passed to us they have witnessed considerable tampering; in fact it would be easier to unscramble an egg than to untangle the history of this textual and interpretive tampering, particularly in those texts dealing with the nature of God.

The King James translators, in an attempt to sort out some of the confusion in the Hebrew text as it refers to Deity, devised a system. Whenever we find the name "GOD" or "LORD" printed in capitals, the original is "Jehovah." In more recent years the consensus of scholars seems to be that the name "Jehovah" is a mistaken rendering and that it ought to have been pronounced "Yahweh." "Jehovah" or "Yahweh" is the personal or proper name of Deity. Thus, as an illustration, the Twenty-third Psalm, which begins with the familiar phrase, "The Lord is my shepherd," ought to be rendered, "Jehovah is my shepherd." Its conclusion, "I will dwell in the house of the Lord for ever," should be, "I will dwell in the house of Jehovah for ever."

Whenever we find "God" in the King James translation (as, for instance, we do throughout the entire first chapter of Genesis and in countless other places), it represents the translation of the word *Elohim*. This is a generic rather than a personal name. Where we find "Lord" (it is first used of God in Genesis 15:2, 8; its appearance is rare in the Pentateuch and historical books but is frequent in the Psalms, Isaiah, Jeremiah, Ezekiel, Daniel, and Amos), it is a rendering of the Hebrew "Adonai." *Adon* is the general Hebrew word for lord, master, or owner. *Adonai* ("my Lords"), like *Elohim,* is plural, though not rendered as such by translators. Thus "Lord God" (in Genesis 2:4, 5, 7, 8, and elsewhere) is "Jehovah Elohim," while "Lord God" is "Adonai Jehovah."[17]

When the name "Jehovah" stood alone in a scriptural text or was joined with the name "Elohim," the Jewish scribes substituted the vowel points for "Adonai." Where "Adonai" was joined with "Jehovah," the vowel points for "Elohim" were used as the substitute. Thus they scrupulously avoided pronouncing the name "Jehovah" or "Yahweh." The effect of this was to depersonalize God. Only the high priest could utter his name and that only on Yom Kippur, the Day of Atonement. With the loss of the temple during the Babylonian captivity, even that ceremonial utterance was temporarily lost.

How God Became Invisible in the Meridian Church

The Jews having cut the path, Christians found it easy to follow. Both used the Septuagint to lay the groundwork for the Hellenization of their people. For the Jews it was a matter of adopting Plato into the law and the law into Plato. This included the transformation, on Philo's part, of God as "Father" and "Lord" into the "Eternal Negation of dialectics," meaning a mysterious God known only by reason or intellect. The new God of Judaism, after whom the Christian God would be patterned, was both immaterial and passionless.[18]

Among the first Christians in the East were those who espoused asceticism, or the practice of physical denial. These despisers of the mortal body also found it necessary to tamper with both scriptural and apocryphal texts in order to sustain their dogma of a bodiless God. In a study on the subject, Catherine Thomas observes that "sexual behavior was not the only practice affected by asceticism. The rise of the institution of penance likely derived from the fact that a suffering Christ did not harmonize with the early Christians' Hellenistic conceptions of godliness; therefore the doctrine of Christ's atonement for men early fell into disuse and was soon replaced by the practice (and then sacrament) of penance in which men found suffering to be the road to heaven. They submitted to humiliating punishments for their own sins and bodily shame, not only at their own instigation but also under the increasing authority of the episcopacy." This reflected another of the arguments over monotheism and the efforts of the church fathers to merge the Father and the Son into one being. The role of Christ as mediator was "filled by holy relics, holy virgins, holy martyrs, and celibate bishops."[19]

The Christian writers of the first two centuries after the deaths of the Apostles sustained the notion that marriage was ordained of God but that virginity and celibacy were superior. The books constituting the New Testament had not yet been agreed upon, so works that would ultimately be rejected as nonscriptural had considerable influence among the Christians of that period. The apocryphal Acts of the Apostles (second-third centuries) taught that marriage and procreation were not compatible with the message of Christ. The Apocryphon of John, a Gnostic work, defined the highest Deity in abstract terms, which excluded anthropomorphism, and maintained that evil powers put man in a material body to keep him imprisoned.[20] The role of the

Gnostic Christ was one of teaching esoteric knowledge rather than making an atoning sacrifice. In the book the Shepherd of Hermas, the shepherd is instructed to live with his wife as a "sister" and receives a promise of greater revelation after proving his purity.[21] Should a spouse die, one could remarry but obtained greater honor with the Lord by not doing so. Justin Martyr wrote that Jesus was born of a virgin to destroy the act of begetting by lawless desire and that Jesus himself did not submit to sexual function. Among some of the Gnostics, marriage was equated with fornication. Others felt they sided with Paul, agreeing that it was better to marry than to burn but that marriage was an obstruction to those seeking perfection.

Paradoxically, Jesus Christ, who is the hope of resurrection for all mankind, is presented by traditional Christianity as the prime witness to prove that there was no resurrection, if by resurrection is meant obtaining some kind of a corporeal body in the world to come. This strange chain of thought centers in the supposition that Christ never married. It is enhanced by the argument that he never had any personal possessions. These two supposed facts are used to prove his disdain for all material things but primarily the body, which the ascetics view as a prison to the soul. The overriding notion is that marriage and, heaven forbid, conceiving children are ungodly and demeaning, as are all corporeal things. But whence did such a notion come? Christ quoted, with approbation, the declaration of his Father that a man should leave father and mother and cleave unto his wife and none else (see Matthew 19:5–6). A major part of his ministry was spent healing the sick and infirm. Among his greatest miracles were the feeding of the five thousand and again the feeding of the four thousand. What is there in all of this, and in the countless other things he did, to suggest an abhorrence of the body or to sustain a doctrine of physical penitence? He it was who marked the path of salvation with the words "Follow me" (Matthew 4:19; 8:22; 9:9; 16:24; 19:21). When, pray tell, did he impose upon himself physical punishments? And if his gospel was to embrace celibacy and regard conceiving children as a sin, why did he not tell someone so instead of giving them the commandment to multiply and replenish the earth?

The strongly held tradition that Christ was not married is necessitated in traditional Christianity by the notion that in his resurrected state he eschewed his body and became immaterial. On the matter of his marriage the New Testament is silent. As to his resurrection the

Gospel writers are united in the testimony that he was corporeal. So the argument for Christ's being celibate is scriptural silence on the one hand and denying the plain meaning of words on the other. As to the notion of an immaterial God, it was pirated from Greek intellectuals. It was simply the fashionable thing to believe.

The New Testament evidences considerable effort on the part of its writers to oppose the influence of ascetic reformers who preferred a bodiless God. Describing Jesus' experience in Gethsemane, Luke said that "his sweat was as it were great drops of blood falling down to the ground" (Luke 22:44). In future years these verses would slip in and out of manuscript copies. They were an obvious annoyance to those attempting to develop the doctrine of a passionless God.[22] In other passages Luke dramatized the physical nature of the resurrected Christ. "Behold my hands and my feet, that it is I myself: handle me, and see; for a spirit hath not flesh and bones, as ye see me have" (Luke 24:39). And again, "Have ye here any meat? And they gave him a piece of a broiled fish, and of an honeycomb. And he took it, and did eat before them." (Luke 24:41–43.) Luke concluded his Gospel with an account of the physical ascension of Christ into the heavens (see Luke 24:51). John is believed to have been responding to the influence of Gnostic doceticism—the belief that Jesus appeared to men in a spirit body, and that since he had no actual human body, he only "seemed to" suffer and die on the cross—when he wrote, "Every spirit that confesseth not that Jesus Christ is come in the *flesh* is not of God: and this is that spirit of antichrist" (1 John 4:3, emphasis added).

Catherine Thomas observes that "ascetic renunciation of the flesh and rejection of an anthropomorphic God developed concomitantly in Christianity; both represented a clear break with Old Testament religion and with the tenor of Christ's and the apostles' teachings on the Father and the Son, and on the body with its associated functions of marriage and reproduction. The higher the level of asceticism climbed, the greater rose the degree of the dematerialization of God." This was a process, she observes, which is understandable in view of the Genesis announcement that man was made in the image of God. Thus as man became increasingly ascetic, so did his God.[23]

Following the pattern that we have seen so well, those who were offended with an anthropomorphic view of God espoused by the scriptures set about their work to make "biblical modifications."[24] For when God said to the children of Israel, "I will dwell in your midst," he had really meant to say, "I shall cause you to dwell." "To behold the face of God" became, by means of a slight vowel change, "to appear before God." Phrases like "he saw" or "he went down" were changed to "he revealed himself"; "he heard" became "it was heard before him."[25] The "image of God" in the LXX became "the glory of the Lord"; the "mouth of God" became the "the voice of the Lord."

Thus we find Origen writing that the Father, who he maintains is whole and indivisible, gives birth to the Son without any act of separation. For him to have embraced an act of separation, it is reasoned, would imply that God had a body and carry with it the onerous system of reproduction known to animals. Thus the Son was not a part of God's substance, nor was he created out of nothing, for then there would have been a time when he was not. Rather the Son was created by an act of will from the mind of God, one independent of either body or feeling.

And thus the stage was set for the grand Council of Nicaea. Here it was declared that Father and Son were one substance while yet being two divided persons. This obvious impossibility is covered with the simple explanation that it is a mystery surpassing both reason and understanding. We will come to that story in its course. It must suffice at this point to say that Christian asceticism was Hellenistic in origin, though it often came to the infant church through Jewish sources, for they had chosen to imbibe of the wine of the same vine many years before. Asceticism and docetism, each with its aversion to the body, emerged as traveling companions and together succeeded in transforming the teachings of the New Testament Church concerning the nature of the Father and the Son. Plato and Philo posed as Moses and Aaron to lead the children of Israel into a philosophical wilderness. And thus it was that the once anthropomorphic God of heaven and his Only Begotten Son became incorporeal, invisible, passionless, and ascetic. It then followed, as it inevitably would, that as God was de-materialized and de-passionized he became more distant. With that distancing came a greater freedom from divine restraint.[26]

In What Sense Is God Invisible?

For the mystic, God so completely transcends the temporal world of which we are a part that he is above bodily form. Thus he does not see, hear, speak, or touch, and of course he is not visible. Any reference to his having been seen or heard by prophets is figurative. Making God more remote, however, has the advantage of making the path of worship correspondingly broader, so that it can accommodate all manner of things that would otherwise be regarded as sin.

The biblical God, by contrast, generally remains unseen. This, however, does not argue that he is incorporeal, only that it is contrary to his purpose to be constantly visible. Perhaps the fact that Hebrew has no word for "invisible" suggests that such an adjective was not necessary to describe their God. The purpose of mortality as a place where faith is to be tested precludes his doing more than appearing to specially chosen witnesses upon specially chosen occasions. Should a people properly prepare themselves for the society of Deity, however, he could dwell in the midst of them. Among the faithful, there have always been perfect witnesses of the reality of God. John stated the principle thus: "That which was from the beginning, which we have heard, which we have seen with our eyes, which we have looked upon, and our hands have handled, of the Word of life" (1 John 1:1).

In What Sense Is God Changeless?

The mystic's God is "infinite," meaning that he is beyond all "finite" categories, beyond time and space. To admit any change in such a God would be to admit imperfection in him. That which is perfect cannot change and still be perfect. The God of revelation is also changeless: "From eternity to eternity he is the same" (D&C 76:4). Yet at one time he was the helpless infant in Mary's arms. How, then, do we declare of him that he "is not a partial God, neither a changeable being; but he is unchangeable from all eternity to all eternity"? (Moroni 8:18.) The God of the prophets is changeless in the sense that he is perfectly trustworthy and steadfast. One scholar notes, "The Hebrew word *chesed*, often translated as 'loving-kindness,' means that God is 'steady and sure, firm and reliable.'"[27]

In What Sense Is God Transcendent?

The term *transcendent,* as generally used, means "beyond space and time." Since the God of the mystics and the philosophers must be unlimited, he must be transcendent, that is, "beyond space and time." Such a God can be everywhere at once, while a God with body and form, it is argued, could be in only one place at a time.

It is true that God's body can be in only one place at a time. It does not necessarily follow, however, that he cannot be everywhere at once. Where, for instance, can one go to hide from God's presence? Your presence is not confined to the space occupied by your body, nor is God's. The presence of a speaker in general conference is not limited to the space immediately behind the pulpit. His presence is known to all within the Tabernacle. Now, what of those tuned in on a worldwide television broadcast? Could we not rightfully say that they were in the speaker's presence, given that they were being influenced by him? Could we not properly say that a God with a body, spatially located somewhere in the universe, who has the power from that location to influence everything that is going on is omnipresent?[28] It is through the Light of Christ that God's presence is universally present.

An Immaterial World

Were it not for irrevocable and unalterable laws, all things in their present state would cease to be. Everything in the world of which we are a part testifies of the existence of laws. One of those irrevocable laws is that something cannot be created out of nothing. Philosophers and theologians argue against this eternal verity, stating that God created all things *ex nihilo,* meaning out of nothing. We would remind them that a law recognized by them holds that two plus two is four, and that in all the endless expanses of eternity two plus two can never be eight, nor can it be nothing. The law also holds that nothing plus nothing remains nothing. Indeed, a thousand nothings multiplied together remains nothing. That being so, Elder Parley P. Pratt asked, "If it still be argued that something can be made from nothing, we would inquire how many solid feet of nonentity it would require to make one solid foot of material substance? The very idea," he asserts, "is the climax of absurdity."[29]

In the Creation account wherein we are told that God created the heavens and the earth, the Hebrew word *baurau,* which is translated *created,* does not imply that things were created out of nothing. The word means, as Joseph Smith taught us, "to organize; the same as a man would organize materials and build a ship."[30] Elder Pratt explains, "When we read that God made the heavens and the earth, we understand that he made them out of eternal elements, by organizing, combining, creating and arranging them in such manner as to form earth, air, water, light, etc., each in their respective place, proportion and order."[31] Indeed, the combined experience of all mankind has not witnessed a single instance in which something has been produced out of nothing.

We have it by revelation that the elements are eternal (see D&C 93:33). It therefore must follow that they cannot cease to exist. No material substance can be annihilated. Traditional Christianity let its philosopher-theologians talk it into adopting the notion of a formless God whose center is everywhere and whose circumference is nowhere. This in turn leads to the idea that in order for us to be like him we must become immaterial beings. Thus the material world of which we are a part is viewed as a temporary and fleeting thing. Such is the declaration of the creeds of Christendom. "I here confess," said Elder Pratt, "that a God without body or parts as described in the Church of England Confession of Faith, in the Presbyterian Articles, and in the Methodist Discipline; and as worshipped by a large portion of Christendom, is not with me an object of veneration, fear, or love. It is not in his power to hate or love, or to do good or evil to any being whatever. But when this same God is said to have 'his center everywhere and his circumference nowhere,' it forms in the rational mind a monster so inconceivably absurd, that I am almost tempted to indulge in irony and compare it to the Paddy's definition of the term nothing, '*a footless stocking without a leg.*'"[32]

A Past and Future Existence

Most men have but a faint idea as to where they came from or what becomes of them at the time of death. Nothing in the Western world has done more to obscure inspired thinking on such matters as the creeds of Christendom. Men are taught to look upon birth as the origin of both body and the spirit. In biblical times and for some five hundred years thereafter the knowledge of a premortal existence was commonly held. It was in A.D. 553 that an edict known as the Anathema Against Origen, promulgated by the Roman emperor Justinian and consented to by the pope under extreme duress, abolished the doctrine of our premortal existence.[33] Up until that point in time it was understood that we were born the spirit children of God in a pre-earth estate.[34] Such knowledge is inseparable with the understanding that God is a personal being. A God who is a spirit essence can hardly be the Father of spirit children in any but the most mystical of senses. Thus when the one doctrine is lost, the other will be lost also. In its place came the notion that each individual spirit was created from nothing at or about the time of the creation of the physical body of the infant in its mother's womb. Thus it was, we are expected to believe, that we awoke, as Elder Orson Pratt described the notion, "from nothing to consciousness, from non-existence to existence, from vacancy to substance, that thoughts and perceptions sprang into being, assumed identity, and began their career as movable intelligent souls."[35] Such is the inheritance bequeathed us by a corrupt priesthood hundreds of years removed from the spirit of revelation and the companionship of the Holy Ghost.

What we are being asked to believe is that all life, be it plant, animal, or human, springs into existence from nothing. Is it not more consistent to believe that the substance of our spirits, like the substance of our bodies and that of all forms of life, had a premortal existence, that all are eternal? indeed, that not so much as a single particle of anything ever sprang from nothing? That all things were created spiritually first is the declaration of scriptures; that they were created from nothing is the speculation of men who believed in a God of their own making.

Consider the nature of a heaven that is ruled over by an immaterial God. It would have to be as immaterial as the God who created it. Thus it would be without time and relationship to space. It would have neither whole nor parts. It would have nothing in common with matter. It would be colorless, shapeless, and bodiless. There would be no way to tell when you were there and when you were not. There would be nothing in it that was ugly nor anything that was beautiful. Like the invisible God who ruled it, it would be devoid of passions. There would be no hatred there, and in like manner it would be completely without love. It would be without quiet or noise. It would be without light and without darkness. As Elder Orson Pratt suggested, the devil himself could not have invented ideas more atheistic than these.[36]

By contrast, this same Elder Pratt described the heaven of the true Saint as one in which there will be

lands, houses, cities, vegetation, rivers, and animals. . . . Indeed, the Saints' heaven is a redeemed, glorified, celestial, material creation, inhabited by glorified material beings, male and female, organized into families, embracing all the relationships of husbands and wives, parents and children, where sorrow, crying, pain, and death will be known no more. Or to speak still more definitely, this earth, when glorified, is the Saints' eternal heaven. On it they expect to live, with body, parts, and holy passions; on it they expect to move and have their being; to eat, drink, converse, worship, sing, play on musical instruments, engage in joyful, innocent, social amusements. . . ; indeed, matter and its qualities and properties are the only beings or things with which they expect to associate. If they embrace the Father, they expect to embrace a glorified, immortal, spiritual,[37] material Personage; if they embrace the Son of God, they expect to embrace a spiritual Being of material, flesh and bones, whose image is in the likeness of the Father; if they enjoy the society of the Holy Ghost, they expect to behold a glorious spiritual Personage, a material body of spirit; if they associate with the spirits of men or angels, they expect to find them material.[38]

The absurdities of the Christian creeds are such that Elder Pratt wondered why it was that the heathens had not sent missionaries to labor among them. "But," he said, "it is evident that the frightful, disgusting picture of the modern Christians' creed would have disheartened the most zealous among them, from undertaking so hopeless a task. There are none, perhaps, who would have courage and fortitude to attack so formidable a monster, unless he were armed, like the Latter-day Saints' missionaries, with divine authority from heaven."[39]

How sweet it is to share the faith of the ancient Saints, when God and angels had bodies and form, when they were personal beings and could appear to those of the household of faith to bless and instruct them! To those who say they cannot believe in such things, we feel but to echo the response of my teaching colleague of years past, "But don't you wish you could!"

7

They seek not the Lord to establish his righteousness, but every man walketh in his own way, and after the image of his own god, whose image is in the likeness of the world, and whose substance is that of an idol, which waxeth old and shall perish in Babylon, even Babylon the great, which shall fall.

—D&C 1:16

How God Lost His Body

It was after nine o'clock at night when Steven stopped by my office. He wanted to sell me a photograph of the mission home and grounds. Normally I would not have been interested, but his was a little different angle. It was an aerial photograph taken from a helicopter. We talked size and price and came to an agreement. Then came one of my favorite questions, "How do you differ from the major faiths?" he asked.

"We believe in the same God you do," I responded. My purpose in so answering was to catch his interest, which I did.

He got a really puzzled look on his face and asked, "What do you mean?"

"Well, let me ask you a question," I said. "When you think about God and when you pray, do you have in your mind's eye a formless spirit essence, or do you see a loving Father, a personal being?"

"A loving Father," he responded without hesitation.

"Well, so do we," I said. "That is where we differ with the major faiths, and that is why we are here. We have an important message about God, about his speaking to prophets in our day. We know he is a personal being, a loving Father, and that he is as anxious to speak to us and bless us with counsel and direction as he was in Bible times when he used to appear to prophets."

"That," Steve said—and he did it with some emphasis and excitement—"is an important message!"

"It is the most important message in the world," I affirmed.

"How do people respond to it?" he asked with genuine interest.

"Very well," I responded, "when we can get them to listen. Our experience is that the great majority of people who will give us even a brief hearing immediately know that what we are saying is both important and true. Our only problem is getting past their lethargy to be heard."

He said, "That is a real shame!"

We talked for fifteen or twenty minutes about the importance of such a message. As he stood to go, I said, "Now, Steve, our message is one that will bless you and your family. How about letting a couple of our young missionaries sit down with you and tell you more about it?"

"Oh, no," he said, "I just wouldn't be interested."

Like Steve, the great majority of people whom our missionaries talk to innately believe in a God who is a personal being. They picture him in their mind's eye as a loving Father. At the same time most of these people claim membership in a church that professes allegiance to the dogma of the Holy Trinity. They seem unaware that their creeds obligate them to worship a God who is without body, parts, passions, or gender and who is not properly thought of in the way they have naturally believed in.

We have seen how the God of the ancients who appeared to so many became invisible. Let us now consider how he lost his body. We will begin with the issue of biblical interpretation.

The Grand Key of Mischief

The Bible is the most quoted and misquoted book ever written. It is the most translated and mistranslated book in earth's history. It exists in more versions than any book ever published. In the Christian world its interpretations are so diverse that it has been suggested that Christianity could more properly be called Christianities. Even to this day the various religious denominations cannot even agree on the books that it should include. Yet, bibliolaters tell us that the Bible is both inerrant and infallible. The argument is that the hand of the Lord has been over the Bible to preserve it from influences that would taint or distort its message. Perhaps this is the reason that it has been the subject of so many pious frauds. People have been easily duped when someone has started quoting from the Good Book. Ought it not be

observed that devils quote scripture as fluently as prophets and certainly more frequently, for there are far more devils than prophets?

In it all—and we have said it before—the grand key of scriptural
mischief is simply to declare all that is literal to be figurative and that
which is figurative to be literal. Thus, while professing reverence and
devotion to the Bible, clever devils can turn upside down, misdirect,
and distort everything within its covers. Nowhere is this more evident
than in what has been said about the nature of God.

Heretics Unaware

There can be no question that anyone reading the Bible without a
preconditioned notion as to the nature of Deity would come away
with the understanding that he is an anthropomorphic being. That is,
they would conceive God to be a personal being with the form and
likeness of a man. They would describe him with the use of personal
pronouns and think of his relationship with mortals in terms of transi-
tive verbs such as *love, promise, bless, forgive,* and *chasten.* Such is the
language of the prophets. It is the way the scriptures have been
written. Anthropomorphic language—that is, language which likens
God to men—is the language in which the message of heaven, known
to us as scripture, has been clothed. At issue is whether it was intended that the plain meaning of this language be trusted, as maintained by the Latter-day Saints, or if we are to set aside such notions as
childish, recognizing that God is the ultimate mystery and that no language can adequately convey understanding of him, as held by traditional Christianity.

The interpretation of virtually every scriptural text requires answering the questions, Was this intended to be understood figuratively
or literally? And how do we know? We will be hard pressed to find any
meaningful instance in which we as Latter-day Saints have given the
same answer to those questions that Christian theologians have. Indeed,
it would be hard to imagine how, taking the same book as a point of
origin, we could stand farther apart. As Latter-day Saints we have
chosen to embrace the plain meaning of words. Those who have embraced the conclusions of traditional Christianity ridicule such a stance
while announcing the meaning of most scriptural texts, particularly as
they deal with the nature of God, to be metaphorical. Significantly, those
who argue that the Bible is inerrant are as committed to a metaphorical

reading of the passages that describe the nature of God and to the creeds of Christendom as anyone else. In fact, the more defensive one becomes about the perfection of the Bible, the more frequently one will find it necessary to resort to metaphorical or allegorical explanations.

In so saying, I readily admit that most professing Christians think of God in terms of biblical imagery. Either they are unaware of the dichotomy between their understanding and the theological position of their churches or they have chosen to wear blinders and ignore that difference. Ministers use a language in common with their congregation but have an entirely different meaning behind the words they are using. If my experience is representative, most of the people that our missionaries talk to share the same conception of God that we do without being aware that it is at odds with their creeds and their churches' formal doctrinal pronouncements.

Our experience in talking to people of other faiths suggests that the great majority of them would be stunned to learn that their personal beliefs are an embarrassment to those who have spelled out their denominational beliefs. They are unaware that their intuitive and innate understanding is wholly at odds with the creeds that they profess. They are heretics unaware. For instance, it is universal to the faith of Bible-reading Christians that God (meaning the Son) was incarnate in the person of Jesus of Nazareth and that he now exists everlastingly with a resurrected body. It is further believed that this same Jesus loves those who profess and accept him as their Savior. In fact, the God of all who profess an allegiance to the doctrine of the Holy Trinity is that God, meaning Jesus of Nazareth, in his resurrected state is without body or form, that he is devoid of parts, and that he transcends all passions and is thus above the notion of love for humankind. As one Christian theologian notes, "In hymns like 'Blessed assurance, Jesus is mine,' and 'What a friend we have in Jesus,' or in 'choruses' like 'Jesus loves me, this I know,' we find in practice what would be hotly denied in theory, a unitarianism of the second person of the Trinity."[1]

The Traditional Argument

Far and away the greater part of biblical language which refers to God is anthropomorphic. That is, it ascribes human characteristics to him. It depicts Deity as having body, parts, and passions, all of which are quite human. An anthropomorphic God is one who sees, hears, knows, and loves. The purists, particularly those addicted to etymology, may desire to distinguish between anthropomorphism (Greek *anthropos*, a human being; *morphic*, shape or form) and anthropopathism (Greek *pathos*, susceptible to pain and suffering). The former describes a God of form like man's; the latter attributes feelings to him.

At issue is whether form and feelings demean or enhance the nature of God. Latter-day Saints know God as an exalted, resurrected, and glorified Man. We believe him to have meant what he said, according to the plain meaning of words, in the Genesis text wherein he said that he created us in his image and likeness. Out of this belief grows the idea that we can, in the course of eternity, become as he is. If God is an exalted, resurrected man, we can in the resurrection become like him. We will enjoy all the blessings of individuality and of body and form known to us here but in a perfect and glorified sense. To so believe is essential to the attendant belief that marriage and family associations continue in the worlds to come. Every doctrine that is meaningful to a Latter-day Saint centers in the nature of God, for his nature is our nature, we are his offspring. When our critics attack our faith in a God with body, parts, and passions, they attack every principle that we hold dear. Conversely, for us to suggest to those espousing traditional Christianity that God is not without body, parts, and passions is to attack the premise of the creeds upon which they have built their theological temple. There is no middle ground here.

In teaching about God, our missionaries have traditionally quoted various passages from the Old or New Testament to illustrate God's corporeal and anthropomorphic nature. Typically the debate begins at the simplest level, with the missionary quoting texts describing God as a being of body and form. Various passages can be quoted which refer to his face, eyes, eyelids, ears, nostrils, mouth, voice, arm, hand, palm, fingers, foot, heart, bosom, and bowels. The missionaries' antagonist responds by declaring all such references to be metaphors. He illustrates his point by quoting texts that liken God to the sun (see Psalm 84:11), a rock (see Deuteronomy 32:15), a spring (see Jeremiah 2:13), or a consuming fire (see Deuteronomy 4:24). His voice is likened to a mighty torrent (see Ezekiel 43:2) or thunder (see Psalm 29:3), his spirit to the wind (see John 3:8), his justice to the depth of the ocean (see Psalm 36:6), and his wisdom to a river (see the Apocrypha, Ecclesiasticus 24:25–29). There is even animal imagery in which God descends on Israel or Judah like a lion, panther, leopard, or bear (see Hosea 5:14; 13:7–8; Lamentations 3:10), or carries us in his wings (see Exodus 19:4).

In his published debate with B. H. Roberts, the Reverend D. Van Der Donckt objected to a literal interpretation of the scriptures, saying that if we accept the idea that we are literally in the image of God and that God has a body, "then we must hold that the *real hand* of God is meant by David in (Psalm 138). . . : 'If I take my wings early in the morning, and dwell in the uttermost part of the sea, even there shall *thy hand* lead me, and *thy right hand* shall hold me.' And as the Psalmist says also: 'Whither shall I flee from *thy face?* If I ascend into heaven, thou art there; if I descend into hell, thou art there' (Psalm 139:7, 8). Have we then according to 'Mormon' standards, not the right to infer that God has such a long hand as to extend to the uttermost parts of the sea, and such an extremely long face, reaching from heaven to hell? To this, I am sure, even the gloomiest Protestants would object. By the way, should we not also conclude that David had wings? ('If I take my wings early in the morning, and fly,' etc.)"[2]

Anthropomorphisms are used simply to make spiritual things intelligible. But to say that God has a body was certainly not intended to convey the idea that this is actually so.

Elder Roberts raises the question as to what authority placed Mr. V. in the position to determine that the plain meaning of scriptures is to be disregarded when it applies to God. He goes on to say:

> The "inspired writings" plainly and most forcibly attribute to Deity a form like man's, with limbs, organs, etc., but the Bible does not teach that this ascription of form, limbs, organs and passions to God, is unreal, and "simply to make spiritual things or certain truths more intelligible to man." On the contrary, the Bible emphasizes the doctrine of anthropomorphism by declaring in its very first chapter that man was created in the image of God: "So God created man in his own image, in the image of God created he him." The explanation is offered that it was necessary to attribute human form, members and passions, to God, in order to make spiritual things intelligible to man; *but what is the reason for ascribing the divine form to man,* as in the passage just quoted? Was that done to make human beings or certain truths more intelligible to God? Or was it placed in the word of God because it is simply true?

The truth that God in form is like man is further emphasized by the fact that Jesus is declared to have been in "the express image" of the Father's person (Hebrews 1:3); and until Mr. V. or some other person of his school of thought, can prove very clearly that the word of God supports his theory of the unreality of the Bible's ascription of form, organs, proportions, passions and feelings, to God and other heavenly beings the truth that God in form is like man will stand secure on the foundation of the revelations it has pleased God to give of his own being and nature.[3]

The real issue here is one of authority. Not the authority of the Bible, but authority to interpret the Bible. If we are in agreement that it is the word of God, should we not then accept its plain meaning as it teaches us of God, at least until someone can establish credentials that would entitle them to say otherwise? Such credentials would of necessity have to be equal to or greater than those of the ancient prophets and Apostles who originally wrote or spoke its sacred message. Thus it would require the authority to pen scripture, for surely to modify the meaning of scripture is no different than writing scripture. And surely such authority could not be had by any who claim the canon complete and the heavens sealed, which is the very position maintained by those who take the license to change it.

The Faith of the Meridian Saints

The meridian Saints worshipped a God who was corporeal. A classic evidence is found in the writings of Celsus, a bitter anti-Christian writer of the second century:

> The Christians say that God has hands, a mouth, and a voice; they are always proclaiming that "God said this" or "God spoke." "The heavens declare the work of his hands," they say. I can only comment that such a God is no god at all, for God has neither hands, mouth, nor voice, nor any characteristics of which we know. And they say that God made man in his own image, failing to realize that God is not at all like a man, nor vice versa; God resembles no form known to us. They say that God has form, namely the form of the Logos, who became flesh in Jesus Christ.

But we know that God is without shape, without color. They say that God moved above the waters he created—but we know that it is contrary to the nature of God to move. Their absurd doctrines even contain reference to God walking about in the garden he created for man; and they speak of him being angry, jealous, moved to repentance, sorry, sleepy—in short, as being in every respect more a man than a God. They have not read Plato, who teaches us in the *Republic* that God (the Good) does not even participate in being.[4]

So now we get to the heart of the matter. The problem with these poor ignorant Christians is that they have been reading the words of the prophets instead of the teachings of Plato. The God of the philosophers, Celsus explains, is "underivable," "unnameable"; he "cannot be reached by reason." All attributes of human nature are distinct from the nature of God, Celsus says. Indeed, "he cannot be comprehended in terms of attributes or human experience, contrary to what the Christians teach; moreover, he is outside any emotional experience," or, as more commonly stated, he is without passions.[5]

Philosopher-Theologians and the Demise of True Christianity

From the criticism of Celsus, we know that the Christians of his day still espoused a God who was both corporeal and personal. This may well have been the case with the ordinary Christians for at least the first three centuries of the current era. Their God was the God of the scriptures, and their trust was in the language of the prophets.[6] "It is only after divine corporeality is rejected on philosophical (Neoplatonist) grounds," states David L. Paulsen, "that these passages [those indicating God's corporeality] are given figurative or allegorical interpretations."[7] Paulsen sustains his case by examining two reluctant witnesses, Origen, one of the most influential of early church writers, and Augustine, the man who did more than any other to shape Catholic theology. Let us briefly consider the testimony of each man.

Origen was a Hellenistic Christian philosopher born in Egypt, probably Alexandria, about A.D. 185 (this was about the time that Celsus was writing). He was the early church's great apostle for the dogma of a bodiless God. The fact that he devoted considerable energy to arguments to prove God to be incorporeal evidences that the general membership of the church needed converting to such a view. In his discussions of the issue, Origen concedes that there is no place in the Bible in which God is explicitly described as being incorporeal. Paradoxically it is from his writings that we learn that today's most often used proof text to show that God is formless, John 4:24 ("God is a Spirit"), was initially understood by some as evidence against that proposition. Origen wrote as follows: "I know that some will attempt to say that, even according to the declarations of our own Scriptures, God is a body, because . . . they find it said . . . in the Gospel according to John, that 'God is a Spirit, and they who worship Him must worship Him in spirit and in truth.' . . . Spirit according to them [is] to be regarded as nothing else than a body."[8] The chain of thought here is that *pneuma* (translated "spirit") literally meant "air" or "breath," thus implying that spirit is both material and corporeal; thus God would have a pure body, but a body nonetheless.

Origen explicitly acknowledges that the issue of God's corporeality had not been settled in the church. In his writings he was at pains to show that a corporeal God was incompatible with Platonist conceptions of the divine nature and that the scriptures, properly viewed, do not disprove divine incorporeality.[9] His efforts here were simply to show that the scriptures were intended to be understood metaphorically. Read literally, they were of "little use."[10] God, he held, did not need a mouth to speak to his creations. He could simply inspire the heart of the saint with the sound of his voice. When we have done something that is unjust, he need only communicate a feeling of anger to us. No body parts are needed. Significantly, it is Origen whom we thank for preserving the writings of his fellow Platonist, Celsus.[11]

Regarding the second writer under consideration here, David Paulsen states: "In his *Confessions,* St. Augustine provides substantial evidence that belief in a corporeal deity was still commonly held at least in some Christian quarters as late as the fourth century."[12] Born of a Christian mother at Thagaste in North Africa in A.D. 354, Augustine grew up with the understanding that the Christian God was an embodied being. The doctrine, he said, was for him a stumbling block. He was plainly embarrassed by it and readily embraced the arguments of those who maligned it.

Eventually his career as a teacher of rhetoric took him to Italy, first to Rome and then to Milan, where, under the tutelage of Bishop Ambrose, he became acquainted with Latin translations of Platonist writings and learned of the possibility of God's being a totally immaterial, invisible, and incorporeal being. With his long-standing stumbling block removed, he converted to the faith in 386 and was baptized the following year at the age of thirty-two. Now firmly founded on a Neoplatonic reinterpretation of Christian doctrine, he could write:

> But when I understood withal that "man, created by Thee, after Thine own image," was not so understood by Thy spiritual sons . . . as though they believed and conceived of Thee as bounded by human shape . . . with joy I blushed at having so many years barked not against the Catholic faith, but against the fictions of carnal imaginations. . . . For Thou, Most High, and most near; most secret, and most present; Who hast not limbs some larger, some smaller, but art wholly every where and no where in space, art not of such corporeal shape. . . . Thy Catholic Church . . . I now discovered . . . not to teach that for which I had grievously censured her. So I was confounded, and converted; and I joyed, O my God, that the One Only Church . . . had no taste for infantine conceits; not, in her sound doctrine, maintained any tenet which should confine Thee, the Creator of all, in space, however great and large, yet bounded every where by the limits of a human form.[13]

The Arguments Against a Corporeal God

One of the earliest known attacks on anthropomorphism reaches back to the latter half of the sixth century B.C. when Xenophanes stated, "If oxen or lions had hands to write or to make works of art like men, horses would represent the gods in the likeness of horses, oxen in the likeness of oxen; they would provide them with a bodily form similar to their own."[14] Some five centuries later, Cicero echoed that sentiment, stating:

> This tendency has been fostered by the poets, painters and image-makers, as it was not easy to show the gods in life and action under any other guise. We also no doubt have to allow for the

prejudice by which mankind conceive of themselves as the most noble of all creatures. But surely you . . . can see how fond a matchmaker is Nature and how she can play the pander to her own charms? Come now, do you believe that there is any creature on land or sea which does not find its greatest pleasure in other creatures of its own kind? If it were otherwise, why should not a bull take his pleasure with a mare, or a stallion with a cow? Do you imagine that an eagle, or a lion, or a dolphin prefers any other shape to his own? So is it any wonder if in the same way nature prescribes that mankind should consider no shape to be more beautiful than theirs? This I think is the reason why we think the gods are similar to men. If the beasts could speak, do you not think that each would award the palm of excellence to its own kind?[15]

What is generally thought to be the wittiest barb thrown at the conception of a God with form is attributed to Voltaire, who is reputed to have quipped that God did not make man in his image, but vice versa.

The best scriptural argument that Origen could muster to defend his immaterial, invisible, and incorporeal God was that the scriptures did not disprove it. That may have been so in his day; it is not in ours. It would be a misconception to suppose that the scriptures constituted a sure standard for him or any of the ante-Nicene Fathers. Be it remembered that there had been no agreement in that day as to what writings constituted the canon of scripture. The New Testament, as we now have it, was not formulated until long after the Council of Nicaea. Indeed, there is considerable question as to the state of the manuscripts from which it comes. At best they would have been fragmentary and often corrupted. But it must also be remembered that scripture did not stand at the heart of the Christian church even before its Hellenization. For that matter, the books of the Old Testament had not been formally agreed upon either. A church once governed by Apostles, prophets, and the spirit of revelation now decided the most significant doctrinal matters without even reference to prayer, let alone the direction of the Holy Ghost. The voice of heaven was eloquent in its absence.

As to the scriptures, nowhere do they suggest that their plain and simple meaning be disregarded in favor of an allegorical or metaphorical interpretation. Further, we note Edmond Cherbonnier's observation in the *Harvard Theological Review* that "the prophets do not charge the pagan deities with being anthropomorphic, but with being insufficiently anthropomorphic. At their best, they are counterfeit persons. At their worst, they are frankly impersonal."[16]

Hosea 11:9 supposedly represents one of the best scriptural arguments against a corporeal God. It states, "For I am God, and not man; the Holy One in the midst of thee." The argument is obvious. God and man have been contrasted and anthropomorphism has been repudiated. But as Cherbonnier points out, the context argues otherwise. In fact, Hosea is one of the most emphatic anthropomorphic writers in the Bible. Cherbonnier writes:

> He attributes to God Himself the feelings and emotions of the husband whose wife has "played the harlot." The contrast between God and man concerns their respective ways of dealing with the situation. Instead of destroying Israel for her faithlessness, as might be expected of man, God is not vindictive. He has resources of mercy and forgiveness for the softening of Israel's heart. This difference between God and man is not a difference "in principle." It is merely *de facto*—a difference which God means eventually to overcome. . . .
>
> . . . From Anaximander to Feuerbach to Freud, philosophers have charged that to conceive God as personal must, by definition, be wishful thinking. The fallacy in such a claim is two-fold. In the first place, the validity of a belief is unaffected by a given person's motives for holding it. He might employ poor reasons, or none at all, in support of a position which is, on other grounds, impregnable. To disparage the position solely on the basis of the person's motives is to argue *ad hominem*.
>
> The second fallacy is the assumption that only those who believe in a personal God are liable to project themselves into their beliefs.[17]

The even more common form this argument takes is the old standard charge that religion is a crutch for those who need to believe. Perhaps it is; but is it not equally true that irreligion is a crutch for those who need to disbelieve? One Christian writer thoughtfully observed that "when fear of anthropomorphism induces men to reject the idea of a personal God, and to substitute for it some product of abstract thinking, they simply delude themselves. What they propose is just as anthropomorphic as what they reject."[18] Consider this example: Krister Stendahl, in his final convocation address as dean of the Harvard Divinity School, stressed the appropriateness of our worshipping a wholly abstract God and avoiding the "I-Thou" language of prayer. "To speak about God," he said, "is a rather arrogant thing, bordering on the ridiculous." He described it as "wholly arrogant and holy arrogance." This because God is beyond our ability to comprehend. "A god comprehended," he declared, "is by definition no god." So the counsel was to avoid sexist language when we pray. "Our Father which art in heaven" is out. "Thou eternal wisdom" is in. Other suggested phrases included, "Thou eternal justice" and "Thou eternal love."[19] But now we have come full circle and embraced once again the anthropomorphic God we were attempting to divorce ourselves of. Surely "wisdom," "justice," and "love" are all anthropomorphisms known to humankind.

We are guilty, according to Stendahl, of arrogant presumption to suppose that we can know something about God. This is what Cherbonnier calls the "moralistic fallacy." It is an attempt to settle the question as to what we can and cannot know about God by recourse to a moral censure. The thing is a boomerang. Stendahl accuses me of arrogance in supposing I can know something about God. In so doing he is really saying that his refusal to know anything about God makes him morally superior to me, which quite frankly is an arrogant presumption on his part.

The Argument About Divine Infinity

The philosopher and humble believer alike want an infinite God. To be infinite is to be unlimited. It is a little hard to get overly excited about a God with territorial bounds. The line of reasoning was enunciated by St. Anselm in the eleventh century. God, he reasoned, is the greatest conceivable being. He is that for which nothing greater is logically possible. Thus God lacks nothing that is "good," and he is whatever is better to be than not to be. He is the "most worthy object of religious worship." He cannot be limited in any way. To be limited in any way is to be relative in that way, which would in turn create the possibility of being dwarfed by something else that is greater. God, this chain of thought holds, must tower infinitely above all other objects. Thus, Anselm reasons that God cannot have body or parts. Anything that is bounded by place is less than that which is not limited by place. Since nothing is greater than God, he can be in no place but rather must be in all places at all times.

The flaw in this line of reasoning is that it mistakenly supposes that a limitation is a defect. As David Paulsen observes, surely this depends on the nature of the limitation. For example, limitations in negative attributes—ignorance, selfishness, cruelty, and so on—would be desirable. Anselm makes it clear that God would be absolutely unlimited only in every admirable attribute. Still the problem remains that a virtue overdone can be a tragic flaw. One may be too trusting, too generous, too helpful, Paulsen points out. Indeed, all godly attributes assume value only as they complement and harmonize with each other. Each must retain its proper weight and balance. Each has its proper place, and each can be very much out of place if applied improperly. Mercy cannot deny justice, nor can justice dominate mercy.[20]

Cherbonnier argues that "there are two distinct kinds of limitation, each of which excludes the other, and between which the theologian is obliged to choose." The first meaning deals with logical predication. A thing is limited the moment any characteristic is attributed to it. Thus any positive statement about God automatically restricts, or limits, him. If he is all-knowing he cannot be unknowing. If he is personal he cannot be impersonal. Now the philosopher enters on the scene with the announcement that everything that has a name is thereby limited. So God can be unlimited or infinite only if he is unknown to us by name, only if he is beyond predication, only if he is indeterminate.[21]

The God who appeared to Joseph Smith is obviously a determinate God. "I, the Lord, am bound when ye do what I say; but when ye do not what I say, ye have no promise" (D&C 82:10). He has limits and bounds. He cannot do a single thing that is ungodly. He cannot lack wisdom; he cannot lack knowledge; he cannot lack goodness or virtue, or patience, or love. Furthermore he has announced himself as being unchangeable (that being another thing he cannot do) and as being the same yesterday, today, and forever. This is the same God known to the prophets of both the Old and New Testaments. Their attention, however, as Cherbonnier notes, was centered on the reality that God could accomplish his purposes. If he could not, he was not a God. If he could, he was anthropomorphic. "The gods of Canaan and Babylon were at least good imitations," says Cherbonnier. "The prophets do not charge them with being anthropomorphic, but with being frauds."

Continuing, Cherbonnier explains:

> As an illustration one may cite another of the passages which superficially appears to "transcend" anthropomorphism: "To whom will you liken me and make me equal, and compare me, that we may be alike? . . . For I am God, and there is no other; I am God, and there is none like me" (Isaiah 46:5, 9). Again, however, the context reverses the interpretation. It contrasts the mighty acts of Yahweh with the impotence of every false god: "They lift it upon their shoulders, they carry it; . . . it cannot move from its place, . . . it does not answer" (v. 7). The true God, however, does move and speak; he announces his purpose and brings it to pass (v. 11).
>
> The intent of such passages is to distinguish Yahweh from idols by precisely these anthropomorphic activities: "They have mouths, but do not speak; eyes, but do not see; they have ears, but do not hear; noses, but do not smell" (Psalm 115:5, 6). Pagan gods are contemptible because of their impotence. They cannot even do the things a man can do, whereas Yahweh does these things *par excellence.*[22]

So the issue here is whether we have a God that can do things or one that is beyond that. The God of the Bible did things. Plato's God is above that. The choice is between an anthropomorphic God and an impotent God. This answers the question as to why the kinds of miracles common to the Old and New Testaments have ceased in the Christian world. Their God doesn't work them. This is why they don't have prophets or Apostles; their God doesn't call them. This is why they don't have continuous revelation; their God doesn't speak.

The Unity of God

No truth about the nature of God has done more to teach and clarify the system of salvation than the scriptural declarations relative to God's unity, or oneness. Conversely, among those who have abandoned revelation as a reliable source from which they take their bearings, no concept has led to greater confusion. The unity of God was not intended to teach monism. Its purpose is to attest that salvation consists in our becoming one with God. "If ye are not one ye are not mine," he declared (D&C 38:27). Paul stated it thus: "He that is joined unto the Lord is one spirit" (1 Corinthians 6:17). Obtaining salvation is the process of learning to think as God thinks, believe as he believes, feel as he feels, and act as he would act. There is no divergence among those who are saved. All are equally loyal to the cause of heaven.

By contrast, no dogma has done more to confuse true theology than the mystics' concept of monism. The mystics can tolerate but one God. To suppose that two beings exist, each equal in power, might, and dominion, causes their world to shatter like crystal under hot water. For the mystics' God to be absolute he must be the sole existent being. He cannot be compromised by the existence of anything to which he can relate. "It is precisely this conception of unity which the Bible opposes," Cherbonnier states. "When the prophet cried, 'Hear, O Israel, the Lord thy God is one God,' he was not referring to 'the one without a second.' He was calling attention to God's constancy of purpose, his integrity of character. Precisely because God is anthropomorphic, with an unmistakable personal identity, He could not be represented by a bull or a baal or a solar disc."[23]

The notion of a sole God does not represent the purity of scriptural intent. As we have seen, it was "only in later Judaism" that this notion appeared. It is the mystic, however, in his attempt to have an absolute God, who "puts Him in quarantine." Cherbonnier further observes: "The mystic finds himself in the embarrassing position of prescribing what God may and may not do. In fact, by denying that God is anthropomorphic, he denies Him the power to act at all." The biblical God, by contrast, is as "absolute" and as "related" as he chooses to be. He can choose to create a universe distinct from himself.[24] He can people it with children created in his image and likeness and endow them with agency and power to become as he is.

Discerning the Figurative and the Literal

We turn again to the issue of figurative versus literal. Do we trust the literalness of the Bible as it gives descriptions of God, or do we suppose that all such references are figurative on the basis of the philosophers' speculative theology? And if we are to be consistent, will not the same rule apply to all else within the covers of the Holy Book? Are words ever to be trusted to mean what they say, and if so, how are we to know? The issue is one that we decide at the peril of our eternal life, at least it is if we take the Savior seriously. "This is life eternal," he said, "that they might know thee the only true God, and Jesus Christ, whom thou hast sent" (John 17:3). But this too might be a figurative expression. If we abandon the notion that God is a personal being, we change the meaning of everything else that is said about him. This in turn changes the nature of our relationship with him and the meaning of everything that we understand to be a part of the plan of salvation.

To worship God correctly we must answer the figurative-versus-literal issue correctly. There is no saving power in bad doctrine. Therefore God himself must be the source of our authority on this matter. Opinion will not do. This makes the genealogy of the idea that biblical anthropomorphisms are to be interpreted figuratively of great importance. Who decided the issue?

The *Encyclopaedia Judaica* acknowledges that biblical anthropomorphism was "a major problem" for Jewish theologians. As we have already seen, in the second century B.C. the Septuagint translators removed many of the anthropomorphisms from the Hebrew Bible. Philo was also very affronted by them. Anthropomorphisms were, he held, introduced into scripture for the instruction of the many, those "whose natural wit is dense or dull, whose childhood training has been mismanaged, and are incapable of seeing clearly."[25] According to the *Encyclopaedia Judaica,* three basic trends of thought existed in the Middle Ages among Jews relative to this matter: (1) That all anthropomorphisms used to describe God were metaphorical. "This approach developed chiefly through the influence of Greek and Arabic philosophy." (2) That allegorical exegesis was a danger that could cause the meaning of all biblical truths to evaporate. (3) That all anthropomorphic references point to those beings (Logoi) that stood between God and man.[26] By the nineteenth century, however, it was argued that an understanding of the nature of God had evolved from anthropomorphic concepts to "a more purified spiritual faith" among the Jews. This argument of evolving revelation reasoned that corporeal representations of Deity were more common to the older portions of the Bible than its later books. However, the *Encyclopaedia Judaica* concedes that "in fact, both personifications of the Deity as well as attempts to avoid them are found side by side in all parts of the Bible." It is also acknowledged that the scarcity of anthropomorphisms in some narratives may be due to their being "designed to express the growing distance between God and man."[27]

The Christian world followed the path marked by their Jewish counterparts. *The Oxford Dictionary of the Christian Church* discusses the issue thus: "This tendency [of attributing human characteristics to God] arises out of the conditions of human knowledge which originates in sense-perception. In its crudest forms it is most prominent in primitive and polytheistic religions, and from the point of view of Greek philosophy it was already ridiculed by Xenophanes. Scripture, esp. in the earlier books of the OT . . . , in order to be intelligible to less developed minds, frequently uses anthropomorphic language, which is in most cases clearly metaphorical."[28]

This is as good as the argument gets, and there is that sense that we have heard it all before. Christian and Jew alike were embarrassed by the simplicity of their faith when confronted by their more sophisticated Greek neighbors. They were told that their concept of God was vulgar and crude. A God with bodily functions came to be an embarrassment to them. For Christians, Origen and Augustine were chief among their spokesmen, but virtually all their intellectuals have been quick to follow suit. As Cherbonnier describes it, these intellectuals see their purpose as preserving "the integrity of human reason against the credulity and superstition which often accompany religion. They want to show the thinking man that Christianity does not insult his intelligence."[29] Thus they mingled scripture with the philosophies of men and in so doing formed an alliance not unlike that of Solomon, who took wives of another faith and found himself worshipping at the shrine of unknown gods. The new God of Christianity became the old god of Greek philosophy.

The issue is clearly set. To the prophets, God was always a person, and he is portrayed by them in the most anthropomorphic of language. To the intellectual, the testimony of the prophets is crude and embarrassing. The choice is now ours as to whether we feel more secure in company with prophets or with self-styled intellects.

8

And wo unto them that seek deep to hide their counsel from the Lord! And their works are in the dark; and they say: Who seeth us, and who knoweth us? And they also say: Surely, your turning of things upside down shall be esteemed as the potter's clay. But behold, I will show unto them, saith the Lord of Hosts, that I know all their works. For shall the work say of him that made it, he made me not? Or shall the thing framed say of him that framed it, he had no understanding?

—2 Nephi 27:27

A Fight in the Dark

I spoke one evening in a missionary fireside on the topic of the divine sonship of Christ. I was able to identify the investigators present and watched their eyes carefully as I spoke. I remember one lady in particular. She was seated on the second row toward the middle of the chapel. She was subconsciously nodding in agreement with each point that I made. After the meeting the missionaries introduced us. Before I had the chance to say anything to her she said, "I have really enjoyed the evening. There was a good, warm feeling here."

"Yes, there was," I responded.

Then she said, "I understood every word you said."

"Good," I said, with some feeling, "because it is very important."

"You know what is interesting," she continued, "I have been a member of the Church of the Holy Trinity for thirty years and have never understood a word they said."

"We have both room for you here and a doctrine that you can understand," I responded.

"Oh, I could never leave them," she replied, raising her voice a little as she said it. "I have been drinking coffee with them for thirty years."

Whenever a truth of salvation has been taught, both mentor and disciple will rejoice together and both will be edified. Such was the experience that this good woman and I shared that night. Equally true is the fact that "that which doth not edify is not of God, and is darkness. That which is of God is light; and he that receiveth light, and continueth in God, receiveth more light; and that light groweth brighter and brighter until the perfect day." (D&C 50:23–24.) Conversely, an unknowable truth is no truth, and an unknowable God is no God. Should another thirty years pass and that good woman and I meet again, she will know nothing more about God than she does now, save she chooses to stand in the light. The seed of truth does not grow in the dark. Let us now construct an important part of the story of how the great night of darkness was ushered in.

The Arian Controversy

In the traditional Christian faith the doctrine of divine sonship was formally supplanted by the dogma of the Holy Trinity at the Council of Nicaea held under the direction of Constantine, emperor of Rome, in A.D. 325. Historians refer to it as the church's first ecumenical conference. The very fact that such a council was called to determine a doctrinal matter evidences that the biblical system of prophets speaking in the name of the Lord no longer existed. It enables us to point to a time and a place where revelation was officially replaced by deliberation and manipulation. Authentic records of what took place are scanty. Most of what calls itself church history is legend. Virtually all that has survived comes from the pens of those who have adopted the prevailing view of the Council and write in its defense.

Important antecedents to the council include the fact that by A.D. 312—only nine years since Diocletian, emperor of Rome, had begun his persecution of the Christians—the political situation had entirely changed. Diocletian had abdicated; Galerius was dead; Constantine's father, Constantius, was dead; and in the West, only Maximian's son, Maxentius, lay between Constantine and control of the western half of the Roman Empire. Constantine was ready to march on Rome, though the odds of victory were not favorable.

Maxentius, fortified behind the walls of Rome, commanded superior numbers, which included the Praetorian Guard, whose power had for centuries determined who would be Caesar in Rome. Nor could Constantine, as aggressor, expect much help from the citizens of Rome, who, weary of the continuous trouble of the previous years, could hardly be expected to enthusiastically embrace yet another Roman's bid for power. Constantine was badly in need of something to give his cause extra purpose and justification. According to Christian legend, on the afternoon before the battle, Constantine saw a flaming cross in the sky, with the Greek words *en toutoi nika*—"in this sign conquer." Early the next morning he dreamed that a voice directed him to have his soldiers mark the letter X with a line drawn through it and curled around the top—the symbol of Christ—on their shields.[1] The order was given to have the new logo painted on every soldier's shield. Another version of the story is that on the "night before the battle Constantine had a dream in which he was shown a sign, accompanied by the words: *Hoc signo victor eris!* 'By this sign you shall be the victor!' The sign consisted of the Greek letters Chi-Rho, the first two letters of the name Christ, in a monogram form" as they had been adopted by the Christians.[2]

To give credence to the vision of Constantine, which some hold was seen by all of his army and attended by the personal visit of Christ to Constantine that night,[3] we must accept the idea that the heavens are sealed as far as Apostles and prophets are concerned but still open to the direction of pagan generals—in this instance, one who only six years before had hundreds of Frankish rebel prisoners torn to pieces in an arena. Further, we must believe that the cause of Christ is now to be advanced by the sword in an unholy alliance between church and state.

Secular history declares Constantine to have been the victor that day, while religious histories grant the victory to Christ and the church. The triumphal arch, which commemorates Constantine's victory, stands to this day alongside the Coliseum in Rome. It is adorned with traditional pagan symbols. A commemorative medallion struck by Constantine in A.D. 313 portrays him as Invictus Constantius alongside the image of Sol Invictus, the god of a pagan cult imported from Syria decades earlier.[4]

At the time of the council, Constantine was unpopular in Rome and was struggling to rule a divided empire. A unifying force was needed, and Constantine saw it in the church, but the church was also seriously divided. Three clouds marred the brilliance of this otherwise cloudless day: the monastic secession, the Donatist schism, and the Arian heresy. With the end of the Great Persecution in A.D. 304—which began with Diocletian's edict that Christian churches be destroyed, their congregations forbidden to meet, and their Bibles and liturgical books surrendered—the church had quickly become the richest religious organization in the empire. This in turn brought a dramatic change in the church's attitude about earthly possessions and the use of political power. Will Durant said it well: "While Christianity converted the world, the world converted Christianity."[5]

Some among the clergy opposing these indulgences of the flesh countered with a new allegiance to asceticism. They surrendered all worldly goods and exchanged their silks and fine-twined linens for the ragged robes of the philosopher. Virginity and celibacy were placed above family life, while the desert and the monastery became the places of salvation. These ascetics had considerable influence in refashioning the God of the prophets into the ephemeral God of the Greek philosophers. Their rejection of all physical comfort and pleasure was reflected in their disdain for the body, which they viewed as a prison into which the spirit had been placed as a result of the fall of Adam. As their God was without body, parts, or passions, it naturally followed that they viewed everything in the scriptures that spoke of an anthropomorphic God as an unfortunate metaphor, and for many martyrdom became a sought-after crown, one by which they could free themselves from the prison of the flesh.

In North Africa the Donatist dispute raged. Donatus, bishop of Carthage, Will Durant explains, "insisted that Christian bishops who had surrendered the Scriptures to the pagan police during the persecutions had forfeited their office and powers; that baptisms or ordinations performed by such bishops were null and void; and that the validity of sacraments depended in part upon the spiritual state of the ministrant. When the Church refused to adopt this stringent creed, the Donatists set up rival bishops wherever the existing prelate failed to meet their tests."[6]

These same years witnessed the most challenging doctrinal issue in the history of the traditional Christian church, known to us as the Arian heresy. The views of Arius sprang from the difficulty of reconciling the idea of the unity of the Godhead with the doctrine of the true Deity of Jesus Christ. Arius, a priest laboring in Baucalis, a parish near Alexandria, Egypt, maintained that the Savior was totally distinct from his Father, that he was the first and noblest of those beings whom God the Father had created (out of nothing), and that he, under the direction of his Father, was the creator of this universe.

Arius's major opponent in this argument was his own bishop, Alexander of Alexandria. Upon learning that one of his priests was teaching some novel doctrines about Deity, he conferred with him. Arius, we are told, subtly hid the full implication of his teachings from his superior. Upon receiving further complaints, Alexander determined to excommunicate Arius. To make the action more authoritative he convoked a council of the bishops of Egypt and Libya numbering nearly a hundred. He then sent an account of the proceedings to other bishops, that they might be warned against this heresy.

Despite the fact that he had been unfrocked, Arius continued to conduct services and seek support for his views. Since Alexandria had been the home of philosophical debates for more than a century, its people zealously threw themselves into the fray. Many priests disagreed with the decision of the bishop, and "tumult and disorder" began to spread from city to city.

Constantine, who was greatly vexed by all of this dissension, particularly as it preoccupied the Eastern church, wrote a letter to Arius and Bishop Alexander seeking to ameliorate the situation. His advisers on the matter were Eusebius of Nicomedia, who favored Arius's position, if for no other reason than his rivalry with the Egyptian bishop Alexander, and Eusebius of Caesarea, who was regarded as the greatest church scholar of his day. These men saw the issue as nothing more than a disagreement over speculative matters which lay beyond the sphere of church doctrine. The letter, which has survived, is now pointed to as evidence that Constantine did not grasp the importance of the theological issues at hand or he would have censured Arius. Such reasoning assumes that it is the prerogative of a pagan emperor to correct the Christian priesthood when they err. Instead he sought peace and offered his assistance as arbitrator and intermediary. Not only did the letter and his personal envoy fail in their purpose, but they were greeted with tumultuous assemblages in the streets of Alexandria, where statues of the emperor were broken. Arius then responded to the emperor with a vain and intemperate letter.

Constantine was enraged. He responded with another letter in which he called Arius a serpent, the image of the devil, and made a bad pun on the priest's name. He then challenged Arius to meet him face-to-face and let him judge the issue. Arius accepted the challenge. He came, and (as those who record the story tell it) with his skill in evasions and ambiguities he succeeded in perplexing the untheological mind of the emperor. Constantine simply concluded the interview by saying that if Arius was deceiving him or concealing things from him, the God of whom he witnessed would confound him as an imposture. The controversy continued to grow more loud and bitter. Constantine determined to convoke a general council of the bishops of all the world to give judgment on the matter.

The Council of Nicaea

The Turkish city of Iznik now occupies the place where Nicaea once stood. It was located southeast of Constantinople (now Istanbul), across the Sea of Marmonra, at a distance of some forty-four miles. It was situated along the banks of a long inland lake, which also now bears the name Iznik. The city was built on the same general plan as the other cities with which the Greek dynasties had enriched their conquests—a square, intersected by four broad straight streets, adorned with long lines of columns, which turned the whole length of their walkways into broad porticoes; thus screened from the heat of the Eastern sun, people could comfortably gather and talk. The great council itself was held in a large rectangular hall at the center of a palace.

The number of bishops, priests, and deacons present in Nicaea is thought to have been about two thousand. Of the 318 bishops present, only 6 were from the West.[7] Europe was far behind the East in intellectual development at the time. Other guests of the city included philosophers, some of them pagan, who sought, if only informally, to be a part of the event. They would gather with the participants of the council in casual groups under the shade of the colonnades in the main streets to debate the issues.[8]

As survivors of the Great Persecution, some of the bishops were a sobering sight. Egypt's two Coptic bishops were sightless in the right eye, it having been dug out with a sword, and the empty socket seared with a red-hot iron. From Neocaesarea, a border fortress on the Euphrates, came a bishop whose hands were paralyzed by the scorching from a similar iron;[9] others had been deprived of the right arm.[10] Their number also included emaciated ascetics. For instance, there was Jacob, bishop of Nisibis, who had lived for years as a hermit on the mountains, staying in the forests during the summer and in caverns during the winter. He had survived by browsing on roots and leaves like a wild beast, clothed in a rough goat-hair cloak.[11]

Legend casts its characters well. A leading role went to the bishop of Alexandria, Alexander by name. He was the official accuser, an old man clothed in the shadow of death. He is referred to as the pope. He is the only bishop officially referred to by that title at that time.[12] Alexander is described as a man of apostolic virtues. He was attended by the deacon Athanasius, small in stature but large in intellect. Though but twenty-five years of age, Athanasius was to shortly assume the office vacated by the death of Alexander (A.D. 328) and become the great champion of his cause. The description given of him is patterned after that of an angel of light. He is said to have been lively of manners and speech and to have been bright and serene of countenance.

As to Arius, the heretic, he is described as being in the image of a twisted snake—tall, very thin, a body that could not support its stature, causing him to twist and contort as he walked. He was, we are told, emaciated and pale of countenance, and he had a downcast look. At times his veins would throb and swell, while his limbs would tremble. He was to die suddenly eleven years later, quite possibly by poison. There was a wild look about him, which at first sight was startling. His dress and demeanor were those of a rigid ascetic. He wore a long coat with short sleeves, and a scarf of only half size, such as was the mark of an austere life; his hair hung in a tangled mass over his head. He was usually silent, but broke out into fierce excitement, giving the impression of madness.

The leading role in this drama, appropriately enough, went to the emperor Constantine, Pontifex Maximus, head of the pagan state cult. Peter de Rosa gives this description; "Born in 274 to Constantius and a mere concubine Helena, he should not have been eligible for imperial honours. He won his consecration by the sword. Twice married, he murdered Cripus, his son by his first wife, in 326. He had his second wife drowned in the bath; killed his eleven-year-old nephew, then his brother-in-law, after giving him assurances of safe-conduct under oath. He did not persecute Christians, only his family and friends."[13]

The council commenced meeting, at least informally, for a few weeks before the arrival of the emperor, who was delayed by commemorative events in Nicomedia. Constantine arrived on the fourth or fifth of July, and the solemn opening of the synod took place the following day.[14] "He caused the council to be removed to the palace," writes Edward Backhouse, "where a large hall was prepared, in which the bishops and other delegates took their places according to their rank."[15] Constantine was a man of imposing presence—tall, muscular, and handsome. It is said that he resembled Apollo. His entrance into the assembly is described thus: "First came some of the officers of the household, then some of the court, then some of the imperial family; lastly, the officer who usually immediately preceded the Emperor appeared at the door, the whole assembly rose, and Constantine entered. His lofty, broad, imposing person was clad in a robe of purple embroidered with gold and colours, and sparkling with precious stones; his long, carefully arranged golden hair was partly covered by a light helmet, encircled by the jewelled diadem of the East. . . . His grand person, with his embroidered robes and flashing jewels, in the midst of the white-robed assembly, was very striking and splendid, and, says Eusebius [of Caesarea], was like the appearance of an angel."[16]

It is argued by some apologists that this unbaptized worshiper of Zeus played no significant role in the council. Yet, all present were there at his expense and by his order. He had chosen the time, the place, and the agenda. He sat at the upper end of the hall in a golden chair and held in his hand a six-foot spear gilded in gold and studded with jewels as a scepter of power. He addressed and charged the assembly, and "then gave those who presided in the council an opportunity of speaking, and permitted the members to examine matters of doctrine and religious differences."[17] At the conclusion of the council he richly rewarded those who had decided properly and banished those who had not.

The Matter to Be Decided

It is a difficult thing to clearly state the issue to be determined at the Council of Nicaea.[18] It is generally conceded that the apostolic messengers who initially took the message of Christ to the nations of the earth would not have been able to understand the subtleties involved. It is reasoned that because the meridian Church anticipated the destruction of the world and the imminent return of Christ, little concern was given to the development of the detailed and systematic theology of later years.[19] It is also conceded that the large majority of the council did not perceive the exact point of the controversy. In his *History of the Christian Church,* F. J. Foakes-Jackson observes that a remark by Socrates, a fifth-century church historian, illustrated well the situation of the council's majority. Apparently referring to a later phase of the Arian controversy, Socrates remarked: "What took place resembled a fight in the dark, no man knew whether he struck at friend or foe."[20] Most of those at the Council of Nicaea were men who had a strong distaste for innovation on the one hand and who were fearful of being branded heretics on the other; yet it was by their vote that the matter was to be decided.

Let it be said that the Christ of modern Christianity was not born of Mary in a stable in Bethlehem; he was created by the vote of a council in a palace hall in Nicaea. "The great attraction of Christianity for the men of the third and fourth centuries was, not its doctrines of Atonement and Redemption, but its Monotheism," writes Foakes-Jackson. "The Faith had given life and reality to the unity of God, which even heathen philosophy had pronounced to be a necessary belief. Nor had the Christian teachers been less influenced by Neo-Platonism than that philosophy by Christianity. The Church teachers of the fourth century very frequently appeal to Philo, to Porphyry, to Plotinus, and other Neo-Platonists, in their belief that they could find in their writings the Christian conception of God. Certainly the Neo-Platonists had constructed a kind of doctrine of the Trinity."[21]

Two key doctrines made this birth of Christ in Nicaea possible: allegorical interpretation of scripture and the Greek doctrine of the Logos. In his work *The Story of Christianity,* Justo L. González explains: "Allegorical interpretation was fairly simple to apply. Wherever Scripture says something 'unworthy' of God—that is, something that is not worthy of the perfection of the supreme being—such words are not to be taken literally. Thus, for instance, if the Bible says that God walked in the garden, or that God spoke, one is to remember that an immutable being does not really walk or speak. Intellectually, this satisfied many minds. But emotionally it left much to be desired, for the life of the church was based on the faith that it was possible to have a direct relationship with a personal God, and the supreme being of the philosophers was in no way personal."

The chasm between the God of the philosophers and the God of the scriptures was bridged with the doctrine of the Logos, as developed by Justin, Clement, Origen, and others. González explains further: "According to this view, although it is true that the supreme being—the 'Father'—is immutable, impassible, and so on, there is also a Logos, Word, or Reason of God, and this is personal, capable of direct relations with the world and with humans. Thus, according to Justin, when the Bible says that God spoke to Moses, what it means is that the Logos of God spoke to him."[22]

These ideas were widespread in the Eastern wing of the church—that portion of the church that spoke Greek rather than Latin. Among them, the generally accepted view was that between the immutable (meaning unchangeable) One and the mutable world stood the Logos of God. Such was the setting for the Arian controversy.

The debate centered on the issue of Logos. This issue in turn centered on the interpretation of the Greek term *gennētos* as it applied to Christ. Traditionally translated "begotten," in Greek philosophical terminology it had a broader and hence vaguer sense. It denoted anything which "came to be" and hence anything that was derived or generated.[23] The place of beginning for both Arius and Alexander is with the God of the philosophers, that is, with a God who is immutable and uncreatable. Both are in agreement that such a God cannot have body, parts, or passions; nor can he speak to his creations by way of revelation. Their God is far beyond and above such things. Everything in the Bible to that effect is "unworthy" of him and hence is an allegory. Both agree that in order for God to communicate with man, a mediator is needed. That mediator is the Logos, or Son, of God. Like the Greek use of the word *begotten,* the denomination *Son* as applied to Christ is also used in a broad and vague sense. To suppose that God actually had a Son would, according to this school of philosophical thought, be unworthy of God. For that matter, a God without body and parts does not conceive a Son who has body and parts. The issue at Nicaea was whether Logos is really also the Father, thus assuring that Christians are pure monotheists, or whether Logos was begotten in some way by the Father and is thus separate from and subordinate to him.

Accounts differ as to Arius's role at the council. Edward Cutts maintains that Arius threw all caution to the wind and spoke forth boldly, declaring that the Word was not co-eternal with the Father and was not of the same substance as the Father, that in the beginning the

Father was alone, and that the Son was created out of nothing by an act of the Father's will. Further, our source tells us that these statements produced such a sensation that the majority of the bishops "stopped their ears with the lively gesture of Eastern disapprobation, and cried out aloud against such blasphemies." From that moment the condemnation of Arius was a foregone conclusion; all that remained was to draw up an authoritative statement or creed.[24] Another source states "Arius reaffirmed his view," but then "clever questioners forced him to admit that if Christ was a creature, and had had a beginning, he could change; and that if he could change he might pass from virtue to vice. The answers were logical, honest, and suicidal." This source also tells us that Athanasius, supporter of Alexander, "made it clear that if Christ and the Holy Spirit were not of one substance with the Father, polytheism would triumph. He conceded the difficulty of picturing three distinct persons in one God, but argued that reason must bow to the mystery of the Trinity."[25] Yet another source maintains that neither Arius nor Athanasius were allowed to sit in the council, not being bishops. According to this view, Eusebius of Nicomedia "spoke for [Arius] and for the position that he represented."[26]

In any case, having rejected the position of Arius, the council now devoted its labor to the formulation of a creed to assure a uniformity of faith among all believers. To find suitable language to represent the decision of the council, question after question was put to the Eusebian party (Eusebius of Nicomedia and those aligned with him), who had represented Arius's views. In one way or another they found it possible to agree with the various expressions. Finally someone hit upon the word *consubstantial* (meaning "of the same substance") to identify those who believed in the true Deity of Jesus. The Eusebians opposed its use and argued that it was unscriptural. The more they opposed it, the more convinced the assembly became that it was precisely the word they sought. Thus the pivotal question of the council became that of "consubstantiality."

Cutts states the issue thus: "The Catholics asserted that Jesus Christ was very and eternal God; the Arians, however high in creation they might place Him, yet placed Him among the creatures. If the Catholics were right, it was sin not to worship Him; if the Arians were right, to worship him was idolatry. If Jesus must be brought down from the Catholic altitude of God to the Arian level of a creature, the whole Christian scheme must undergo a corresponding degradation."[27]

A vote was taken. Only seventeen voices objected to the use of *consubstantiality*. The creed was given as follows:

> We believe in one God, the Father Almighty, the Maker of all things visible and invisible.
> And in one Lord Jesus Christ, the Son of God, only-begotten of the Father, that is, of the substance of the Father, God of God, Light of Light, very God of very God, begotten not made, being of one substance with the Father, by Whom all things were made of things in heaven and in earth; Who for us men and for our salvation came down from heaven, was incarnate, was made man, suffered, rose again the third day, ascended into the heavens, and He will come to judge the living and the dead.
> And in the Holy Ghost.

Appended to these creedal statements was the following canon:

> As for those who say that "there was a time when the Son was not," or that "He was not before He was begotten," or that He was "made out of nothing," or that He is of another "hypostasis" or of another "substance" than God, or that He is "created" or "mutable," and "subject to change," those the Holy Catholic Apostolic Church of God declares to be anathema.[28]

The council condemned Arius as a heretic. Constantine in turn issued an edict branding him as infamous and condemning his books to be burnt; any found possessing them were to be put to death. This addition of a civil sentence to an ecclesiastical one was to have serious consequences, for it established the precedent for the intervention of secular authority in behalf of the church.

The decision of the council was of some importance to Constantine. If the Godhead could be divided into separate personages, if holiness was not the exclusive province of one God, then, as John Romer writes, "fractions of this sacredness might still run throughout man's world just as Jesus, the Son had once done. And if sacredness could run unchecked through the order of the world, the role of emperors in such a universe of democratic holiness would come but a poor second! Constantine wanted *his* Imperium to resemble the order of heaven, with the role of emperor echoing the role of God in heaven. Arguments about the nature of God were far from being theological abstractions: they were about power in this world and the next."[29]

As to the seventeen negative votes, these bishops were undoubtedly advocates of the Arian view, but when they understood that the creed was to be published under imperial authority, and that the penalty of recusancy would be the loss of place and favor, all but two submitted. The two were banished. Eusebius of Nicomedia and Theognis of Nicaea subscribed the creed, but refused to put their hands to the anathema, holding that from what they had read and heard, they did not know that Arius had actually taught the doctrines of which he was accused. Three months later they too were banished.

Where historical sources are scanty, which is very much the case in the telling of the story of Nicaea, popular imagination is quick to make up the difference. It is said that a fountain sprang up in the square of Nicaea where the synod had united in a public prayer, the waters of which had a healing power. Another legend centers around the signing of the creed. Two of the bishops died during the council and were buried at Nicaea. When the creed, we are told, was subscribed by the others, the document was left on the graves of the two bishops, with this invocation: "O fathers and brothers, you have fought the good fight, you have finished your course, you have kept the faith; if what we have done is pleasing to God, you who now see Him face to face, add your names to ours." The next morning, the story goes, their signatures were appended to it.[30]

At the conclusion of the council, Constantine invited all the signers of the creed to a grand banquet, the magnificence of which is said to have surpassed all imagination. He awarded presents to each according to his station, and also gave them letters to present to the proper officers of their provinces, ordering a quantity of corn to be put at the disposition of the churches every year for their sustenance and that of the church widows, virgins, and the poor.[31] He then dismissed them with the request that they not tear one another to pieces, counsel that was not followed.[32] Constantine was mistaken if he thought the controversy ended, or if he supposed that he would not change his own view of it.

The Controversy Continued

It may well be that what agreement existed in Nicaea was made possible by the ambiguous nature of the creed.[33] Neander observes that "it was nothing but the influence of the emperor Constantine, which induced the eastern bishops, at the council of Nice, to suffer the imposition of a doctrinal formula which they detested, and from which, indeed, they sought immediately to rid themselves."[34] Whatever the reasons, the commotion excited by the controversy remained in the minds of many. "The spirit of dissension triumphed both over the decrees of the council and the authority of the emperor," observes Mosheim. "For those who, in the main, were far from being attached to the party of Arius, found many things reprehensible, both in the decrees of the council, and in the forms of expression which it employed to explain the controverted points; while the Arians, on the other hand, left no means untried to heal their wounds, and to recover their place and their credit in the church."[35] Their efforts were crowned with success, as the emperor's sister, Constantia, was in frequent communication with Eusebius of Nicomedia. She also had an Arian presbyter for her spiritual guide who convinced her that Arius had been unjustly condemned. Constantia possessed great influence over her brother, and on her deathbed in 327 she earnestly commended the Arian priest to his attention. Thereafter the priest rapidly gained the emperor's confidence and succeeded in persuading him that personal motives and passions had much more to do with the decision of the late council than any concern for sound doctrine. Constantine accordingly sent Arius a message giving him permission to return to Alexandria.

The readmission of Arius was like dry grass on a smoldering flame. Athanasius refused to receive the heretic back. Constantine threatened Athanasius with banishment. Athanasius would not yield to the emperor's threat. Enemies then brought a grievous charge against him. Athanasius was required to appear before Constantine, who, greatly impressed by the little giant, acquitted him. Athanasius still continued his opposition to the desires of the emperor. More charges followed. The second time, the emperor was not as patient with the intractable bishop and had him banished.

Arius was now triumphant. He returned to Alexandria, only to find the church community there too devoted to their exiled bishop to allow place for his antagonist. Disturbances arose, and Arius was called to give an accounting to the emperor. He did so successfully. Constantine directed that he be reinstated with all proper solemnities in Constantinople. But the bishop of that city, whose name ironically enough was Alexander and who was a zealous champion of the one-essence doctrine, refused to open the church doors. Friends of Arius threatened to obtain an imperial order and effect a forcible entry. Alexander, it is said, prostrated himself before the altar and prayed that either he or Arius might be removed. That night "a violent disorder seized" Arius, followed by hemorrhaging. Arius died almost immediately.[36]

Of Arius's death, Edward Gibbon observes, "The strange and horrid circumstances of his death might excite a suspicion that the orthodox saints had contributed more efficaciously than by their prayers to deliver the church from the most formidable of her enemies."[37] Archibald MacLaine says, "After having considered this matter with the utmost care, it appears to me extremely probable, that this unhappy man was a victim to the resentment of his enemies, and was destroyed by poison, or some such violent method."[38]

Constantine expired in A.D. 337. A few days before his death he received a Christian baptism at the hand of the once banished Eusebius of Nicomedia.[39] At Rome he was enrolled with his predecessors among the gods of the heathen Olympus, and incense was offered before his statue. While in Constantinople he had prepared himself a tomb in a magnificent church he had built. His tomb was placed in the midst of twelve pillars representing the twelve Apostles. The church canonized him and his mother empress, Helena, under the title, "Equal to the Apostles."[40]

Implications of the Arian Controversy

For nearly seventeen hundred years apologists have represented the Council of Nicaea as a venerable assembly, full of wisdom and heavenly grace, guided by the hand of the Lord to solve a difficult doctrinal question and thereby save the church. I am reminded again that it is the victors, not the vanquished, who write history. Those assembled claimed to be the lawful successors of the Apostles of Christ and had in this council the opportunity of showing to the world how men anointed with the Holy Spirit are able to handle and resolve the Lord's business. Most, if not all, of the fathers there assembled would have been men of extensive experience in the church; many had in times past shown their courage in holding to the faith in the hour of trial, and bore as stripes of honor the scars of their fidelity. Yet the story of the council is not one of importuning the heavens; it is not one where the voice of God is heard; it is not one of dignity, or of patience, or of charity. Rather it is one of strife, envy, and debate. There is no semblance in it of anything that is divine; there is nothing about it that even vaguely imitates anything in holy writ. The very notion of the council and the attendant debate is that of a church staggering along blindly, putting its foot in and out of damnation until it was rescued by the formulation of a creed that Christ had somehow neglected to give them. In fact, it is a dramatic evidence that the apostasy from the meridian Church was complete.

The true significance of the Nicene Council was not in its anathematizing the doctrine of Arius or in the other peripheral issues that were decided.[41] As the future would attest, the Arian controversy was far from settled. The council's greater significance lay in the only true unity evidenced in it, that of, to use a phrase of Thomas Paine's, "the adulterous connection of church and state."[42] The church sought imperial patronage, and Constantine sought the power of the church for political purposes. The great feast with which the council concluded might well be thought of as the wedding feast celebrating the union of throne and altar. Incalculable atrocities would follow down through the centuries almost to the present day, as the throne enforced decrees of the church, and all this would be done in the name of Christ.

One immediate illustration of the new spirit of Christianity is found in Constantine's chastity laws. Among other things, these laws held that when a female ward grew up and wished to marry, her guardian must furnish proof that she was a virgin inviolate; if the guardian had seduced her, he was to be deported and all his property confiscated. Rapists were burned alive. A man who carried off a girl against her parents' wishes could no longer marry her, even if she was willing; on the contrary, her acquiescence rendered her liable to be burned alive. Nurses who encouraged girls to elope were to have boiling lead poured down their throats, while anyone of either sex who aided the lover was to be burned alive. Seduction was treated like a ritual impurity that could not be cleansed. If parents of those seduced concealed the crime, they too became liable to deportation.[43] Surely this was a theology that Christ would not have recognized.

The Mainspring of All Corruption

The creeds of Christendom constitute the perfect evidence of the darkness and apostasy which engulfed the earth following the death of the Apostles. Born of contention and nurtured in bitterness, these creeds all trace themselves back to Nicaea. Joseph Smith stated that the "hand of murder, tyranny, and oppression" under which the early Saints of this dispensation were made to suffer was "supported and urged on and upheld by the influence of that spirit which hath so strongly riveted the creeds of the fathers, who have inherited lies, upon the hearts of the children, and filled the world with confusion." That spirit "has been growing stronger and stronger, and is now the very mainspring of all corruption, and the whole earth groans under the weight of its iniquity." The Prophet described the spirit that promulgated and enforced the creeds of Christendom as "an iron yoke," "a strong band," and as "the very handcuffs, and chains, and shackles, and fetters of hell." (D&C 123:7–8.) The Lord himself declared the creeds of Christendom "an abomination in his sight," describing those who profess them as "corrupt," for "they draw near to me with their lips, but their hearts are far from me, they teach for doctrines the commandments of men, having a form of godliness, but they deny the power thereof" (Joseph Smith—History 1:19).

The Nicene Creed is not to be found in any Gospel. It derives from no utterance of Christ nor from the words of any of his Apostles. It directly contradicts the plain language of the New Testament. Its ideas cannot even be expressed in scriptural language; they are cloaked in that of the Greek philosopher whence they came. Its best defense is the admission that it is a mystery and as such is indefensible. Gibbon tells us: "The great Athanasius himself, has candidly confessed that whenever he forced his understanding to meditate on the divinity of the Logos, his toilsome and unavailing efforts recoiled on themselves; that the more he thought, the less he comprehended; and the more he wrote, the less capable was he of expressing his thoughts."[44] Of the Athanasian Creed, which was formulated about a century after the Nicene Creed, James E. Talmage said: "It would be difficult to conceive of a greater number of inconsistencies and contradictions expressed in words as few."[45] As to the very notion of a creed, the following observations ought to be made:

1. Four thousand years of scriptural history leave the Bible reader without so much as a vague hint that true religion includes a creed. If a creed is either necessary or appropriate, why did neither Christ nor his Apostles or prophets suggest it?

2. All the creeds of Christendom come after the point in time that their authors declared the heavens to have been sealed and revelation to have ceased. There is no creed that can claim revelation or the spirit of prophecy as its source.

3. The doctrines of the creeds are so far removed from the teachings of the scriptures that scriptural language is not adequate to give expression to them. An advocate of the creeds concedes: "The Bible does not teach the doctrine of the Trinity. Neither the word 'trinity' itself, nor such language as 'one-in-three,' 'three-in-one,' one 'essence' or 'substance,' or three 'persons' is biblical language. The language of the doctrine is the language of the ancient church, taken not from the Bible but from classical Greek philosophy."[46]

4. Having described their God in nonbiblical language, the professors of these creeds find it necessary to warn us against the language that is in the Bible so that we do not falsely suppose that God is the kind of being of whom the Bible writers spoke.

5. The professors of these creeds also concede that their language and doctrine would be so foreign to the original Twelve or the writers of the Bible that none of them would recognize or understand it. The creeds are justified by what is called progressive, or evolutionary, revelation. Thus, as one writer observes, "fourth-century orthodoxy is not the same as what Peter and Paul believed, any more than modern Roman Catholicism or Anglicanism is."[47] The notion here is that "heresy precedes orthodoxy." This is survival of the fittest; the dogma that prevails constitutes orthodoxy. Thus any faithful followers of Christ, were they to return and attend today's worship services, would be both lost and in danger of being declared heretics should they voice their understanding.

6. A fundamental notion of the Nicene Creed is that God is immutable, or that he changes not. How, then, we are left to ask, is he going to demand that those of one age and era profess the dogma of the creed in order to obtain salvation while those of the household of

faith who lived in the preceding four thousand years had no such dogma or even the vaguest notion of it? Can they still be eligible for salvation? And what of us, should we discover in this process of progressive revelation at some future day that that dogma of the creeds was simply another of the heresies that preceded the real orthodoxy, can we be saved? And if we can be saved having given our allegiance to heresy, why can't all heretics in all ages be saved?

7. The ultimate test of the divinity of any doctrine is whether it brings us closer to God or not. The doctrine of the Holy Trinity, the supreme mystery of historical Christian theology, holds that God exists in three persons of one substance. Its purpose and its effect have been and are to make God remote and ineffable.[48] Thomas Jefferson stated the issue well: "When we shall have done away with the incomprehensible jargon of the Trinitarian arithmetic, that three are one, and one is three; when we shall have knocked down the artificial scaffolding, reared to mask from view the very simple structure of Jesus; when, in short, we shall have unlearned everything which has been taught since his day, and got back to the pure and simple doctrines he inculcated, we shall then be truly and worthily his disciples."[49]

9

*Therefore whosoever heareth these sayings of mine, and doeth
them, I will liken him unto a wise man, which built his house upon
a rock:*
*And the rain descended, and the floods came, and the winds
blew, and beat upon that house; and it fell not: for it was founded
upon a rock.*
*And every one that heareth these sayings of mine, and doeth
them not, shall be likened unto a foolish man, which built his house
upon the sand:*
*And the rain descended, and the floods came, and the winds blew,
and beat upon that house; and it fell: and great was the fall of it.*
—Matthew 7:24–27

A House Built
upon the Sand

I had expected to meet a man in ministerial garb; instead he was
dressed in a handsome kilt and Prince Charley jacket. He was very
direct. "I came to ask some hard questions," he said.

"That is where Mormonism looks best," I responded. "Sit down
and ask away."

Our conversation lasted for some hours. He was frankly surprised
at how good our answers were. At one point he said, "For a small
church you sure have a big theology."

He was a good man, open and honest. We liked each other. At the
appropriate time I said, "Now it is my turn to ask the hard questions. I
want you to tell me how you justify your creed."

He buried his head in his hands and said, "Our creed is responsible for the Dark Ages."

The Shifting Sands of Man-made Theology

As Christ anointed with clay the eyes of a man born blind and then directed him to wash it away in the pool of Siloam, similarly all men who would see with the eyes of the Spirit must wash away all that is earthly or temporal. The mind of man unaided by the Spirit of God is earthbound, and theologies woven out of the philosophies of men neither exalt nor enlighten. The promulgators of such theologies seek legitimacy in scripture but inevitably find it necessary to twist and contort the scriptures to conform to their views. Men have created nearly countless images of Jesus, none of which would be recognizable to those he knew as disciples and called friends during his mortal ministry. One prominent Christian minister observed: "If it could ever be proved that the Gospels consisted throughout of completely accurate material for a biography of Jesus, the traditional Christian faith would collapse in ruins. This can hardly be stressed too strongly, especially to those Christians who are convinced that an orthodox faith rests on the factual reliability of the Bible in general and on the status of the Gospels in particular as precise records of the words and acts of Jesus, and of the incidents of his life. Such a conviction is very nearly the reverse of the truth. Every one of the systematic edifices of belief, both orthodox and heretical, which have marked the history of Christianity has depended in the last analysis on an edited, expanded, or artificially interpreted version of the Gospel text."[1]

What the good bishop is telling us is that all religious denominations that profess Bible history and doctrine as a part of their faith are forcing the sources to conform to their system of belief. While none of them would give credence to a coerced testimony from a living Apostle or prophet, all feel quite comfortable resting their salvation on the contrived testimony of the dead. One writer observed that "there are a thousand interpretations of the one book, often justifying diametrically opposite views."[2] Now, what ought to dawn on us at some point is that this strained sense of Bible loyalty is entirely at odds with the Bible pattern. Often those of whom we read in the Bible story were without access to any form of written revelation. The common bond between the faithful in the various generations of the Bible was a belief in personal revelation suited to their own circumstances and needs. None of them would ever have supposed that revelations given to others were sufficient for them. Yet, as a monument to irony, the claim to immediate and personal revelation is labeled heresy today and seen as a great threat to the Bible. While the theological architecture of the various churches of the world in our time is remarkably diverse, the ground common to all is the sand upon which they have built, for none can admit a God who has sufficient authority to say anything worthy of admission to the ancient canon. Thus the authority to identify the path men ought to follow where there are so many divergent views is, we are told, no longer in the heavens.

Common Sense

In January of 1776, the American colonies were involved in armed conflict with Great Britain, though there was no universal understanding among their citizens as to why. Men like John and Samuel Adams of Massachusetts and Benjamin Franklin saw the hostilities as a war of independence. Others, like John Dickinson of Philadelphia, simply wanted to force the English Parliament to acknowledge the justice of colonial claims, and to obtain redress for the long litany of grievances that had led to the shedding of blood. Indeed, this was the dominant view when Thomas Paine, in his pamphlet *Common Sense,* argued with great persuasiveness for the necessity of breaking all ties with a corrupt and tyrannical parent nation to stand independent.[3] In the introduction to his pamphlet Paine observed that "a long habit of not thinking a thing *wrong,* gives it a superficial appearance of being *right,* and raises at first a formidable outcry in defence of custom. But the tumult soon subsides. Time makes more converts than reason."[4]

Let us speak of common sense where matters of religious faith are concerned. It was seen as necessary in what we know as the Protestant Reformation to break all ties with a corrupt and tyrannical parent, the old mother church. Living in a tamer age, most Latter-day Saints are only vaguely aware of the acute struggle that was involved in this reformation. For instance, many Saints dutifully carry a copy of the Bible with them to church unaware that it is a remnant of that struggle. Were they to read the preface, they would discover a letter of effusive praise addressed to King James by the translators. In that epistle they rightfully anticipate that they will be "traduced by Popish Persons" at home and abroad for freeing the sacred book from its papal prison. Within the lifetime of some of their number, William Tyndale had been burned at the stake for the crime of translating the Bible into English. Nor had they forgotten that John Wycliffe had been accused of heresy by the Roman church for his English translation and that many Christian martyrs had been burned to death with Wycliffe's Bible tied around their necks. They knew that their translation had been bought with blood. They also anticipated harsh criticism from those of their own nation and faith. In this they were not to be disappointed either, for more than a hundred years would pass before the book gained general acceptance among English-speaking people. Tradition is a powerful opponent, and all efforts to break the chains of ignorance and darkness are met with considerable opposition.

In another of his works, *The Age of Reason,* Paine observed that soon after he had written *Common Sense,* he saw "the exceeding probability that a revolution in the system of government would be followed by a revolution in the system of religion. The adulterous connection of church and state, wherever it had taken place, whether Jewish, Christian, or Turkish, had so effectually prohibited by pains and penalties, every discussion upon established creeds, and upon first principles of religion, that until the system of government should be changed, those subjects could not be brought fairly and openly before the world; but that whenever this should be done, a revolution in the system of religion would follow. Human inventions and priestcraft would be detected; and man would return to the pure, unmixed and unadulterated belief of one God, and no more."[5]

The separation of church and state was essential to the restoration of the gospel. Two of the greatest contributions to the concept of government made by the Constitution of the United States were religious freedom and the separation of church and state. Civil and ecclesiastical tyranny had shared the same bed from the time that a church which had long since lost its virtue was seduced by Constantine. Each reinforced the other in a swelling flow of blood. From that time until the American Revolution, true religion was an impossibility. Religious liberty was unknown. The creeds of Christendom, like chains forged in the fires of hell, kept the souls of men captive in the dark dungeon of theological mysteries, where they were guarded and abused by those wearing clerical robes, who in turn were sustained by the power of the state.

The line of reasoning was simple: error has no rights, any more than deadly viruses have rights, and any that opposed the state church were in error. Thus you either embraced the tenets of the prevailing faith or were labeled an enemy to the state. Thomas Jefferson responded that such a condition made "one half the world fools, and the other half hypocrites."[6] He reasoned that if an all-wise and all-powerful God restrained himself from coercing either the bodies or the minds of men and women, how utterly absurd it must then be for "fallible and uninspired men" to assume "dominion over the faith of others."[7]

"All national institutions of churches," wrote Thomas Paine, "whether Jewish, Christian or Turkish, appear to me no other than human inventions, set up to terrify and enslave mankind, and monopolize power and profit." In rejecting the churches of his day, Paine was not rejecting their adherents. He was entirely comfortable in allowing all men to worship as they chose, for only in according that privilege to them could he legitimately claim it for himself. But he did maintain that to enjoy happiness a man must be true to himself. To Paine, infidelity was not the refusal to believe a particular thing but rather the profession of believing what one did not. "It is impossible to calculate the moral mischief," he said, "if I may so express it, that mental lying has produced in society. When a man has so far corrupted and prostituted the chastity of his mind, as to subscribe his professional belief to things he does not believe, he has prepared himself for the commission of every other crime. He takes up the trade of a priest for the sake of gain, and in order to qualify himself for that trade, he begins with a perjury."[8]

That perjury, Paine felt, included the notion of a national church, "as if the way to God was not open to every man alike."[9] The idea of a Church of Scotland suggests that salvation is available to the Scots alone, while a Church of England suggests that salvation is the rightful inheritance of those wise enough to have been born as Englishmen, and so forth.

The greater difficulty, however, is the intolerance that the union of church and state breeds. Creeds know no tolerance. Consider the early history of Maryland as an example. Settlers of various faiths spread into its wilderness before the middle of the seventeenth century. Though governed by a benevolent Catholic ruler, the Protestants of Maryland carried with them from England an intense hatred of Catholicism, and, as Milton V. Backman Jr. explains, "this cancerous enmity ignited the flames of persecution." Faced with the threat of a revocation of their charter, the Maryland assembly passed the first toleration act in American history. Backman writes: "By the Act of 1649, toleration was to be continued for all Trinitarian Christians, and the state was authorized to protect the religious rights of such citizens. But anyone who denied 'the Holy Trinity, the Father, Son, and Holy Ghost, . . . or the unity of the Godhead' was to be 'punished with death and confiscation or forfeiture of all his or her lands and goods to the Lord Proprietary and his heirs.'"[10] The struggle for religious freedom did not come easily, even in the New World. Vermont did not enjoy a separation of church and state until 1807, Connecticut until 1818, New Hampshire until 1819, and Maine until 1820. Massachusetts was the last of the states to divorce herself from such an entanglement with religion, not doing so until 1833.[11]

Freedom from state-imposed creeds made the restoration of the gospel possible and created a climate in which man could again enjoy the privilege of uncensored prayers. Speaking of this freedom, Joseph Smith said that the "most prominent difference in sentiment between the Latter-day Saints and sectarians was, that the latter were all circumscribed by some peculiar creed, which deprived its members the privilege of believing anything not contained therein, whereas the Latter-day Saints have no creed, but are ready to believe all true principles that exist, as they are made manifest from time to time."[12]

Religious Mysteries

As to the matter of religious mysteries, Thomas Paine observed that "the word mystery cannot be applied to *moral truth,* any more than obscurity can be applied to light. The God in whom we believe is a God of moral truth, and not a God of mystery or obscurity. Mystery is the antagonist of truth. It is a fog of human invention, that obscures truth, and represents it in distortion. Truth never envelops *itself* in mystery, and the mystery in which it is at any time enveloped is the work of its antagonist, and never of itself."[13]

By definition, true religion, being the work of God, cannot have any connection with mystery. Paine wrote: "The very nature and design of religion, if I may so express it, prove even to demonstration that it must be free from everything of mystery, and unencumbered with everything that is mysterious." Given that the proper worship of God is a duty shared equally by all humankind, the comprehension of those duties must be shared equally also. It is only when religion has

been reduced to a pious fraud that it is necessary to hide the sub-
terfuge under the fog of mystery. Only when such religion cannot bear
examination do men place a bar to questions and investigation.[14]
"Man once surrendering his reason," said Thomas Jefferson, "has no
remaining guard against absurdities the most monstrous, and like a
ship without a rudder, is the sport of every wind."[15]

As used in the scriptures, the word *mystery* has reference to re-
vealing rather than concealing truth. This finds expression in two
ways: in some instances the term *mystery* is used in reference to rituals
or rites, that is, sacred knowledge granted to initiates (see Alma
12:9–10; D&C 84:19–22); in other instances it is used in reference to
those truths (and now are reaching beyond the comprehension of
Thomas Paine) which can be known only by revelation (see D&C
89:18–19; 121:26–32).[16] Speaking of the biblical age, Joseph Priestley,
in his *History of the Corruptions of Christianity,* which work greatly influenced Thomas Jefferson, observed: "Everything, indeed, in that age,
was called a *mystery* that was reputed *sacred,* and the knowledge of
which was confined to a few; but the idea of *unintelligible,* or *inexplic-
able,* was not then affixed to the word mystery. The heathen mysteries,
from which the Christians borrowed the term, were things perfectly
well known and understood by those who were *initiated,* though concealed from the vulgar."[17]

Thus the word *mystery,* which once described that understanding
which was most cherished and sacred to the Saints, was gainsaid as
the cloak for an incomprehensible contradiction. This word once associated with surety became the harbinger of bewilderment. Faith, in
turn, which is born of knowledge and must be inseparably sealed to
truth to bear good seeds, was forced to deny its parentage and disavow its union with veracity. In his *History of Dogma,* Adolph Harnack
points out that the doctrine of the Logos—which is intelligible only to
a few who have been "trained in philosophical speculations"—was
"equivalent for the great mass of Christians to the setting up of a mystery, which in the first place could only make an impression through
its high-pitched formulas and the glamour of the incomprehensible."
He then observes:

> But as soon as a religion expresses the loftiest contents of its creed
> in formulas which must remain mysterious and unintelligible to
> the great mass of its adherents, those adherents come under

guardians. In other words, the multitude must believe in the creed; at the same time they no longer derive from it directly the motives of their religious and moral life; and they are dependent on the theologians, who, as professors of the mysterious, alone understand and are capable of interpreting and practically applying the creed. The necessary consequence of this development was that the mysterious creed, being no longer in a position practically to control life, was superseded by *the authority of the Church, the cultus, and prescribed duties,* in determining the religious life of the laity; while the theologians, or the priests, appeared alone as the possessors of an independent faith and knowledge.[18]

Like all other false doctrines, the concept of mysteries as they are espoused by traditional Christianity have the effect of making God more abstract and of moving him farther from the realm of the experience and understanding of the generality of people. Rather than hide behind a bold voice and a veil of mystery like the Wizard of Oz, true religion lifts men to heights of understanding that otherwise could not be theirs. For instance, of those who serve him in righteousness and truth, the Lord has said:

> And to them will I reveal all mysteries, yea, all the hidden mysteries of my kingdom from days of old, and for ages to come, will I make known unto them the good pleasure of my will concerning all things pertaining to my kingdom.
> Yea, even the wonders of eternity shall they know, and things to come will I show them, even the things of many generations.
> And their wisdom shall be great, and their understanding reach to heaven; and before them the wisdom of the wise shall perish, and the understanding of the prudent shall come to naught.
> For by my Spirit will I enlighten them, and by my power will I make known unto them the secrets of my will—yea, even those things which eye has not seen, nor ear heard, nor yet entered into the heart of man. (D&C 76:7–10.)

Such is the true doctrine of mysteries. The God of heaven will reveal all his secrets to those who seek to know them. The quest is one of righteousness and truth. Nothing is to be withheld, and nothing is to be incomprehensible. All are invited to make the journey. How perfect the contrast with theologies born in the minds of men! "A God understood is no God at all," they declare, and well might they add, "A doctrine understood is no doctrine at all."

We return to Thomas Jefferson and John Adams, two of the great minds that gave this nation both political and religious freedom. Jefferson, having read Plato, reports on his reading to his dear friend Adams:

> His [Plato's] foggy mind, is forever presenting the semblances of objects which, half seen thro' a mist, can be defined neither in form or dimension. Yet this which should have consigned him to early oblivion really procured him immortality of fame and reverence. The Christian priesthood, finding the doctrines of Christ levelled to every understanding, and too plain to need explanation, saw, in the mysticisms of Plato, materials with which they might build up an artificial system which might, from its indistinctness, admit everlasting controversy, give employment for their order, and introduce it to profit, power and pre-eminence. The doctrines which flowed from the lips of Jesus himself are within the comprehension of a child; but thousands of volumes have not yet explained the Platonisms engrafted on them: and for this obvious reason that nonsense can never be explained. Their purposes however are answered. Plato is canonized; and it is now deemed as impious to question his merits as those of an Apostle of Jesus. He is peculiarly appealed to as an advocate of the immortality of the soul; and yet I will venture to say that were there no better arguments than his in proof of it, not a man in the world would believe it. It is fortunate for us that Platonic republicanism has not obtained the same favor as Platonic Christianity; or we should now have been all living, men, women and children, pell mell together, like beasts of the field or forest.[19]

The Trinity

Thomas Jefferson attributed the absurdity of the notion of the Trinity to Athanasius, stating that he would "as soon undertake to bring the crazy skulls of Bedlam to sound understanding, as to inculcate reason into that of an Athanasian." According to Jefferson, the doctrine of the Trinity, a "mere Abracadabra," was only the unhappiest example of what happens when one gave up "morals for mysteries, Jesus for Plato."[20] Priestley noted that from the plain doctrine of the scriptures, "a doctrine so consonant to reason and the ancient prophecies, Christians have at length come to believe what they do not pretend to have any conception of, and than which it is not possible to frame a more express contradiction. For, while they consider Christ as the supreme, eternal God, the maker of heaven and earth, and of all things visible and invisible, they moreover acknowledge the Father and the Holy Spirit to be equally *God* in the same exalted sense, all three equal in power and glory, and yet all three constituting no more than one God."[21] An eighteenth-century writer in Britain observed: "A Christian is one who believes things which his reason cannot comprehend, who hopes for that which neither he nor any man alive ever saw, who labours for that which he knows he can never attain; yet in the issue his belief appears not to have been false, his hopes make him not ashamed, his labour is not in vain. He believes three to be one, and one to be three; a Father not to be older than his Son, and the Son to be equal with his Father; and One proceeding from both to be fully equal to both."[22] Jefferson observed that "had there never been a Commentator, there never would have been an infidel."[23]

No one who ever sought God thought to do so by seeking the Trinity. Virtually every Christian you meet will think and speak of Christ and God in ways entirely incompatible with the doctrines of their creeds. In speech and thought they are more the disciples of Arian than Athanasius, but in fact are the disciples of neither. Their natural inclination is to the pure and simple doctrines that are written in the scripture of their hearts as surely as they are found on the pages of holy writ.

How Creeds Supplanted Truth and Righteousness

The creeds of Christendom have covered the heavens like clouds of darkness. They did not bring with them the gentle and refreshing rains of revelation that would call forth life from the seeds so newly planted by Christ and his disciples. Theirs has been a merciless torrent, washing away seeds and uprooting tender plants while scattering the seeds of noxious weeds in their place. The very meaning of faith was changed. The principle of continuous revelation was taken. The idea of accepting the testimony of a specially called witness was lost. The notion that spiritual truths could be known by feelings in the breast, or heart, was no longer held. In their stead came deductions from metaphysical premises which noticeably lacked the sense of assurance and spiritual confidence once enjoyed by the multitude of believers. The words *faith* and *belief* are interchangeable as used in both the Old and New Testaments. At the heart of the meaning of the Hebrew word for *faith* is the idea of certainty. In the verb form, it is to cause to be certain, sure, or assured. Thus biblical faith constitutes an assurance or certainty, in contrast with modern concepts of faith which hold it to be akin to the hope of a certain possibility or the optimism that something will prove to be true. Jesus frequently used the word to stress the certainty of a matter.[24]

As modified by Greek thought, the scriptural concept of faith, like the new God of Christianity, became more abstract and impersonal. The Greek words which designate *faith* and *belief* as used in the Old Testament carry the idea of a sense of trust or assurance, primarily trust in a person. The emphasis is as much moral as intellectual. As these words were used by the Greek philosopher, however, the emphasis shifted to that of an intellectual conviction. Whereas a belief in God had once implied an acceptance of what the prophets taught as those things are recorded in the scriptures, as refashioned by the philosopher it became more vague and mystical. Theory replaced certainty.[25]

For post–New Testament Christianity, "acceptance of these philosophical speculations was as important as the belief in God," says Edwin Hatch.[26] "The habit of defining and of making inferences from definitions," Hatch tells us, "grew the more as the philosophers passed over into the Christian lines, and logicians and metaphysicians presided over Christian churches. The speculations which were then agreed upon [at the Council of Nicaea] became stamped as a body of truth, and with the still deeper speculations of the Councils of Constantinople and Chalcedon,[27] the resolutions of the Nicene Fathers have come to be looked upon as almost a new revelation, and the rejection of them as a greater bar to Christian fellowship than the rejection of the New Testament itself."[28]

Members of The Church of Jesus Christ of Latter-day Saints are often surprised to discover that some in the "Christian world" regard them as a non-Christian cult. The initial thought on the part of the Latter-day Saint is that such expressions represent either a misunderstanding or misinformation and that once our faith in Christ is explained the issue will be resolved. This is not the case. The fact that our faith is entirely Christ-centered, that we seek salvation in his name and by compliance to the principles of his gospel and in no other way has nothing to do with it. The fact that we use the New Testament as scripture and believe it more completely and literally than any people on earth has nothing to do with it. The fact that we would have no faith nor existence as a people had not both the Father and the Son appeared to Joseph Smith in the spring of 1820 has nothing to do with it. The fact that we do not accept the clearly uninspired conclusions of the Council of Nicaea has everything to do with it, and nothing else matters! Such is the standard of orthodoxy that is being used, and it does not matter how large the paintings of Christ are that greet the patrons to our visitors' centers, nor does it matter how loyal we are to him. Adherents of historical or traditional Christianity have defined Christianity as loyalty to the determinations of the Council of Nicaea, and until we are willing to deny that Jesus Christ is literally the Son of God we will not be accepted as Christian by them.

Significantly, too, the issue has nothing to do with behavior. The Latter-day Saint people can be fully committed to living Christlike lives while their critics may share no such interest. How a people choose to live, however, is not the issue. The issue is what you believe. This represents what Hatch called "the change in the centre of gravity" that took place when the gospel was taken from the Semitic to the Greek world.[29] To the Hebrew mind a person's faith was manifest in what he did. Illustrating the point, John writes: "For every one that doeth evil hateth the light, neither cometh to the light, lest his deeds should be reproved. But he that *doeth truth* cometh to the light, that his deeds may be made manifest, that they are wrought in God." (John 3:20–21, emphasis added.) Again, John said that if we "walk in darkness, we lie, and *do not the truth*" (1 John 1:6, emphasis added). How you lived determined your spiritual understanding. To the Hebrew, truth was what you did. Conversely, the Greek tradition held that the gospel was what you "believed"; conduct was not the issue. Such was the view that prevailed, and so down through the ages heresy consisted in failure to believe the prescribed creed, not in un-Christian conduct. Thus a faithful, Christlike Latter-day Saint is not—by this narrow, creed-based definition—Christian. Part of the irony of such a theological position lies in the fact that neither Christ nor his disciples professed belief in the doctrines of Nicaea. Their doctrine was, "Ye shall know them by their fruits" (Matthew 7:16). Thus the same defin- ition that excludes the Latter-day Saints from being called Christians also excludes Christ and his New Testament disciples.

Revelation Versus Speculation

The spirit of prophecy did not die a sudden death as was the case with other doctrines in the early church. It died rather gradually, and then too of natural causes. The fact that it could be counterfeited was a contributing factor. The claim to revelation could be a trump card in any argument. If extant scripture or church tradition did not sustain your position, you simply claimed a revelation on the matter. In a church without legal administrators or ordained channels of revelation there is no way to handle such claims other than to simply ban all fur- ther revelation, which is eventually what happened. Another dimen- sion of the same problem was the forging of manuscripts that were then attributed to authority figures. Hatch observes that "there were many writings attributed to apostles and apostolic men which were of doubtful authority."[30] With the death of the Apostles the church was without the ability to discern the same.

A new principle was necessary to give the church the advantage with splinter groups, and that was the determination to deny the right of private interpretation of scripture. Scriptural interpretation was to rest with the church. So the meaning of scripture and the determina- tion of what was scripture came to rest with the bishops of what claimed to be apostolic churches. The system they used to determine doctrinal matters was the same they had been using to ensure disci- pline. They would call a council of bishops and form resolutions. Orthodoxy was determined by the vote of the bishops, or majority rule, and at the same time, formalizing their theological speculations strengthened their authority. Thus belief became belief in accepted speculations which have carried down to our own day. Because they are not a matter of revelation and thus do not have inherent within them the spiritual power that the truths of heaven do, it has been nec- essary to sustain them with legislation and by the sword. The idea that every man had the right to worship God according to the dictates of his own conscience was supplanted by the idea that the officers of the church were the guardians of the faith. This assumption "soon began to breed its offspring of venom and abuse," says Hatch. Torrents of abuse were to follow in this war of doctrines as those with greater followings traduced the others. So it was that the idea of certainty and trust in God that had been the basis of all true religion was, as Hatch puts it, "changed into the idea of a creed, blending theory with fact, and metaphysical speculation with spiritual truth."[31]

There are three historical and undeniable facts that should not be lost to the understanding of every professor of the traditional Christian creeds: First, that they are based on philosophical speculations that are at best unprovable and that are not sustained by revelation. Second, that they represent the determination of the majority in attendance at the particular meeting at which the matter was decided. As Hatch points out, this procedure "assumes that God never speaks to men except through the voice of the majority. It is a large assumption."[32] It is an assumption that must recall the fact that Christianity began as a tiny sect in Palestine that was itself labeled a heresy by the majority of its nation and even today exists in a world in which it is a minority religion. Surely the founder of every heretical sect, so called, lives in the hope that time will prove him to be right and the established churches to be in error. It need also be added that if the majority of Christian bishops (or their equivalent) reject the Virgin Birth, as an illustration, which may already be the case, then by the above reasoning that doctrine ceases to be true.

The third fact is that the creeds are founded on the premise that the definitions and interpretations of the majority are not only true but final. Such a view is predicated on the assumption that once, and only once, did God speak to men, and that the revelation of himself as found in the Gospels is a unique fact in the history of the universe. This assumption stands in opposition to the possibility that there was never any intention on the part of God to quit speaking to his children and that each generation is entitled to immediate and personal communication with him. A difficulty in the assumption that revelations of the New Testament were final is the notion that the inspired interpretation of that revelation developed gradually through three centuries and was then suddenly arrested. This difficulty has sometimes been circumvented with the argument that there was no new development of truth after New Testament times and that the Nicene theology was part of the original revelation—something not evident in scripture but communicated to the Apostles by Christ. Responding to this argument, Hatch observes that the elements that are distinctive to "Nicene theology were gradually formed" and that "the whole temper and frame of mind which led to the formation of those elements were extraneous to the first form of Christianity, and were added to it by the operation of causes which can be traced." Thus he reasons that "the assumption of the finality of the Nicene theology is the hypothesis of a development which went on for three centuries, and was then suddenly and for ever arrested. Such a hypothesis, even if it be *a priori* conceivable, would require an overwhelming amount of positive testimony. Of such testimony there is absolutely none."[33]

Drinking at the Fountainhead

In a remarkable and powerful conclusion to his 350-page commentary on the influence of Greek ideas on Christianity, Hatch observes that rather than travel again "the beaten tracks of these ancient controversies as to particular speculations," we would be better served by determining the proper place of speculation in true religion. For the highest knowledge, he suggests, "we must go alone upon the mountain-top"; and he states further that we need to learn "that though the moral law is thundered forth so that even the deaf may hear, the deepest secrets of God's nature and of our own are whispered still in the silence of the night to the individual soul."[34]

It is to that knowledge that can be obtained only on the mountaintop or in the quiet grove that we now turn our attention.

10

When Jesus came into the coasts of Caesarea Philippi, he asked his disciples, saying, Whom do men say that I the Son of man am? And they said, Some say that thou art John the Baptist: some, Elias; and others, Jeremias, or one of the prophets. He saith unto them, But whom say ye that I am? And Simon Peter answered and said, Thou art the Christ, the Son of the living God. And Jesus answered and said unto him, Blessed art thou, Simon Bar-jona: for flesh and blood hath not revealed it unto thee, but my Father which is in heaven.

—Matthew 16:13–17

The Fatherhood of God

While attending a stake conference in the beautiful city of Aberdeen, Scotland, I was called on to speak extemporaneously. Since my invitation was impromptu, I decided to share it in like manner with someone else. Seated on the front row of the congregation was a young lady with a newly born child in her arms. She radiated the joyful delight that the heavens reserve for new mothers. I asked if she and her newborn child would assist me. She was somewhat embarrassed but agreed. As she stood by my side, I first asked her which was the more pure and sacred, her newly born child or the Holy Bible which I held in my hands.

She was hesitant to answer. I reassured her, pointing out that there was a General Authority sitting behind her and that whatever she said could be used against her. After a few moments of hesitation she said, in a very soft voice, "I think my child is."

She could hardly have answered otherwise, for every feeling of her heart so dictated. I assured her that she had answered correctly, observing that her child was a more perfect witness that there was a God in heaven than any written revelation could possibly be. I then asked a second question: At birth did her child have a distinct personality and spirit peculiar to itself, or was her little daughter more like a blank piece of paper waiting to be written upon?

Feeling more comfortable and confident now, she answered without hesitation. Her child, she explained, was unique and special, differing from all other children even from the moment of its birth. Again I concurred with her conclusion. My observations and experience assure me that none of us is born like a blank piece of paper.

Mothers gain an awareness of the distinctive natures of their children even during pregnancy. Among the things we bring with us into this world is a knowledge of the most important truths of eternity, foremost among them being that God is a personal being and loving Father. Such truth rests quietly and securely within the souls of all of God's children, save it has been forced to take refuge by actions offensive to the Spirit of truth.

All May Enjoy the Spirit of Revelation

As we share a common right to breath, so we share the right to implore the heavens in seeking to know God and his purposes in our creation. Who would dare say some were born with the right to pray while others were not? When Christ said, "Ask, and it shall be given you; seek, and ye shall find; knock, and it shall be opened unto you," he did not have in mind some exclusive group or limited time period, for he also said, "Every one that asketh receiveth; and he that seeketh findeth; and to him that knocketh it shall be opened" (Matthew 7:7–8). Both the principle and the promises are universal.

An understanding of the saving principles of the gospel of Jesus Christ must be within the capacity of all accountable persons. If this were not so, then God could not be God, for there could be no justice in the dispensing of the blessings of heaven. We could hardly argue that it was justice that one man be saved because he had the good fortune to be born Catholic and another damned because he had the bad fortune to be born Protestant, or vice versa. Salvation, to mean something, ought to be a matter of faith and works, not a matter of the community or family into which one was born. There could be no justice in a God creating some to be saved and others to be damned, notwithstanding the fact that some have argued for that principle.

Such a belief would be little different from a system of laws that protected some and abused others. Earth's history has known enough of such injustice. We hardly need to extend it to the heavens. All, either in this life or the next, must have equal opportunity to accept or reject the principles of salvation before their day of judgment, or we are forced back to the admission that God has ceased to be God because he is no longer just.

Salvation is a path that each must choose and trod for him or herself. In order to do so, everyone must have the right to obtain by the spirit of revelation a personal confirmation of the principles of salvation. Unless such an opportunity is extended to all, the justice of God would again be called in question. Thus if answers are to be found in the Bible, an understanding of its saving truths must be equally evident to all honest truth seekers. What it cannot mean is that its truths are available exclusively to those who are indoctrinated in some system by which they filter out the plain meaning of words, giving everything a new, symbolic meaning. That simply brings us back to the notion of an exclusive salvation extended to those who have the good fortune to learn the cryptic code by which the scriptures are to be interpreted. It is a form of predestination, with some having the good fortune to know saving truths and others not. Another version of the same inequitable system of dispensing the gospel is the claim that the truths of salvation are in the Bible but are to be understood and interpreted by apostolic tradition that is the exclusive province of a particular church. Once more this makes the church the beginning point of acceptable understanding and not the scriptures, for the scriptures, according to such a system, have meaning only as it is assigned to them by the church.

Again, if we are to maintain that God is just, then we are committed to the position that the invitation to embrace the truths of salvation must be extended to everyone on an equitable basis. All must be invited to drink at the fountainhead. All must have the capacity to discern and know the truth. All must have the freedom, or agency, to accept or reject it. This means that the whole system of salvation must center in the manifestation of God's love and trust. It means that all must be agents unto themselves. This means that the beginning point for each person must be personal prayer, their own mountaintop or their own private grove. It is to say that all true religion must be immediate and personal.

All Christian denominations profess that the scriptures are the foundation of their faith. To do so, however, each has its set of a priori conditions by which the scriptures must be read. What no one wants to do is to trust people to determine the course they should follow with the scriptures alone. The reason for this is obvious: without the cryptic code or the claim to apostolic traditions, the untutored reader would never end up with what has been determined by a given denomination to be the appropriate understanding. Suppose, for instance, we were to take the Bible to a people in another world, giving it to them without commentary save to say that they would find the truths of salvation in it. Could they, worlds without end, ever come up with the doctrine of salvation by grace alone or the doctrine of the Holy Trinity? The first demands reading the scriptures with a blind eye; the second demands that they be filtered through a course in Greek philosophy. The best evidence that no one reading them could come up with such conclusions is the simple fact that no one within the covers of the Bible ever did. Such notions simply never occurred to them.

No one is satisfied to say the waters of everlasting life are in the Bible, read it, you are on your own. The preferred way is to say here is a version of the Bible we have decided is reliable, now we will take you through it and show you what it really means.

Now, it ought to be freely confessed that as Latter-day Saints we also read the Bible with an a priori condition of our choosing. Rather than argue that words don't mean what they say or that we are the possessors of otherwise unknown apostolic traditions, we maintain that revelations can be properly understood only by the same Spirit by which they were originally given. Thus it takes prophets to understand prophets and revelation to understand revelation. As Latter-day Saints we maintain that without prophets and revelation original to our day, the prophets and revelations of a past day cannot be fully understood. Unlike the rest of Christendom, we are not arguing that our faith came first from scripture, for to do so is unscriptural. Nobody in the Bible did it that way. What seems to have been generally overlooked is that no one in Bible times had a Bible. What they had was the spirit of revelation. True, some of them had extant scripture, but their understanding of it came by way of additional scripture. The ancients were of the understanding that the best way to obtain truth was not to ask it of books but to ask it of God. They had no aversion to books, but they sought the proper understanding of such from the heavens. They dealt in primary, not secondary, sources.[1] They dealt in personal, not secondary, experiences. Neither priest, nor mystery, nor scripture stood between them and their God, whom they knew to be their Eternal Father. Such is the system Mormonism seeks to restore.

We approach an examination of the scriptures relative to their testimony on the matter of the fatherhood of God with the faith that the verity of their message is within the grasp of all honest truth seekers; that the scriptures were intended to be understood according to the plain and obvious meaning of words; that no a priori system is necessary to comprehend their message; and that all truths declared within them are subject to an immediate and personal confirmation by the same Spirit that revealed them originally.

"Come, . . . Let Us Reason Together"

In Caesarea Philippi, Jesus introduced a discussion with his disciples by asking, "Whom do men say that I the Son of man am?" By so doing he has attested that he is the son of a man. Peter, however, in response to his question, said, "Thou art the Christ, the Son of the living God." Christ, in turn, commends Peter for his answer, declaring that Peter will be blessed because he did not get his answer from "flesh and blood," meaning the mind of mortal man, but by revelation from "my Father which is in heaven." (Matthew 16:13, 16–17.)

For the honest truth seeker it would be hard to imagine a more instructive text. It declares that Jesus of Nazareth is "the Christ," meaning the Messiah, he who will redeem his people. It contains his witness that his Father is a man, and the words of Peter, which Christ accepts as true, that he is "the Son of the living God." Further, Jesus here affirms that his Father abides in heaven. From such a text one can only conclude that the God of Peter and Christ is also the Father of Christ, that he resides in heaven and that he is an exalted man.

Having noted Christ's reference to himself as the "Son of man" and Peter's testimony that he was the Son of God, Elder John Taylor asked: "O, ye great men, and wise men, and ye who wear the sacerdotal robes, how can Jesus have two fathers; or how can the scriptures be true without he has two?"[2]

The response of historical Christianity to that question is that neither expression is to be understood literally. Christ declares himself to
be the "Son of man," we are told, to emphasize his humanity, and calls
himself the "Son of God" to emphasize his divinity.[3] It is essential to
such theology that we understand that the Son of God, as one source
states, "is not so entitled because He at any time began to derive His
being from the Father (in which case He could not be co-eternal with
the Father), but because He is and ever has been the expression of
what the Father is."[4] This is the point to which our study consistently
returns. The word *Father* as it refers to the God of heaven and the
word *Son* as it refers to Christ are never, scholarly sources tell us, used
in the New Testament so as to suggest that one is actually a father and
the other actually a son.[5] And how is the reader to know this? Simply
because it is the decision of Nicaea. But what of those who lived before Nicaea? What of Peter and the other disciples of Christ, those
from whom both the scripture and the apostolic tradition were to have
come—what, we are left to ask, was their understanding?

The Savior never once said that he begot himself. He did, however, consistently declare himself to be the Son of the Father and affirm that the Father was a man. In the eighth chapter of John, Christ
declares himself to be the light of the world. The Pharisees challenge
his testimony on the grounds that he stood alone in bearing it. Their
objection was based on the ancient law of witnesses, which required
the testimony of two or more men to establish a thing as true. "Thou
bearest record of thyself," they said, and thus "thy record is not true."
In response Jesus said, in part: "I am not alone, but I and the Father
that sent me" are your witnesses. "It is also written in your law," he
said, "that the testimony of two men is true. I am one that bear witness
of myself, and the Father that sent me beareth witness of me." (John
8:12–13, 16–18.) Let us not miss what Christ has said. To paraphrase:
"Your law requires the testimony of two men. I am one man and my
Father is the other man, and thus my testimony is binding."[6]

Interrogating Christ, the corrupt high priest Caiaphas said: "I ad-
jure thee by the living God, that thou tell us whether thou be the
Christ, the Son of God. Jesus saith unto him, Thou hast said: nevertheless I say unto you, Hereafter shall ye see the Son of man sitting on
the right hand of power, and coming in the clouds of heaven."
(Matthew 26:63–64.) Again Christ has declared himself to be God's

Son while testifying that his Father is a man. Only if the text is read with the predetermination that it does not mean what it says can its plain meaning be missed.

The first occurrence of the designation "the Son of man" in Mark's Gospel is in the account of the healing of the man stricken with palsy. Rather than give him a blessing of healing, Jesus simply said to him, "Thy sins be forgiven thee." His expression greatly troubled those who witnessed the event. Sins are committed against God, and he alone can forgive them. In their minds, Christ had clearly arrogated to himself the right to speak in the first person for Deity. His action was designed to evidence his authority. The mortal eye does not witness the forgiveness of sins, but it could see the effects of Jesus' words on the stricken man. Knowing their thoughts, Jesus said: "Why reason ye these things in your hearts? Whether is it easier to say to the sick of the palsy, Thy sins be forgiven thee; or to say, Arise, and take up thy bed, and walk? But that ye may know that the Son of man hath power on earth to forgive sins, (he saith to the sick of the palsy,) I say unto thee, Arise, and take up thy bed, and go thy way into thine house." (Mark 2:5–11.) Now we are left to ask why Christ refers to himself as the "Son of man" in a situation that he deliberately concocted for the purposes of emphasizing that his heirship was divine. As in the previous examples, was he not telling them that his Father was an exalted, glorified man?

In the conclusion of the same chapter in Mark, we have Christ's well-known statement that "the sabbath was made for man, and not man for the sabbath: therefore the Son of man is Lord also of the sabbath" (Mark 2:27–28). Using the argument of traditional Christianity, that the title "Son of man" was intended to emphasize Christ's nature as man, we would have to say that the mortal, or corruptible, nature of Christ was given rule over the Sabbath, or holy, day. Is it not better theology to say that the Holy One of Israel, the Son of the Eternal Father, is master of the Sabbath day?

The title "Son of man," or more correctly "Son of Man" (as it is rendered in the JST), is the favorite self-designation of Jesus in the Gospels. We have him recorded as using it eighty times. He undoubtedly used it on countless occasions that are unrecorded. Joseph Smith restored understanding that came from the days of Adam. Deity was known by the title Man of Holiness, and thus his Son would properly be known as the Son of Man, meaning the Son of Man of Holiness. "In the language of Adam," we are told, "Man of Holiness is his name, and the name of his Only Begotten is the Son of Man, even Jesus Christ, a righteous Judge, who shall come in the meridian of time" (Moses 6:57; see also 7:35). There are two revelations in the Doctrine and Covenants in which Christ is referred to as "Son Ahman" (see D&C 78:20; 95:17). We have it from Elder Orson Pratt that in an unpublished revelation the name of the Father was designated as *Ahman* in the pure, or ancient, tongue. The name of the Son was given as *Son Ahman,* the name of men as *Sons Ahman,* and the name of angels as *Anglo-man* in that same language.[7] Elder Bruce R. McConkie suggested that the Father's name could possibly have been rendered *Ah Man* and have carried the same meaning as Man of Holiness.[8]

The Sons of God

A parade of problems attends the inability to allow plain language to mean what it says. As scholars and theologians have spilt an ocean of ink attempting to explain the title "Son of man," they have, in like manner, wrestled to obscure the plain and obvious meaning of the title "Son of God." This is accomplished by their reviewing the various ways the title is used in scripture and then throwing their arms in the air as if in total despair, asking, How could they possibly know which of these, if any, were to apply to Jesus of Nazareth? Their chain of thought is as follows:

1. In the book of Job, the angels in the councils of heaven and those who sang for joy upon learning of the creation of the earth are called "sons of God" (see Job 2:1; 38:7).

2. In his genealogy of Christ, Luke traces that genealogy back to Adam, who he says is "the son of God" (Luke 3:38); and to make matters worse, the parable of the prodigal son suggests that this designation applies to all men (see Luke 15:11–32).

3. The whole house of Israel is referred to as the "son of God"; for instance, in Exodus 4:22, Jehovah says, "Israel is my son, even my first-born."

4. The title is also applied to the kings of Israel as representatives of the chosen nation (see 2 Samuel 7:14; Psalm 2:7).

5. In the New Testament the title is applied to faithful members of the Church. For instance, John wrote: "But as many as receive him, to

them gave he power to become the sons of God, even to them that be-lieve on his name" (John 1:12).[9]

Singularly, the cobweb of confusion or uncertainty is swept away by simply allowing the phrases "son of God" or "sons of God" to mean what they say. "I bow my knees," wrote the Apostle Paul, "unto the Father of our Lord Jesus Christ, of whom the whole family in heaven and earth is named" (Ephesians 3:14–15). If we dare, with the Apostle Paul, assume that language can be trusted, then we understand that we have been directed to pray to our Father in Heaven because he is our Father and he resides in heaven. Thus we read that "the morning stars sang together, and all the sons of God shouted for joy" (Job 38:7). Why the songs of joy? Because the foundations of the earth had been laid (see Job 38:4–6) and the promise given that they, the spirit children of God, might come to the earth to obtain a physical body and prove themselves worthy of God's presence in the endless worlds to come (see Abraham 3:24–26). That none might forget their heavenly kinship, "a genealogy was kept of the children of God. And this was the book of the generations of Adam, saying: In the day that God created man, in the likeness of God made he him; in the image of his own body, male and female, created he them, and blessed them, and called their name Adam, in the day when they were created and became living souls in the land upon the footstool of God." (Moses 6:8–9.)

Thus Adam was first begotten as a spirit son of God and, according to the testimony of Luke, received his physical body from the same Father (see Luke 3:38; see also JST, Luke 3:45). Of this text in Luke, Elder Bruce R. McConkie said: "This statement, found also in Moses 6:22, has a deep and profound significance and also means what it says. Father Adam came, as indicated, to this sphere, gaining an im-mortal body, because death had not yet entered the world. (2 Nephi 2:22.) Jesus, on the other hand, was the Only Begotten in the flesh, meaning into a world of mortality where death already reigned."[10]

All have rightful claim on an inheritance in the family of heaven. Such was the testimony of Christ, who on the morning of his resurrec-tion instructed Mary, saying, "Go to my brethren, and say unto them, I ascend unto my Father, and your Father; and to my God, and your God" (John 20:17). Ultimately we are all children of the same Father, and thus all address him by the same title in prayer, "Our Father who art in heaven." How, then, does Christ's kinship with the Father differ from our own? In that we inherited our physical bodies from others of the sons and daughters of Adam, while Christ had God as a Father. Mary was his mother, and from her he inherited blood, or the ability to die. God was his Father, and from him he inherited immortality, or the ability to live. Thus it is that of all the souls who ever drew breath on this earth, Christ alone could say of his life: "No man taketh it from me, but I lay it down of myself. I have power to lay it down, and I have power to take it again." (John 10:18.) That is, to paraphrase, "I have the power to die, which I inherited from my mother, Mary, and I have the power to live, or take up my life again, which I inherited from God, who is my Father." Thus it is that Christ is the Only Begotten in the flesh, meaning the only child begotten of the immortal Father and a mortal mother.

Only by letting words mean what they say can the scriptural picture as it speaks of sons and daughters of God hang together. Scriptural references to Israel being the children of God, or to its kings, or to the Saints of New Testament times all fit perfectly with our understanding, and none infringe on the divine sonship of Christ. Nor does that understanding rob us of our own divine heritage.

Elder John Taylor stated:

> Let us reflect that Jesus Christ, as Lord of Lords, and king of kings, must have a noble race in the heavens, or upon the earth, or else he can never be as great in power, dominion, might, and authority as the scriptures declare. But hear; the mystery is solved. John says: "And I looked, and, lo, a Lamb stood on the mount Sion, and with him an hundred forty and four thousand, having his Father's name written in their foreheads" [Revelation 14:1].
>
> "Their Father's name," bless me! that is GOD! Well done for Mormonism; *one hundred and forty four thousand* Gods, among the tribes of Israel, and, two living Gods and the Holy Ghost, for this world! Such knowledge is too wonderful for men, unless they possess the spirit of Gods. It unravels the little mysteries, which like a fog, hides the serene atmosphere of heaven, and looks from world to world; from system to system; from universe to universe; and from eternity to eternity, where, in each, and all, there is a presidency of Gods, and Gods many, and Lords many; and from time to time, or from eternity to eternity, Jesus Christ shall bring in another world regulated and saved as this will be when he delivers it up to the Father; and God becomes *all in all.* "And," as

John the Revelator said: "there shall be no more curse: but the throne of God and of the Lamb shall be in it; and his servants shall serve him. And they shall see his face; and his name shall be in their foreheads." [Revelation 22:3–4.]

"His name in their foreheads," undoubtedly means *"God"* on the front of their crowns; for, when all things are created new, in the celestial kingdom, the servants of God, the innumerable multitude, are crowned, and, are perfect men and women in the Lord, one in glory, one in knowledge, and one in image: they are like Christ, and he is like God: then, O, then, they are all "Living Gods," having passed from Death unto Life, and possess the power of eternal lives![11]

The Knowledge of the Heart and the Mind

"For as many as are led by the Spirit of God," Paul wrote in his Epistle to the Romans, "they are the sons of God." The reference here is obviously to those who have been adopted anew into the family of the Father. This is a natural extension of the doctrine of a new birth, or being born again. Such a doctrine does not deny our first birth; it simply draws upon it to emphasize the need of our being born into a state of spiritual sensitivity. Extending that analogy, both the scriptures and our prophets speak of the necessity of our being adopted into the family of our Eternal Father. Thus Paul, continuing his thought, writes, "For ye have not received the spirit of bondage again to fear; but ye have received the Spirit of adoption, whereby we cry, Abba, Father. The Spirit itself beareth witness with our spirit, that we are the children of God: and if children, then heirs; heirs of God, and joint-heirs with Christ; if so be that we suffer with him, that we may be also glorified together." (Romans 8:14–17.)

Paul's testimony, one echoed by the experience of countless people, is that once we attune ourselves with spiritual things we draw closer to God, and as the Spirit becomes our teacher and as it recalls to our memory feelings and knowledge planted deep within our souls, we recognize God as a personal being and as a loving Father and reach out to him, crying, "Abba, Father." *Abba* is an Aramaic word meaning "Daddy," or "Papa."[12] It bespeaks the most gentle and sacred of feelings. It represents such intimacy that slaves were forbidden to use it in addressing the head of the family.[13] It is a perfect attestation that our souls long for a relationship with a God who is accepting, loving, and personal and that this is the God of whom the Spirit bears witness. True principles always bring us closer to God.

The old traditional classic *A Dictionary of Christ and the Gospels* notes that at the time of Christ the "Jewish conception of God was based on the traditional interpretation of the Law, not on the spiritual teaching of the Prophets. God was put further and further away; the conception of Him became increasingly abstract and transcendental."[14] While the writer of this entry sees so clearly how the Jews removed themselves from an understanding of the God of the prophets, he fails to observe that the Christian world trod the same path with precisely the same results. Their God became equally impersonal, abstract, and transcendental.

The more closely we look at the nature of God as presented to us by the Savior, the sharper the contrast becomes between the Judaism of his day and the Christianity of ours. In the most trying moment of his life we find him praying: "Abba, Father, all things are possible unto thee; take away this cup from me: nevertheless not what I will, but what thou wilt" (Mark 14:36). We are left to ask, Does one address a bodiless and formless essence, an essence that transcends one's understanding and experience, as "Abba, Father"? Does one plead with an essence, of which one is an inseparable part, to be excused from drinking the bitter cup? And how is it that the Son surrenders his will to the Father if there never was a difference between the will of the two?

To ask such questions is but to spawn countless others. In Mark 13:32, speaking of a time in the future, Jesus says, "But of that day and that hour knoweth no man, no, not the angels which are in heaven, neither the Son, but the Father." If they are of the same essence, their knowledge must also be the same. Christ cannot be unknowing of things his Father knows.

What are we to understand by the many declarations like the following?

"I seek not mine own will, but the will of the Father which hath sent me" (John 5:30; see also 6:38).

"If any man will do his will, he shall know of the doctrine, whether it be of God, or whether I speak of myself" (John 7:17).

"I do nothing of myself; but as my Father hath taught me, I speak these things" (John 8:28).

"And he that sent me is with me: the Father hath not left me alone; for I do always those things that please him" (John 8:29).

"For my Father is greater than I" (John 14:28).

And of course we are left to question Christ's motive in prayer. Was he in fact praying to himself? To whom was he speaking when he said, "My God, my God, why hast thou forsaken me?" (Matthew 27:46.) Attempts to harmonize these statements, and the scores of others like them in the Gospels, with the dogma of the Trinity constitute an exercise in both spiritual and intellectual perjury. One has to deny the plain meaning of words and the obvious implications of plain statements.

Surely true religion must demand that its adherents exercise faith. There is, however, a difference between perjuring reason and substituting faith for that which is beyond our reach for the present moment. True religion sees faith and reason as not only compatible companions but also complementary ones. Thus it is that the Lord said he reveals things to the "mind" and the "heart" (D&C 8:2). The gospel contains neither mindless revelations nor heartless ones. Such an omission, however, is frequently prostituted in academic settings. The classical historical and theological illustration of this is the very story this work is telling. We must not lose sight of the fact that it was only when the ancient church sought to justify its faith in terms chosen to be congenial to the prevailing philosophy, chosen because they represented "common ground," chosen because they had an aura of respectability in intellectual circles, that the church sold her birthright for a mess of pottage. Such is the true prostitution of reason.

The Testimony of Scripture

Again, and we cannot overstate it, the ruling thought in all that Christ did was to establish the truth of God's fatherhood. His first recorded utterance in the New Testament comes at the age of twelve when his earthly guardians, Joseph and Mary, found him teaching in the temple: "Wist ye not that I must be about my Father's business?" he said. (Luke 2:49.) The last words known to have fallen from his lips were, "Father, into thy hands I commend my spirit" (Luke 23:46). The heavenly messenger who heralded his birth to Mary spoke of him as "the Son of the Highest" and as "the Son of God" (Luke 1:32, 35). It had been revealed to many that he would "be born of Mary, . . . she being a virgin, a precious and chosen vessel," who would "be overshadowed and conceive by the power of the Holy Ghost, and bring forth a son, yea, even the Son of God" (Alma 7:10).

When the relation between Christ and the heavens is involved, Jesus virtually never employs any name but "Father." In all of his prayers of which we have record in either the Old World or the New, this is the case. (See Matthew 11:25–26; 26:39; Luke 23:34, 46; 3 Nephi 17:14; 19:20.) The abstract designations—like the "Blessed One," or the "Holy One," common to the synagogue or to the writings of Philo—are nonexistent.[15] Christ always addressed Deity as "God" or "Father," while the Father did not address him as "Jesus" or "Christ" or "Emanuel" or by any other title or name save "Son" only.

In a work written nearly a hundred years ago, the author observes that "the Fatherhood of God . . . was the characteristic revelation of the New Testament, and determined the whole teaching of our Lord and of His chief apostles as to the relationship and dealings of God with men in Christ. This revelation was, moreover, the completion of the religion of the Old Testament. . . . But when we trace the course of theological thought in the Christian Church, all is different. Its history is that of the gradual vanishing away, first from the thought, then from the heart, of the Church of the apprehension of God's Fatherhood, and the substitution of other conceptions for it."[16]

A further description of this movement includes this observation: "God, who is the hope of men in the Old Testament and their Father in the New, was removed by the thought of men, in the darker times and moods of the Middle Ages, to an infinite distance, while the saints and the officers of the Church filled the foreground of His court, and discharged, by delegation, His functions for Him. Or, where God was not thus trifled with, He became for the majority the object of abject dread, which was fostered by ecclesiastical teachers, both for the promotion of religion as then understood, and for the aggrandisement of the Church."[17]

In this movement the sovereignty of God subverted the fatherly love of God as the eminent doctrine. This was, of course, directed at strengthening the position of the church. It is singularly distinctive that the doctrine of the Holy Trinity declares no truth relative to our kinship with Deity or the family in heaven spoken of by Paul. In the Trinity dogma, the doctrine of the fatherhood of God, the most preeminent doctrine in the New Testament, is absent. Nor can it be argued that this doctrine was restored with the Protestant Reformation. Indeed, what the Reformation did was to introduce a new severity into the uncompromising sovereignty of God to save and to damn rather than to unfold his role to love as a Father. A brief conversation with any evangelical will provide adequate proof of this.

Why Christ Was Killed

It was not for his testimony that he was the Christ, the Promised Messiah, that Jesus of Nazareth was killed; it was for his testimony that he was the Son of God. Christ was accused by the Jews before Pilate of being guilty of sedition and rebellion against the power of Rome (see Luke 23:1–5; John 19:12); but as is well known, this was merely a pretext to incite the power of the state against him. Had Jesus any intent of emancipating his nation from Roman rule, he would have solicited the favor of those who sought his death, and in all probability would have gained it.

Nor was he put to death because he claimed to be the Christ. The Jews were anxiously looking for the coming of their Messiah; be it remembered that the delegation from the temple went down to the Jordan River to ask John if he were the Christ (see John 1:19–25); "and all men mused in their hearts of John, whether he were the Christ, or not" (Luke 3:15). Further, it was well known that John was the son of Zacharias and Elisabeth. His was a miraculous birth, given that both parents were "well stricken in years" (Luke 1:7), but there was no pretense here to divine sonship.

The same conclusion can be deduced from the manner in which that generation eagerly welcomed false Christs who promised to deliver them from Roman rule and whom they knew to be mere men making no claim to divine origin, which they certainly would have done if the Christ were generally expected to be of such origin (see Acts 5:36–37).[18]

At the time of his triumphal entry into Jerusalem, Christ was greeted with such acclamations as, "Hosanna to the Son of David" (Matthew 21:9), "Blessed be the kingdom of our father David" (Mark 11:10), "Blessed be the King that cometh in the name of the Lord" (Luke 19:38), and, "Hosanna: Blessed is the King of Israel" (John

12:13). These inspired utterances evidence an acceptance of Christ as the promised Messiah, though they do not affirm an acceptance of his divine sonship. When the Savior put the question to the Pharisees, "What think ye of Christ? whose son is he?" they did not answer by saying, "He is the Son of God," but rather, "The Son of David." They either could not or dared not answer the second question put to them: "How then doth David [speaking] in [the] spirit call him Lord?" (Matthew 22:41–45.) The appearance of the story is that they did not expect their Messiah to be the Son of God; and when he claimed to be such they rejected his claim as their Messiah.

If that understanding was not had by the people, it appears it was had by Caiaphas, who, when Christ refused to dignify the accusations of false witnesses with a response, charged him by the living God to "tell us whether thou be the Christ, the Son of God." Jesus responded, saying, "Thou hast said: nevertheless I say unto you, Hereafter shall ye see the Son of man sitting on the right hand of power, and coming in the clouds of heaven." The record continues: "Then the high priest rent his clothes, saying, He hath spoken blasphemy; what further need have we of witnesses? behold, now ye have heard his blasphemy. What think ye? They answered and said, He is guilty of death." (Matthew 26:63–66.) The key issue, however, remains that of sonship. This is further evidenced by the words of the Jews to Pilate, "We have a law, and by our law he ought to die, because he made himself the Son of God" (John 19:7), and by the previous resolution of the Jewish Sanhedrin: "Then said they all, Art thou then the Son of God? And he said unto them, Ye say that I am. And they said, What need we any further witness? for we ourselves have heard of his own mouth. And the whole multitude of them arose, and led him unto Pilate." (Luke 22:70–71; 23:1.)

Earlier the Jews sought to kill Jesus because he broke the Sabbath by healing a man, and also because he said that God was his Father, thereby making himself "equal with God" (John 5:18); on another occasion, when he claimed a premortal life, saying, "Before Abraham was, I am," the Jews responded by taking "up stones to cast at him" (John 8:58–59); in still another instance, he asserted his own unity with God, saying, "I and my Father are one," whereupon the Jews "took up stones again to stone him" because, they said, "thou, being a man, makest thyself God" (John 10:30–33). It is clear that claiming messiahship is one thing and claiming divine sonship quite another.

All True Doctrines Grow Out of the
Doctrine of the Fatherhood of God

Our conception of the kingdom of heaven, including all of its doctrines and laws, is dependent on our conception of God. Obviously if our vision is clouded by false notions of the nature of Deity, our perception of our relationship with him will be similarly clouded. Every word that Christ uttered, every doctrine that he taught, every work that he performed was a manifestation of his perception of the kingdom of God and the nature of its King. It was his purpose in all things to establish the kingdom of his Father on earth. Thus we find him teaching all men to pray, saying: "Our Father which art in heaven, Hallowed be thy name. Thy kingdom come. Thy will be done in earth, as it is in heaven." (Matthew 6:9–10.)

Jesus professed to be the agent of his Father. The ruling thought in all that he did was to establish the truth of God's fatherhood. He claimed no doctrine or authority save that which he had received from the Father. To the woman of Samaria he said, "The hour cometh, and now is, when the true worshippers shall worship the Father in spirit and in truth: for the Father seeketh such to worship him" (John 4:23).[19] The fatherhood of God is the preeminent doctrine of the Gospels. It finds its purest expression in the writings of John. This is significant because John's is generally agreed to be the most spiritual of the Gospels, the one directed to the Saints, and therefore the one that is often an enigma to scholars. It appears that Matthew's Gospel was written as a missionary tract to the Jews, that Mark's was directed to the Romans, and that Luke was writing to those of the Greek world. John alone seems to have the Saints, those of the household of faith, as his primary audience. The only other scriptural text that matches John's emphasis on the doctrine of the fatherhood of God is 3 Nephi 11 to 27, where Jesus himself is the teacher. In either case, one will find the Savior making over a hundred references to the fatherhood of God in a span of fourteen or fifteen chapters. The phrases "your Father," "my Father," or "the Father" are used repeatedly. Both texts emphasize that the Son is subordinate to the Father. This is particularly significant in 3 Nephi because it is the resurrected and perfected Christ who is doing the teaching there. Two of the most dramatic teaching moments in 3 Nephi, for instance, describe his praying to the Father (see 3 Nephi 17:15–18; 19:31–34).

Indeed, every doctrine and principle of the gospel of Jesus Christ is but an extension of the verity that the God of heaven is our Father. It is out of this soil that all the truths of salvation grow, for as Jesus said: "Every plant, which my heavenly Father hath not planted, shall be rooted up" (Matthew 15:13). The very seed, we are told, from which the tree of everlasting life comes is the claim of Jesus of Nazareth to be the literal Son of God. In the chapter that follows we will turn our attention to that matter.

11

And the Spirit said unto me: Behold, what desirest thou?
And I said: I desire to behold the things which my father saw.
And the Spirit said unto me: Believest thou that thy father saw
the tree of which he hath spoken?
And I said: Yea, thou knowest that I believe all the words of my
father.
And when I had spoken these words, the Spirit cried with a loud
voice, saying: Hosanna to the Lord, the most high God; for he is
God over all the earth, yea, even above all. And blessed art thou,
Nephi, because thou believest in the Son of the most high God;
wherefore, thou shalt behold the things which thou hast desired.
—1 Nephi 11:2–6

The Doctrine of
Divine Sonship

Synod Hedges Bets on Virgin Birth and Resurrection." So read the
headline. The lead sentence was as follows: "Efforts to tie the
Church of England to a literal interpretation of the Virgin Birth and
bodily Resurrection of Christ were resisted by the General Synod after
an emotive debate yesterday." The article explained that though the
amendment that was approved by the synod rejected a commitment to
the idea of "virgin birth" and a "bodily" resurrection, it did affirm the
church's traditional belief in the birth, death, and resurrection of
Christ "as found in the Apostles' and Nicene Creeds." The archbishop
of York explained that what we are dealing with here is an "incomprehensible mystery and unless we see it as that we can't begin to take
account of it. It is foolish to ask our Church to say more than our tradition has already given us."

On the matter of the nature of Christ's conception, Raymond
Brown, the prolific Catholic theologian, observed: "In a certain sense

this is not one of the most relevant problems of theology or exegesis [exposition of scripture]. The solution to it will not help the wretched in the inner city or even the wretched in the suburbs; should it be resolved, there will remain questions of war and peace and even of priestly celibacy. To some the problem will seem a parade example of the purely (or impurely) inquisitive in theology, in short, the 'nosey.'"[1]

As Latter-day Saints we take sharp exception to the conclusions drawn by these distinguished religious leaders. As there are ordinances of salvation, so there are doctrines of salvation, the acceptance or rejection of which determine our destiny both in this world and in the world to come. We, in concert with traditional Christianity, are committed to the belief that all must take upon themselves the name of Christ if they are to be saved. Parting company with them, it is our faith that all are entitled to know with perfect surety upon what principles salvation rests. Those principles cannot be hidden behind the guise of mystery. A just God is obligated to make them available to all and to do so on equal terms. Nor can we agree that it makes no difference to the wretched in the inner city or the downtrodden wherever they may be found. It *is* the difference! Their sorrowful state is the evidence of Adam's fall, and it is the most eloquent of testimonies of the need for the redemption of Christ. It is the reason that he was born of Mary; it is the reason that he suffered and died; it is the reason that he broke the bands of death in a resurrection that was as literal as was his birth.

"The Son of God Was the Messiah"

The airways are full of various and divers voices witnessing for Christ. In their nature those witnesses differ remarkably from each other and also significantly from the testimony born of Christ in the New Testament.

As there are many who accept Jesus as their Savior while either rejecting or ignoring him as Lord and Master, so there are many who have accepted him as the Christ, or Messiah, while rejecting any notion that he was divine. Indeed, as we have seen, the doctrine of the Holy Trinity, which is the dominant doctrine in determining orthodoxy in the Christian world today, denies that Jesus is the Son of God in any but a strictly figurative sense.

How so many have been able to read the doctrine of divine sonship out of the testimony of Christ and his disciples as recorded in the
New Testament baffles those to whom it is such an obvious and important part of that record. It is, however, to the Book of Mormon that
we as Latter-day Saints turn to obtain a testimony of Christ that is
pure and untampered with. Here we find the doctrine of divine sonship declared with a simple eloquence that denies confusion or argument on the part of the honest truth seeker. Can it be stated more
simply than Nephi did, "The Son of God was the Messiah"? By "faith
on the Son of God," Nephi explained, his father, Lehi, had received
great power—indeed, sufficient power to dream dreams and see visions. (See 1 Nephi 10:17.) By application of that same faith, for the
heavens are equally open to all, Nephi learned that the record that
would be kept by his people in conjunction with other scriptural
records would come forth in the last days to restore the "plain and
precious things" which had been taken from the testimony of "the
twelve apostles." Singularly an angel testified to Nephi that these
records would restore the knowledge that the "Lamb of God," he who
worked out the atoning sacrifice, "is the Son of the Eternal Father, and
the Savior of the world." Such would be the testimony, the angel said,
that would go to "all kindreds, tongues, and people," confirming that
this is a doctrine in its true form that has been lost to them. (See 1
Nephi 13:40.)

Indeed, the Book of Mormon declares this to be the pivotal doctrine of the latter-day Restoration. Having explained that the Jews of
the Old World were scattered because of their rejection of "the Only
Begotten of the Father," Nephi announces that they will remain in
"their lost and fallen state" until that day in which they are "persuaded
to believe in Christ, the Son of God, and the atonement," so that they
can "worship the Father in his name, with pure hearts and clean
hands, and look not forward any more for another Messiah." Then
"the Lord will set his hand again the second time to restore" them and
will "proceed to do a marvelous work and a wonder among" them.
Indeed, Nephi states, "there is save one Messiah, . . . he who should be
rejected of the Jews" and whose "name shall be Jesus Christ, the Son
of God." (2 Nephi 25:12,16–17,19.)

Nephi's testimony was that "unless a man shall endure to the end,
in following the example of the Son of the living God, he cannot be

saved" (2 Nephi 31:16). The testimony of Nephi's brother Jacob was that "all the holy prophets which were before us [all the prophets before the days of Jeremiah] . . . believed in Christ and worshiped the Father in his name." Those having the law of Moses understood that it pointed their souls to Christ, even as Abraham offered his son Isaac, "which is a similitude of God and his Only Begotten Son." (Jacob 4:4–5.) Like Nephi, King Benjamin was instructed by an angel that the Messiah "shall be called Jesus Christ, the Son of God" (Mosiah 3:8). None were more direct in teaching the doctrine of divine sonship than Abinadi, who declared that "God himself shall come down among the children of men, and shall redeem his people." With language that plain, it would be hard to argue that Christ did not have a pre-earth life or that he was not divine. Further, Abinadi explained that "because he dwelleth in flesh he shall be called the Son of God"—that is, while he is mortal, while he has blood flowing in his veins, he will not be called God, but rather the Son of God, by whose power, according to Abinadi, he was "conceived." Yet, because "the will of the Son" was perfectly "swallowed up in the will of the Father"—that is, because he so perfectly represented the Father—he would be known as both Father and Son. (Mosiah 15:1–4,7.)

Perhaps the most detailed of messianic prophecies in holy writ are found in the book of Alma, where we read that "the Son of God cometh upon the face of the earth," that he will be born of Mary, she being "a virgin, a precious and chosen vessel, who shall be overshadowed and conceive by the power of the Holy Ghost, and bring forth a son, yea, even the Son of God" (Alma 7:9–10). Thus Alma told his people that "not many days hence the Son of God shall come in his glory; and his glory shall be the glory of the Only Begotten of the Father" (Alma 9:26). From the days of Adam, Alma explains, "God did call on men, in the name of his Son, (this being the plan of redemption which was laid) saying: If ye will repent, and harden not your hearts, then will I have mercy upon you, through mine Only Begotten Son" (Alma 12:33). Alma's testimony was that none who have read the scriptures could "disbelieve on the Son of God" (Alma 33:14). In so testifying he would have had reference to the brass plates, or the scriptures known to those of the Old World obviously before many of the plain and precious things were taken from them. Helaman instructed his sons, Nephi and Lehi, saying, "And now, my sons, remember, remember that it is upon the rock of our Redeemer, who is Christ, the Son of God, that ye must build your foundation" (Helaman 5:12). Thus we find Helaman's son Nephi testifying that the Son of God must come and be lifted up even as Moses had prophesied (see Helaman 8:14–15), again suggesting that Moses' testimony had been tampered with as we shall shortly see.

In perfect harmony with the testimony of the many prophets who had heralded his coming to the nation of the Nephites, Christ spoke from the heavens to those who survived the calamities that attested to his death, saying: "I am Jesus Christ the Son of God. I created the heavens and the earth, and all things that in them are. I was with the Father from the beginning. I am in the Father, and the Father in me; and in me hath the Father glorified his name." (3 Nephi 9:15.) Much of the instruction given by Christ in his ministry among the Nephites centered in the covenants made by their ancient fathers and the promises relative to the gathering of Israel in the last days. In that instruction Christ affirms the promises made by others in his name that it will come to pass that when the fulness of the gospel is preached to his promised seed they will believe in him, that he is "Jesus Christ, the Son of God," and they will "pray unto the Father" in his name (3 Nephi 20:30–31).

Such were the prophecies that were written and preserved to come forth for the benefit of the remnant of the house of Jacob. Mormon, whose name was placed on the book in which this collection of prophecies is preserved, said, "They shall go unto the unbelieving of the Jews; and for this intent shall they go—that they may be persuaded that Jesus is the Christ, the Son of the living God; that the Father may bring about, through his most Beloved, his great and eternal purpose, in restoring the Jews, or all the house of Israel, to the land of their inheritance, which the Lord their God hath given them, unto the fulfilling of his covenant" (Mormon 5:14). If the message of a book or the testimony of a man can be captured in a single sentence, none would represent Mormon better, as he addresses himself to the scattered remnant of Israel, than the following: "Know ye that ye must come to the knowledge of your fathers, and repent of all your sins and iniquities, and believe in Jesus Christ, that he is the Son of God, and that he was slain by the Jews, and by the power of the Father he hath risen again, whereby he hath gained the victory over the grave; and also in him is the sting of death swallowed up" (Mormon 7:5).

The Holy Order of God

According to the Book of Mormon, there was an order, or system, by which the true messengers of God could be identified (see Alma 5:44–47; 6). The system, referred to as the "order of God," or "the holy order of God," has been identified for us in latter-day revelation as "the Holy Priesthood, after the Order of the Son of God" (D&C 107:3). This is, of course, the true and proper name of what we commonly know today as the Melchizedek Priesthood. The name identifies three singular truths that are associated with the power and authority necessary to be a legitimate witness of Christ. They are holiness, order, and the doctrine of divine sonship. Let us lay the matter plain: Where there is no holiness, there is no authority to testify of Christ. Again, where there is no order (that is, ordinances, organization, discipline, and so on), there is no authority to testify of him. And finally, where the doctrine of divine sonship is not understood, there can be no true testimony of him.

Only under the direction of the priesthood, which is the authority by which the gospel and all ordinances of salvation are ministered (D&C 84:19), can a binding and valid testimony of Christ be borne. The elements of a binding testimony are the same in all ages of earth's history. Thus it was that even in the days of Adam an angel of the Lord instructed him relative to the sacrifices he had been offering, saying: "This thing is a similitude of the sacrifice of the Only Begotten of the Father, which is full of grace and truth. Wherefore, thou shalt do all that thou doest in the name of the Son, and thou shalt repent and call upon God in the name of the Son forevermore." (Moses 5:7–8.) From that day forth men were called upon by the Holy Ghost to repent, "and as many as believed in the Son, and repented of their sins," were saved (Moses 5:14–15).

This was the testimony of the brass plates. Nephi, son of Helaman, taught "that Abraham not only knew of these things, but there were many before the days of Abraham who were called by the order of God; yea, even after the order of his Son; and this that it should be shown unto the people, a great many thousand years before his coming, that even redemption should come unto them" (Helaman 8:18). We read that just prior to Christ's visit to the world of the spirits, there were gathered to meet him "an innumerable company of the spirits of the just, who had been faithful in the testimony of Jesus while they lived in mortality; and who had offered sacrifice in the similitude of the great sacrifice of the Son of God, and had suffered tribulation in their Redeemer's name. . . . While this vast multitude waited and conversed, rejoicing in the hour of their deliverance from the chains of death, the Son of God appeared, declaring liberty to the captives who had been faithful." These "bowed the knee and acknowledged the Son of God as their Redeemer and Deliverer from death and the chains of hell." (D&C 138:12–13, 18, 23.) From among their number, messengers were chosen to declare the gospel of salvation to the spirits in the realms of darkness who had died in their sins without a knowledge of the truth and also among those who had rebelled against the prophets in mortality.[2] "These were taught faith in God, repentance from sin, vicarious baptism for the remission of sins, the gift of the Holy Ghost by the laying on of hands, and all other principles of the gospel that were necessary for them to know in order to qualify themselves that they might be judged according to men in the flesh, but live according to God in the spirit. And so it was made known among the dead, both small and great, the unrighteous as well as the faithful, that redemption had been wrought through the sacrifice of the Son of God upon the cross." (D&C 138:31–35.)

The language of such texts is at some pains to emphasize the doctrine of Christ's divine sonship. They illustrate that this doctrine was well established among a great multitude of faithful souls in both the Old and New Worlds, and that its conspicuous absence from the Old Testament as it has been preserved for us is a classic illustration of "plain and precious things" being taken from that record.

The Tree of Life

Few, if any, scriptural texts are more instructive than Nephi's account of the vision he had relative to the tree of life. Motivated by his father's recital of a prophetic dream in which he was invited to partake of the fruit of that tree, Nephi desired to share the same experience. "Having heard all the words of my father, concerning the things which he saw in a vision," he said, "and also the things which he spake by the power of the Holy Ghost, *which power he received by faith on the Son of God*—and the Son of God was the Messiah who should come—I,

Nephi, was desirous also that I might see, and hear, and know of these things, by the power of the Holy Ghost, which is the gift of God unto all those who diligently seek him, as well in times of old as in the time that he should manifest himself unto the children of men" (1 Nephi 10:17, emphasis added).

Nephi knew that what his father had experienced he could experience. He knew that God, who is no respecter of persons, responds to the honest entreaties of all "who diligently seek him." All of God's children have claim on the same heavenly inheritance. Now, it is significant to note that father Lehi had spiritual power because of his "faith on the Son of God." This was not an unanchored faith. It did not stand alone. It was not simply faith that there was a God, or faith in a Messiah, or even faith in Christ as the Savior. More explicitly, Lehi had great spiritual power because of his faith in Christ as the Son of God. His faith centered in the doctrine of Christ's divine sonship. This is the central doctrine of the Book of Mormon. This is the knowledge that needed to be restored to the earth. The idea that there was a God in heaven, or that Christ was the long-promised Messiah, or that his is the only name whereby men can be saved was never lost to the nations of the earth. The doctrine that was lost, and that universally, was the doctrine of divine sonship, and when it was lost, the powers of heaven were lost also.

So it was that Nephi testified that those who diligently seek the truths of heaven will have "the mysteries of God" unfolded to them "by the power of the Holy Ghost," and that the promise is for those of all ages of earth's history (1 Nephi 10:18–19). Such was the setting in which he was "caught away in the Spirit of the Lord" to an "exceedingly high mountain" (1 Nephi 11:1), where he saw the same vision that his father had seen before him. As he recounts the same in 1 Nephi 11, he tells us that he was interviewed by the Spirit. He was first asked what it was he wanted to know. He responded that he wanted to see the things which his father had seen. Then came the key question, "Believest thou that thy father saw the tree of which he hath spoken?" (Verse 4.) Now, of all the things that his father had recited in his vision—the large and spacious field, the tree, the river of water, the iron rod, the strait and narrow path, the mist of darkness, the great and spacious building, and so on—we must ask why Nephi's guide chose to ask whether he believed his father's account of the tree. When

Nephi said, "I believe all the words of my father," the Spirit "cried with a loud voice, saying: Hosanna to the Lord, the most high God; for he is God over all the earth, yea, even above all" (verses 5–6). Now we are left to ask what there was in Nephi's response that evoked such a refrain of praise on the part of the Spirit. The response to our question was immediately forthcoming: "Blessed art thou, Nephi, because thou believest in the Son of the most high God; wherefore, thou shalt behold the things which thou hast desired" (verse 6). Thus the tree is associated with the Son of God; and Nephi's belief in his father's account of the tree and his associated belief in the Son of God qualify him to see the vision his father has seen.

The Spirit further explained: "And behold this thing shall be given unto thee for a sign, that after thou hast beheld the tree which bore the fruit which thy father tasted, thou shalt also behold a man descending out of heaven, and him shall ye witness; and after ye have witnessed him ye shall bear record that it is the Son of God" (verse 7).

Nephi was then shown a tree, the beauty of which exceeded "all beauty," and the whiteness of which exceeded "the whiteness of the driven snow" (verse 8). Knowing that he had seen the tree "which is precious above all" (verse 9), Nephi sought to know the interpretation, or meaning, of it. In response to Nephi's request, the Spirit vanished and Nephi was shown in his stead a vision of the city of Jerusalem and other cities. He then beheld the city of Nazareth, and, as he reports in his account, "in the city of Nazareth I beheld a virgin, and she was exceedingly fair and white" (verse 13). Then the heavens were opened and an angel came down and stood before him and inquired as to what he had seen. Nephi responded that he had seen "a virgin, most beautiful and fair above all other virgins," whereupon the angel asked, "Knowest thou the condescension of God?" Nephi responded, "I know that he loveth his children; nevertheless, I do not know the meaning of all things." (Verses 15, 16, 17.)

Though Nephi did not know the answer to the angel's question relative to God's condescension, his response does indicate that he understood that we are the children of God and as such are loved by him. Obviously, God cannot do that which is ungodly, for in so doing he would cease to be God. Yet, God, in his perfection, can love his children even in their imperfection and can, in order to nurture and bless them, bend to do that which might not otherwise seem godly.

Thus it was that he condescended to father a child in the flesh. The angel explained to Nephi that the virgin whom he had seen was "the mother of the Son of God, after the manner of the flesh" (verse 18). As the vision continued, Nephi "beheld that she was carried away in the Spirit; and after she had been carried away in the Spirit for the space of a time the angel spake unto me, saying: Look! And I looked and beheld the virgin again, bearing a child in her arms. And the angel said unto me: Behold the Lamb of God, yea, even the Son of the Eternal Father! Knowest thou the meaning of the tree which thy father saw?" (Verses 19–21.)

In response to the angel's final question, "Knowest thou the meaning of the tree which they father saw?" Nephi said, "It is the love of God, which sheddeth itself abroad in the hearts of the children of men; wherefore, it is the most desirable above all things." To which the angel responded, "Yea, and the most joyous to the soul." (Verses 21, 22, 23.) In the context of all that has preceded Nephi's expression, we would understand him to be saying that he has now learned that the tree which is "precious above all" represents the greatest manifestation of God's love, the gift of his Son, and that the condescension of God in fathering that Son in mortality is a perfect manifestation of his love for all his children. As John stated it, "For God so loved the world [not meaning that which is worldly, but his children scattered throughout the world], that he gave his only begotten Son [that is, that he allowed the only Son of whom he was the Father in mortality to be offered as a sacrifice for the sins of the rest of his children], that whosoever believeth in him should not perish, but have everlasting life" (John 3:16).

To suppose that Nephi's understanding was limited to the idea of God's love and that it did not embrace the doctrine of divine sonship would make all that preceded it in the previous twenty-one verses, which recount his experience when he was caught away into the high mountain, a meaningless diversion. It would negate all the instruction he received from the Spirit of the Lord and the angel, and also would miss the meaning of the vision he had of Nazareth and the birth of Christ and the testimony of the angel that Christ was the Son of the Eternal Father. It would suggest that when Nephi indicated that he did not know the meaning of the condescension of God and then was shown the vision of the birth of God's Son, the revelation added nothing to his understanding.

Planting the Seed of Faith

All true principles carry within them the evidence of their own truthfulness. Good doctrines carry a good spirit. They taste good and feel good and lead to good. They lift the heart and enlighten the mind. They are food to the soul and as such are delicious to the taste. Thus it was that Alma, knowing the characteristics of the word of God, likened it to a seed which honest truth seekers could plant in their hearts, doing so with the assurance that if they did not crowd it out with unbelief or by resisting the Spirit of the Lord, it would cause their breasts to swell and their souls to enlarge (see Alma 32:28).

Alma taught us that another distinguishing characteristic of the word of God is that, like the good seed, it brings "forth unto its own likeness" (Alma 32:31). That is, the revelations of heaven are never sterile; they are not shrouded in the fog of mystery or found attempting to seal the heavens or silence God in the guise of loyalty to the revelations of the past. Thus when we plant the seed of truth, we do so expecting it to swell and sprout, to grow, and at the appropriate time of harvest to produce good fruits, each of which will have within it a host of seeds whereby the cycle of growth can continue endlessly.

That such was the doctrine of Alma is well known to the reader of the Book of Mormon. What is not as well known is that the specific doctrine to which he makes reference as he speaks of planting the word, or seed, of faith in our hearts is the doctrine of divine sonship. Too often we have supposed that his discourse ended with Alma 32, but it does not. Consider what takes place in the chapter that follows. First we read that those to whom he was directing himself sought of him to know "whether they should believe in one God, that they might obtain this fruit of which he had spoken, or how they should plant the seed, or the word of which he had spoken, which he said must be planted in their hearts; or in what manner they should begin to exercise their faith" (Alma 33:1).

Here we have it, the very issue that Constantine assembled his council of bishops in Nicaea to decide: that is, whether we believe in one God or not. And what does Alma have to say on the matter? Why, he does just exactly what you would expect. He tells the people to search the scriptures, and then he does it with them. He starts by quoting Zenos, an Old World prophet whose writings are recorded in the brass plates. It is a psalm that is quoted, one that concludes with a reference to the mercy that is extended to them by God because of his Son and to the fact that judgments will also be turned away from them because of the Son. By way of commentary, Alma observes that if they believe the scriptures they must believe what Zenos has said, "for, behold he said: Thou hast turned away thy judgments because of thy Son. Now behold, my brethren, I would ask if ye have read the scriptures? If ye have, how can ye disbelieve on the Son of God?" (Alma 33:2–14.)

Alma then observes that Zenos was not alone in speaking of the Son of God but that Zenock, another prophet of old, also spake of him. Alma adds: "And now, my brethren, ye see that a second prophet of old has testified of the Son of God, and because the people would not understand his words they stoned him to death. But behold, this is not all; these are not the only ones who have spoken concerning the Son of God." (Alma 33:17–18). Moses is cited as a third witness of the doctrine of divine sonship (see Alma 33:19).

The Old Testament knows no prophets by the name of Zenos or Zenock. It appears that both of these prophets were slain because of the boldness of their testimonies relative to the coming of the Son of God (see Helaman 8:19–20) and that those testimonies are also to be numbered among those things deliberately taken from the ancient texts.

Now, as Alma concludes his discourse and completes his answer to the question as to whether his questioners should believe in only one God, he directs that they "begin to believe in the Son of God, that he will come to redeem his people, and that he shall suffer and die to atone for their sins; and that he shall rise again from the dead, which shall bring to pass the resurrection, that all men shall stand before him, to be judged at the last and judgment day, according to their works" (Alma 33:22). He then identifies this as the word that they are to plant in their hearts. It is the doctrine of Christ's sonship and thus his role as the atoning one that Alma says will swell in their breasts; this is the doctrine that is to enlighten their minds; this is the seed that he said will become "a tree, springing up in you unto everlasting life." Then he promised that God would lift their burdens through "the joy of his Son." (Alma 33:23.)

The Fruits of the Seed of Faith in the Son of God

All seeds must produce after their own kind. The seeds of Christian creeds and Nicaea produce after their kind, as does the seed of faith once known to those whose story the Bible tells. The seed of Nicaea declares God to be incomprehensible, to be without body and form. What harvest can there be from such a seed? Can such a doctrine actually allow God to have a Son? The decision of the great council thunders a resounding "No!" The God of the creeds cannot be reduced to fatherhood; he cannot condescend to beget a son. To do so suggests that another might claim his name and his power, and thus there would be two Gods instead of one. This in turn would offend Plato and all his disciples who worship Perfection, whom they have denominated as the One God. What, then, does one do with the plain declarations of scripture that in countless instances and scores of ways contradict such a conclusion? How easy the answer—simply declare such scriptural statements to be grand metaphors given to placate and pacify intellectual and spiritual children. Thus the notion of a material and corporeal heaven has no place in creedal thought, for it has no resemblance to the God of heaven who is said to reside there. There is no gender in such a heaven nor purpose for it, nor is there marriage or a family or purpose for them. The citizens of such a heaven have but one purpose in their eternal state, and that is the adoration of their God. How he is glorified by the worship of inferior beings who have no comprehension of his greatness must, we suppose, remain like all else that appertains to him a mystery.

In as sharp a contrast as the eternities afford stands the doctrine of divine sonship. This doctrine centers in a God who is a corporeal being; a God of body, parts, and passions; a God who literally fathers us as his children and thus is properly addressed as "Our Father in Heaven." When we speak of such a God, like the prophets who have testified of him in holy writ we use the word *Father* to mean father. Now, he can hardly give what he doesn't have. We are his children. In using the phrase "Son of God," in reference to Jesus of Nazareth, we understand the word *Son* to mean precisely that. Jesus of Nazareth is actually and literally God's Son. When the Father speaks of Christ as his Only Begotten, we understand the word *begotten* to mean precisely that. Of the great host of our Father's children, Christ is the only child of our Eternal Father who was begotten by him in the flesh. It was this unique inheritance that enabled Christ to work out an atoning sacrifice. From his mortal mother, Mary, he inherited blood, or the capacity to die. From his Eternal Father he inherited immortality, or power over death. Thus he alone among all of the Father's children could say of his life: "No man taketh it from me, but I lay it down of myself. I have power to lay it down, and I have power to take it again. This commandment have I received of my Father." (John 10:18.)

Thus it is according to the doctrine of divine sonship that Adam and Eve and all their posterity were created in the image and likeness of God. As God has form and body, so they have form and body. Scripture declares Christ to be in the "express image" of God's "person" (Hebrews 1:3), and so we believe it to be. Again, the promise of holy writ is that when the Savior shall return "we shall be like him; for we shall see him as he is" (1 John 3:2); or as the psalmist declared, "As for me, I will behold thy face in righteousness: I shall be satisfied, when I awake, with thy likeness" (Psalm 17:15). Elaborating on this doctrine, the Prophet Joseph Smith said: "When the Savior shall appear we shall see him as he is. We shall see that he is a man like ourselves." (D&C 130:1.) As to the nature of society in the worlds to come, he added, "And that same sociality which exists among us here will exist among us there, only it will be coupled with eternal glory, which glory we do not now enjoy" (D&C 130:2).

Only the doctrine of divine sonship provides for a bodily resurrection. The Bible can be searched in vain for a definition of resurrection, while the revelations of the Restoration are abundantly plain. Our "sleeping dust," we are told in the Vision of the Redemption of the Dead, will be "restored unto its perfect frame, bone to his bone, and the sinews and the flesh upon them, the spirit and the body to be united never again to be divided," that we "might receive a fulness of joy" (D&C 138:17). Only the knowledge of a corporeal resurrection can create the possibility of eternal marriage and the continuation of the family unit. In ancient days these doctrines were the exclusive province of those whose faith embraced the words of living prophets. So it is today, for it is from the Book of Mormon that we first learned that resurrection is the inseparable union of body and spirit (see Alma 11:45; 40:23). With the knowledge that in the worlds to come body and spirit are inseparably united comes the assurance that a distinction between the sexes will also exist. If a woman is not resurrected as a woman, whatever she may be she is no longer a woman, and something very precious has been lost. So it is with a man. The purpose of resurrection is not to save us as something different but to save us as we are. Resurrection is to exalt and perfect, not to alter or destroy. Manhood and womanhood were not intended to become extinct in the eternal worlds. Given that we are resurrected as men and women, nothing would be more unnatural than to suppose that marriage and family relationships would no longer exist. So it is that the gospel plan centers in and around the family unit, and so it is that we as Latter-day Saints make the declaration that salvation is a family affair. As our scripture declares that it is only in the eternal union of body and spirit that we can experience a fulness of joy (see D&C 93:33; 138:50), so might we say that it is only in the eternal union of husband and wife and father and mother that we experience that fulness of joy.

When father Lehi partook of the fruit of the tree of life, he found it to be sweet above all that was sweet and that it brought great joy to his soul. Thus it became his immediate desire that his family partake of that fruit with him. (See 1 Nephi 8:10–12.) Nephi, in experiencing the same vision, learned that the tree of life was a symbolic representation of the love of God as manifested by the life and sacrifice of Christ, and thus it naturally follows that the fruits of that tree are the saving principles of Christ's gospel, for no other fruit can bring with it the promise of eternal life. These principles, we are told, are delicious to the taste, bringing joy and happiness with them. Significantly, every gospel principle that is sweet to the taste of a Latter-day Saint grows out of the doctrine of the divine sonship of Christ. Thus it is that Alma speaks of this doctrine as a seed that grows up into the tree of everlasting life. Among the fruits we pluck from this tree are the doctrines of a corporeal resurrection, eternal marriage, the continuation of the family unit, and the promise that we as the children of God are his heirs and as such can become equal with him in power, might, and dominion (see D&C 76:95). Had we not planted the seed of divine sonship but rather the seed of man-made creeds, no such harvest would be available. In the sharpest of irony, some of those who have not found these fruits, not having planted the seed from which they come, have denounced them as unscriptural and labeled the Latter-day Saints as non-Christian cultists. This is an interesting twist, given that the seed of our faith is the testimony that Jesus of Nazareth is the literal Son of God; but then, did not prophets promise that the prince of darkness would stir up the hearts of the children of men "to anger against that which is good"? (2 Nephi 28:20.)

As children of a divine Father we have come to earth to obtain bodies in his image and likeness in order that we might obtain the exaltation that is his. Through the atonement of Christ we lay claim to our bodies in the resurrection, even as he did, and also obtain the opportunity to be born again into the heavenly family. Thus our souls are stirred by the testimony of Joseph Smith and Sidney Rigdon, who said: "And now, after the many testimonies which have been given of him, this is the testimony, last of all, which we give of him: That he lives! For we saw him, even on the right hand of God; and we heard the voice bearing record that he is the Only Begotten of the Father—that by him, and through him, and of him, the worlds are and were created, and the inhabitants thereof are begotten sons and daughters unto God." (D&C 76:22–24.)

12

God himself was once as we are now, and is an exalted man, and sits enthroned in yonder heavens! That is the great secret. If the veil were rent today, and the great God who holds this world in its orbit, and who upholds all worlds and all things by his power, was to make himself visible,—I say, if you were to see him today, you would see him like a man in form—like yourselves in all the person, image, and very form as a man.

—Joseph Smith

The God of Joseph Smith

If there is a God in heaven and if there are truths of salvation, those truths, by their very nature, must be within the grasp of all who are intended to comply with them. Such truths do not and cannot require training in logic to be understood. To so suggest is to deny the justice of God and make of him a partial being. There are three things, Joseph Smith taught, that are "necessary in order that any rational and intelligent being may exercise faith in God unto life and salvation." The first is the idea that he actually exists. In effect, we are being told that knowledge precedes faith. You cannot exercise faith in God if you know nothing of him. Each of us is initially dependent on the testimony, or witness, of another. The second requisite, the Prophet taught, is a *"correct* idea" of God's "character, perfections, and attributes." Thus we learn that you cannot exercise faith in principles that are false (see Alma 32:21). One may be perfectly sincere in worshipping God as a stone, a mountain, the sun, or some other heavenly body, yet in so doing one can only receive the blessings that stones, mountains, or heavenly bodies are capable of giving. Salvation is not born of error, superstition, or ignorance; nor does it have a variety of sources. If we worship a God who is without body, parts, and passions, who is the great immaterial force or intelligence that rules the universe, when in fact he is a personal being with form and body who is literally the Father of our spirits, then we worship an idol that is the creation of mortal intellect. In so doing we would have claim only upon those blessings that a nonexistent God can give. The third principle identified by the Prophet is an actual knowledge that the course we are pursuing is according to God's will. Certainty is an inseparable part of true religion.[1]

It is common in scholarly circles to maintain a sense of disdain for the certainty of religion. We are left to ask, Can the Holy Ghost or those possessing it lack confidence? The truths of heaven are known only by the Spirit of truth, and that Spirit is light. "Wherefore, he that preacheth and he that receiveth, understand one another, and both are edified and rejoice together. And that which doth not edify is not of God, and is darkness. That which is of God is light; and he that receiveth light, and continueth in God, receiveth more light; and that light groweth brighter and brighter until the perfect day." (D&C 50:21–24.)

True Religion Is Always Immediate and Personal

Joseph Smith professed no knowledge of God learned in schools or from the philosophies of men. His knowledge was the result of personal experience. He read the injunction of James, "If any of you lack wisdom, let him ask of God, that giveth to all men liberally, and upbraideth not; and it shall be given him" (James 1:5). He believed what he read. He asked in faith, nothing wavering, and in fulfillment of the divine edict he received. His was not a hearsay knowledge; he was an eyewitness. On one occasion he said, "Could you gaze into heaven five minutes, you would know more than you would by reading all that ever was written on the subject."[2] On a later occasion he stated, "One truth revealed from heaven is worth all the sectarian notions in existence."[3] As to the opinions of men, Joseph Smith said that they were to him "as the crackling of thorns under the pot, or the whistling of the wind."[4] He also counseled, "The best way to obtain truth and wisdom is not to ask it from books, but to go to God in prayer, and obtain divine teaching."[5]

In Isaiah's great prophecy about the Christ, he said that his visage would be more marred than that of any man (see Isaiah 52:14). We know that many have experienced greater physical scarring than did the Savior, suggesting that what Isaiah had in mind was the manner and extent to which the purity of his message would be perverted. The world is full of strange and contradictory images of Christ. This kaleidoscopic theology is without the power of salvation. God is not the author of confusion and our hope of eternal life cannot rest upon uncertainty. These seemingly endless, and in some instances shameless, depictions of Christ and his gospel dramatize the need for a pure source and a pure vessel by which that message might be conveyed to us—one unschooled and unlearned in the notions of the world, one through whom the truths of heaven could be revealed. So it was that Isaiah, who prophesies of the latter-day restoration of the gospel, spoke of one who was "not learned" who would do "a marvellous work and a wonder" (Isaiah 29:12–14).

In the purity and innocence of youth, Joseph Smith sought the truths of heaven. Unlike the great reformers who sought to purge the old church of its excesses and corruptions, unmindful that they in the very act were feeding upon them and clothing themselves in them, Joseph was innocent of all such associations. He knew nothing of the philosophical speculations upon which the theologies of the day rested. Untrained in logic and sophistry, he listened as priest contended against priest, and convert against convert. The "war of words and tumult of opinions" wearied even his youthful soul, and he questioned how he or anyone could know which, if any, of the competing parties was right. It was in such a frame of mind that he was deeply impressed with James's invitation to ask of God. "Never," he said, "did any passage of scripture come with more power to the heart of man than this did at this time to mine. It seemed to enter with great force into every feeling of my heart. I reflected on it again and again, knowing that if any person needed wisdom from God, I did; for how to act I did not know, and unless I could get more wisdom than I then had, I would never know; *for the teachers of religion of the different sects understood the same passages of scripture so differently as to destroy all confidence in settling the question by an appeal to the Bible."* (Joseph Smith—History 1:6–12, emphasis added.) Thus it was that his classroom became a quiet grove and his tutors the God of heaven and his Beloved Son.

It is a curious view of history that in the past God held converse with men but that for well-nigh two thousand years he has kept silent.

Such, however, is the orthodox view, one upon which Catholic, Protestant, Jew, and Muslim alike are agreed. The subject of revelation is approached almost disdainfully in the work *A Dictionary of Christ and the Gospels*. Under the heading "Revelation" we read: "Few theological or philosophical problems have received keener and more industrious examination than the problem which is suggested to us by the word 'revelation.' Does the word stand for any real disclosure of His secrets by the Eternal? Does God stoop to unveil His face to men? And if He does, what is the mode of such manifestations? What are the conditions under which we may believe that a revelation has been given? Is there any room in a rational scheme of the Universe for a revelation?" Then comes the classic doctrinal pronouncement: "It is a part of the claim of Christianity that the revelation of God in Christ is unique and final."[6] Can there be any wonder, then, that neither the learned divines nor those under their tutelage sought direct communication with God in the hopes of receiving an immediate and direct response? It will be recalled that when Joseph Smith attempted to tell of the experience that was his in the Sacred Grove, he was immediately told that it "was all of the devil, that there were no such things as visions or revelations in these days; that all such things had ceased with the apostles, and that there would never be any more of them" (Joseph Smith—History 1:21).

In contrast, Joseph Smith held that true religion required all to ask of God. "Ye are commanded in all things to ask of God, who giveth liberally," states a revelation he recorded in March of 1831 (D&C 46:7). The first paper published by the Church was *The Evening and the Morning Star*. In one of its first issues it set forth the Latter-day Saint source for finding truth: "Search the Scriptures—search the revelations which we publish, and ask your Heavenly Father, in the name of His Son Jesus Christ, to manifest the truth unto you, and if you do it with an eye single to His glory, nothing doubting, He will answer you by the power of His Holy Spirit. You will then know for yourselves and not for another. You will not then be dependent on man for the knowledge of God; nor will there be any room for speculation."[7] Such statements reflected the doctrine of the Book of Mormon, which was published even before the organization of the Church. In it, for instance, we have an epistle written by Mormon to his son Moroni relative to the practice of infant baptism among some of their people. Mormon writes: "Immediately after I had learned these things of you I inquired of the Lord concerning the matter. And the word of the Lord came to me by the power of the Holy Ghost." (Moroni 8:7.) Mormon then gives the word of the Lord as it was revealed to him. As is well known, Moroni follows the same pattern in the concluding chapter of the book. All who read it with an honest heart are enjoined to ask God if it is true, and all who do so are promised that they will have that knowledge revealed to them by the power of the Holy Ghost (see Moroni 10:3–5).

As to the notion that the Bible constitutes the final word of God, Joseph Smith responded:

> We ask, does it remain for a people who never had faith enough to call down one scrap of revelation from heaven, and for all they have now are indebted to the faith of another people who lived hundreds and thousands of years before them, does it remain for them to say how much God has spoken and how much He has not spoken? We have what we have, and the Bible contains what it does contain: but to say that God never said anything more to man than is there recorded, would be saying at once that we have at last received a revelation: for it must require one to advance thus far, because it is nowhere said in that volume by the mouth of God, that He would not, after giving what is there contained, speak again; and if any man has found out for a fact that the Bible contains all that God ever revealed to man he has ascertained it by an immediate revelation, other than has been previously written by the prophets and apostles.[8]

Joseph Smith as a Competent Witness

The number of occasions upon which Joseph Smith personally saw the Savior is unknown to us. Five such instances are preserved for us in scripture. In chronological sequence they are as follows. First, there is the First Vision, which took place in what we have come to call the Sacred Grove in upstate New York in the spring of 1820. On this occasion both the Father and the Son appeared to Joseph Smith. The Father introduced Christ as his "Beloved Son" and directed Joseph to hear him. Christ subsequently told Joseph not to unite himself with any of the churches of the world and denounced their creeds as an abomination. Obviously there are those who are offended with this statement and are at great pains to discredit the vision. It is not the purpose of this work to respond to those efforts, though it ought to be observed that if we were to give credence to the arguments used to discredit Joseph Smith and the First Vision and then apply the same procedures to Christ and the Gospel accounts of his resurrection, they too would have to be judged false. There are those who are so anxious to poison the well at which the Latter-day Saints drink that they forget that they too must drink of the same waters.

Oliver Cowdery recorded a very interesting account of the visit of John the Baptist when he came to restore the Aaronic Priesthood. It is included as a footnote near the end of the Pearl of Great Price. From Oliver's account of that event we learn that he and Joseph "were wrapped in the vision of the Almighty" on that occasion and that they "heard the voice of Jesus."[9] On February 16, 1832, Joseph Smith and Sidney Rigdon, in conjunction with their labors on the Joseph Smith Translation of the Bible, had the heavens opened to them in a series of visions. They saw the Savior on the right hand of God and heard a voice "bearing record that he is the Only Begotten of the Father—that by him, and through him, and of him, the worlds are and were created, and the inhabitants thereof are begotten sons and daughters unto God" (D&C 76:23–24). Thus we learn that his atoning sacrifice made on this earth is infinite in its effects and makes salvation possible to the inhabitants of those countless earths that he created under the direction of the Father. They are saved through obedience to the same laws and ordinances that have been given to us.

On January 21, 1836, Joseph Smith, while in the Kirtland Temple, had a vision of the celestial kingdom in which he was taught the principles which determine who in the world of the spirits is entitled to embrace the fulness of the gospel and thus obtain eternal life. In introducing that vision he records having seen "the blazing throne of God, whereon was seated the Father and the Son" (D&C 137:3). In April of that year, the temple having been dedicated, Christ appeared to Joseph Smith and Oliver Cowdery to acknowledge his acceptance of it as his house (see D&C 110:1–7). Now we ask, Who else in the nearly twenty centuries since the resurrection of Christ has shared such experiences while providing a host of revealed truths to sustain the verity of his claim? Joseph Smith has penned more revelation than the twelve most prolific Bible writers combined.

If the Bible is the issue, then we are bold to proclaim Joseph Smith as the most competent witness, save Jesus only, of its truths in earth's history. A library containing every scrap of knowledge the world has accumulated about this book would not rival his understanding. It is one thing to read the book and quite another to be instructed by its authors. Who among the world's scholars can boast of having stood face-to-face with Adam, Enoch, Noah, a messenger from Abraham's dispensation (most probably Abraham or Melchizedek), Moses, John the Baptist, Peter, James, and John? While religious leaders were claiming that the heavens were sealed to them, Joseph Smith was being tutored by ancient prophets who laid their hands upon his head and conferred upon him every priesthood, key, power, and authority that they held.

Joseph Smith claimed the Holy Ghost as his textbook[10] and made a translation of the Bible from the original language—the language of revelation. Who but Joseph Smith could tell us that Seth was in the perfect likeness of his father (see D&C 107:43), or could give a detailed description of Paul?[11] Joseph Smith knew the Bible; he knew its prophets; he knew its message; and he knew its central character, the Lord Jesus Christ, with whom he also stood face-to-face and by whom he was instructed. Joseph Smith was a living Bible, and he has done more to enhance our understanding of that great book than any other man who ever lived.

A Test of a True Prophet

The prophetic efforts of Joseph Smith did not center in sharing his spiritual experiences but rather in qualifying us to have the same experiences. The emphasis of his ministry was not on what he had seen but on what we could see. "God hath not revealed anything to Joseph," he said, "but what He will make known unto the Twelve, and even the least Saint may know all things as fast as he is able to bear them."[12] Many a pretender to the prophetic office has claimed to entertain angels or to have spoken with God, but who other than Joseph Smith introduced his angels to others? Joseph introduced Moroni to Oliver Cowdery, David Whitmer, and Martin Harris. He was never alone when priesthood or keys were restored. Witnesses were always present. He received many revelations in the presence of others. He and Sidney Rigdon received the revelation on the degrees of glory together. Together they saw legions of angels, along with the Father and the Son (see D&C 76:21–23). Oliver Cowdery was with Joseph Smith when John the Baptist came to restore the Aaronic Priesthood, and when Peter, James, and John came to restore the Melchizedek Priesthood. Oliver was also with Joseph Smith when Christ came to accept the dedication of the Kirtland Temple, and Moses, Elias, and Elijah restored their keys, powers, and authorities.

Joseph Smith not only parted the veil but also extended the invitation for all of us to pass through it. The God of Joseph Smith made glorious promises to all who would serve him in righteousness and truth. "To them," he said, "will I reveal all mysteries, yea, all the hidden mysteries of my kingdom from days of old, and for ages to come, will I make known unto them the good pleasure of my will concerning all things pertaining to my kingdom. Yea, even the wonders of eternity shall they know, and things to come will I show them, even the things of many generations." (D&C 76:5, 7–8.)

Joseph was talking more about what we could do than what he had done. While we have relatively few recorded instances in which Joseph Smith shared his experience in the Sacred Grove, we have a dozen revelations in the Doctrine and Covenants that invite us to have our own sacred grove. The validity of an experiment is if it can be repeated. A good seed not only bears good fruits but always bears the same fruits regardless of who plants it. Thus Joseph Smith taught us that the seed of faith will always bring its train of attendants, including revelations, visions, dreams, and so on, and that all who plant and nurture the seed are entitled to the harvest.[13]

The test of a true prophet and seer does not rest in his conveying his revelations but in his qualifying you to receive your own. Moses did not take the children of Israel to Sinai to tell them that he spoke with God as one man speaks with another but rather to sanctify them and bring them all into the divine presence. With the restoration of the Melchizedek Priesthood came the restoration of the "key of the knowledge of God" (D&C 84:19). "The power and authority of the higher, or Melchizedek Priesthood, is to hold the keys of all the spiritual blessings of the church—to have the privilege of receiving the mysteries of the kingdom of heaven, to have the heavens opened unto them, to commune with the general assembly and church of the Firstborn, and to enjoy the communion and presence of God the Father, and Jesus the mediator of the new covenant" (D&C 107:18–19).

That priesthood restored to Joseph Smith and Oliver Cowdery by Peter, James, and John, that same priesthood given to every worthy male adult in the Church, has as its purpose to prepare all who hold it in worthiness to stand in the presence of the Father and the Son. This was the very doctrine that Moses taught the children of God in the wilderness when he "sought diligently to sanctify his people that they might behold the face of God; but they hardened their hearts and could not endure his presence; therefore, the Lord in his wrath, for his anger was kindled against them, swore that they should not enter into his rest while in the wilderness, which rest is the fulness of his glory" (D&C 84:23–24).

From that point the story is well known, but perhaps the implications are not. The Lord took Moses and the higher priesthood out of their midst. In its stead he gave them the Aaronic, or Lesser, Priesthood, which contains the keys of the ministering of angels. (See D&C 84:24–26.) Paul referred to this story as the provocation in the wilderness (see Hebrews 3:8), as did Lehi's son Jacob (see Jacob 1:7). That is, the children of Israel provoked the Lord in refusing to prepare themselves to see him. Thus the privilege was lost and in its stead they were given the law of Moses. The invitation and its implications are the same in our dispensation. If we reject the privilege and attendant responsibility to prepare to stand in the presence of God, that privilege will be taken from us and a lesser order of things given in its stead.

Doctrine and Covenants 50, given in May of 1831, concludes with the promise that all who will build on the "stone of Israel," that is, Christ, will enjoy a future day in which they shall "hear" and "see" and "know" the Savior (D&C 50:44–45). In Doctrine and Covenants 67, given in November of the same year, the Lord said, "A promise I give unto you that have been ordained unto this ministry, that inasmuch as you strip yourselves from jealousies and fears, and humble yourselves before me, . . . the veil shall be rent and you shall see me and know that I am—not with the carnal neither natural mind, but with the spiritual" (D&C 67:10). The vision of the degrees of glory, recorded in Doctrine and Covenants 76, concludes with the declaration that such things can be seen and known only by the power of the Holy Spirit, "which God bestows on those who love him, and purify themselves before him; to whom he grants this privilege of seeing and knowing for themselves; that through the power and manifestation of the Spirit, while in the flesh, they may be able to bear his presence in the world of glory" (D&C 76:116–18). In December of 1832 the command was given, "Sanctify yourselves that your minds become single to God, and the days will come that you shall see him; for he will unveil his face unto you, and it shall be in his own time, and in his own way, and according to his own will" (D&C 88:68). In May of 1833 came the Lord's promise, "Every soul who forsaketh his sins and cometh unto me, and calleth on my name, and obeyeth my voice, and keepeth my commandments, shall see my face and know that I am" (D&C 93:1). In the summer of 1833 came the commandment that the Saints build a temple in Kirtland, with the promise that if they would keep it undefiled, God's glory would rest upon it. "I will come into it, and all the pure in heart that shall come into it shall see God" (D&C 97:16). In the dedicatory prayer for the temple, the Prophet noted that they had built a house to the Lord, "that the Son of Man might have a place to manifest himself to his people" (D&C 109:5). A week later the Savior appeared in the temple and said to Joseph Smith and Oliver Cowdery, who stood before him, "I will appear unto my servants, and speak unto them with mine own voice, if my people will keep my commandments, and do not pollute this holy house" (D&C 110:8).

The Doctrine and Covenants records the appearance of a veritable host of angels who appeared to the Prophet while in company with others. Their numbers include Moroni; John the Baptist; Peter; James; John; Moses; Elias; Elijah; Michael, or Adam; Gabriel, or Noah; and Raphael, who we assume is Enoch. That angelic ministrations would occur among the Saints is evidenced by the inclusion of a revelation that gives instruction as to the grand keys whereby it can be determined whether messengers are of God or of the devil (see D&C 129).

A Second Test of a True Prophet

A simple test by which we can determine the legitimacy of any purported revelation is to ask, What does it reveal? By definition a revelation must reveal something, and that revelation must be more than a clap of the hands and a shout of hallelujah, for that adds nothing to our knowledge. If God reveals himself to someone, through that experience the person must obtain some sure knowledge about him. All claimants must pass the same test. If traditional Christianity claims no sure knowledge about God, it is because they are without the light of heaven. If they are without that knowledge, they have no business acting as his spokesman. Such is the second test we apply to Joseph Smith. If he is a true prophet, then we can rightfully expect him to be the source of sure knowledge about Deity.

Admitting that history has preserved for us only fragmentary accounts of the teachings of the Savior and his prophets from ages past, we announce that from extant records we have more revealed knowledge from Joseph Smith dealing with the nature of God than we have from any man who ever lived. From the First Vision, which is the foundation for everything he taught, we learn the following:

1. The veil can be parted. God speaks. He reveals himself.

2. The personages of the Godhead are separate and distinct.

3. Those personages have bodies, and men are in their image and likeness.

4. One of those personages denominated the other as his Beloved Son, thus making himself the Father.

5. All doctrines taught relative to the Father and the Son in the creeds of Christendom are false.

Everything that Joseph Smith subsequently taught is a natural extension of these singular truths. Each passes the test of granting us greater certainty about God and our relationship with him. Let us illustrate by briefly reviewing what he taught relative to the corporeal nature of God, the doctrine of joint-heirship, and the anthropomorphic nature of Deity, as well as his observations on the doctrine of the Trinity.

A Corporeal God

The God of the prophets and the God of scripture was always a corporeal being. Singularly, Joseph Smith was the first man in nearly eighteen hundred years to testify of the same God spoken of in holy writ. Considerable effort has been expended on the part of some to sustain the idea that Joseph Smith initially believed in the Trinity. His teachings relative to the corporeal nature of God, spirits, and resurrected beings all stand as a refutation of such a notion.

In her history of the Prophet, Lucy Mack Smith, his mother, recounts a conversation with a Deacon Beckwith in Palmyra while the Book of Mormon was being printed. She told the deacon: "The different denominations are very much opposed to us. The Universalists are alarmed lest their religion should suffer loss, the Presbyterians tremble for their salaries, the Methodists also come, and they rage, for they worship a God without body or parts, and they know that our faith comes in contact with this principle."[14] The Book of Mormon, which was published almost two weeks before the Church was organized, is most emphatic in teaching a corporeal resurrection. Amulek taught that the mortal body would be raised to an immortal body, "that they can die no more; their spirits uniting with their bodies, never to be divided" (Alma 11:45). Alma taught that "the soul shall be restored to the body, and the body to the soul; yea, and every limb and joint shall be restored to its body; yea, even a hair of the head shall not be lost; but all things shall be restored to their proper and perfect frame" (Alma 40:23). Indeed, it was Alma who taught of paradise as an intermediate state where spirits await the day when they will be reunited with their bodies. Quite generally Latter-day Saints take such knowledge for granted, supposing the Bible-believing world to share in it. They do not. You can read the Bible until doomsday and you will never find in it a definition of either *resurrection* (the word is not even used in the Old Testament) or *paradise* or any synonymous phrase. What we are being taught here is the significance of the body in the plan of salvation.

The doctrine of eternal marriage, which is unique to Mormonism, was revealed to Joseph Smith in 1831 (see headnote to D&C 132). Obviously it requires a bodily resurrection and implies that all exalted beings are corporeal. It grew out of Joseph Smith's labors in his translation of the Old Testament. A host of truths were restored to us as a result of this work, many of which enhance our understanding of the nature of Deity and our relationship with him. It was in his work on the book of Genesis that the Prophet first learned about the Grand Council in Heaven where Satan and his followers rebelled (see Moses 4:1–4). Here he was told that Adam was a son of God (see Moses 6:22) and that in the genealogical record that was kept, Adam's posterity were called "the children of God" (Moses 6:8). Here he learned that Cain would rule over Satan because Cain had a body (Moses 5:23, 30). Subsequent to this the Prophet taught that "all beings who have bodies have power over those who have not," and that Satan "has no power over us only as we permit him."[15] Is it not interesting that Satan—who sought the throne of God in a state of rebellion in the heavenly council and was cast out having lost the chance to obtain a body—has been so successful in getting the creeds of men to focus their worship on a bodiless God?

A revelation given through Joseph Smith on May 6, 1833, explained that man had been with God in the beginning, that is, prior to the creation of the earth, but then only in spirit form. The necessity of a body was then explained: "For man is spirit. The elements are eternal, and spirit and element, inseparably connected, receive a fulness of joy; and when separated, man cannot receive a fulness of joy." (D&C 93:29, 33.) While the full implications of this find expression in the doctrine of heirship, to which we will come, it will suffice for the moment to say that the Prophet declared: "That which is without body, parts and passions is nothing. There is no other God in heaven but that God who has flesh and bones. John 5:26. As the Father hath life in himself, even so hath he given to the Son to have life in himself. God the Father took life unto himself precisely as Jesus did." That is to say, he too had father, mother, and a mortal birth in some previous estate prior to his exaltation. The Prophet explained events associated with the Grand Council in Heaven, at which we were all present, these events being prior to the creation of the earth. "We came to this earth," he said, "that we might have a body and present it pure before God in the celestial kingdom. The great principle of happiness consists in having a body. The devil has no body, and herein is his punishment."[16]

"In tracing the thing to the foundation," Joseph said on another occasion, "and looking at it philosophically, we shall find a very material difference between the body and the spirit; the body is supposed to be organized matter, and the spirit, by many, is thought to be immaterial, without substance. With this latter statement we should beg leave to differ, and state the spirit is a substance; that it is material, but that it is more pure, elastic and refined matter than the body; that it existed before the body, can exist in the body; and will exist separate from the body, when the body will be mouldering in the dust; and will in the resurrection, be again united with it."[17]

The Doctrine of Joint-Heirship

The body, the Prophet taught, is essential to obtaining a fulness of joy. There is no salvation without it, he said.[18] The whole system of salvation, according to Joseph Smith, consists of obtaining a fulness of God's grace and his glory. In the revelation on the degrees of glory (1832), salvation was defined as the children of God becoming equal with him "in power, and in might, and in dominion" (D&C 76:95). This is the doctrine of joint-heirship.

Three other revelations given in 1832 contained this same assurance. A revelation dealing with the means of providing for the poor concluded with the vow that Christ would "appoint every man his portion," and that the faithful and wise steward would "inherit all things" (D&C 78:21–22). The same doctrine is found in what we know as the oath and covenant of the priesthood. In this revelation the Lord explains that those who receive the priesthood and who receive his servants have received him, and that to receive him is to receive his Father. He then promises, and does so with an oath, that those who receive his Father will receive his Father's kingdom; therefore, all that his Father has will be given to them. (See D&C 84:35–38.) A revelation called the Olive Leaf was also given that year, and it promised the Saints that they might eventually receive their inheritance and be made equal with God (see D&C 88:106–7).

One of the most significant revelations on this subject came on May 6, 1833. This revelation included the restoration of part of the writings of John the Baptist and the stipulation that the balance would be revealed when men become sufficiently faithful to receive it. The primary purpose of the revelation is to explain "what" and "how" we worship in order that we might obtain the fulness of the Father (see D&C 93:19). It explains that Christ did not enjoy a fulness of the Father's grace at birth but that through the experiences of mortality he advanced "from grace to grace" until he received that fulness (see D&C 93:6–14). Christ's example constitutes the answer to the "what" and "how" of worship. This knowledge, the Lord said, was revealed so that men might be able to worship God correctly and, in due time, also receive of his fulness. The Lord explained that men are to go from grace to grace, as he did, until they have received of his fulness and are glorified in him as he is glorified in the Father. The promise is that if men will keep the commandments and will receive truth and light, they too will know all things and, like Christ, gain all power in heaven and earth. (See D&C 93:17, 19–28.) That is to say, they become joint-heirs with Jesus Christ. A joint-heir is one who inherits equally with all others including Christ himself. Each heir has an equal and undivided portion of the whole of everything. If one knows all things, so do all others who inherit jointly with him. If one heir possesses all things, then each heir possesses all things, and so on.

In the *Lectures on Faith,* Joseph Smith explained[19] again that Christ gained the fulness of his Father, meaning "the same mind, the same wisdom, glory, power, and fullness. . . , possessing all knowledge and glory," by going from grace to grace. He also stated that "all those who keep his commandments shall grow up from grace to grace, and become heirs of the heavenly kingdom, and joint heirs with Jesus Christ." As joint-heirs, he said, they would be "filled with the fullness" of glory. For, he said, as "the Son partakes of the fullness of the Father through the Spirit, so the saints are by the same Spirit, to be partakers of the same fullness, to enjoy the same glory; for as the Father and the Son are one, so, in like manner, the saints are to be one in them."[20]

In the King Follett discourse, the Prophet reviewed these principles, explaining that to be a joint-heir with Jesus Christ means "to inherit the same power, the same glory and the same exaltation, until you arrive at the station of a God, and ascend the throne of eternal power, the same as those who have gone before." He explained that this is what Jesus Christ did in order to gain his fulness and that we are to do the same.[21]

God as an Anthropomorphic Being

The great "mystery" of the Godhead which defies description and definition in the sectarian world, and about which countless volumes have been written that have left even their authors confused, is declared by Joseph Smith in two simple sentences uttered under the influence of the Holy Ghost. "The Father has a body of flesh and bones as tangible as man's; the Son also; but the Holy Ghost has not a body of flesh and bones, but is a personage of Spirit. Were it not so, the Holy Ghost could not dwell in us." (D&C 130:22.)

In the crowning discourse of his life, one that captures the substance of all the great doctrines of the Restoration, Joseph Smith declared: "I will go back to the beginning before the world was, to show what kind of being God is. What sort of a being was God in the beginning? Open your ears and hear, all ye ends of the earth, for I am going to prove it to you by the Bible, and to tell you the designs of God in relation to the human race, and why He interferes with the affairs of man." Then the Prophet parted the heavens for all to see what he had seen:

> God himself was once as we are now, and is an exalted man, and sits enthroned in yonder heavens! That is the great secret. If the veil were rent today, and the great God who holds this world in its orbit, and who upholds all worlds and all things by his power, was to make himself visible,—I say, if you were to see him today, you would see him like a man in form—like yourselves in all the person, image, and very form as a man; for Adam was created in the very fashion, image and likeness of God, and received instruction from, and walked, talked and conversed with him, as one man talks and communes with another.[22]

Joseph was delivering a funeral discourse and as such was announcing the principles of consolation for those who mourn the loss of loved ones. Those principles, he said, centered in understanding the character and being of God and how he came to be so. The ideas, he said, were incomprehensible to some and yet they are simple. *"It is the first principle of the Gospel to know for a certainty the Character of God, and to know that we may converse with him as one man converses with another, and that he was once a man like us; yea, that God himself, the Father of us all, dwelt on an earth, the same as Jesus Christ himself did."*[23] These principles, he said, were taught in the Bible and he would prove his doctrine from that source. He then proceeded to do so, commencing with the first sentence in Genesis, which, properly translated, announces a plurality of Gods and refers to a great council in heaven at which the plan of creation was presented.[24]

The Creeds of Men and the Nature of the Godhead

"Many men say there is one God; the Father, the Son and the Holy Ghost are only one God," Joseph observed. "I say that is a strange God anyhow—three in one, and one in three! It is a curious organization. . . . All are to be crammed into one God, according to sectarianism. It would make the biggest God in all the world. He would be a wonderfully big God—he would be a giant or a monster."[25] Since Joseph's source was always revelation, he volunteered that "any person that had seen the heavens opened knows that there are three personages in the heavens who hold the keys of power, and one presides over all."[26] Earlier he had explained that "everlasting covenant was made between three personages before the organization of this earth, and relates to their dispensation of things to men on the earth; these personages, according to Abraham's record, are called God the first, the Creator; God the second, the Redeemer; and God the third, the witness or Testator."[27] In his last public discourse, Joseph Smith said: "I have always declared God to be a distinct personage, Jesus Christ a separate and distinct personage from God the Father, and that the Holy Ghost was a distinct personage and a Spirit: and these three constitute three distinct personages and three Gods. If this is in accordance with the New Testament, lo and behold! we have three Gods anyhow, and they are plural; and who can contradict it?"[28]

Some Latter-day Saints have felt uncomfortable with the uncompromising directness of the Lord's condemnation of the creeds of Christendom and those who teach them, as it is recorded in Joseph's account of the First Vision. The renowned historian Will Durant was no less direct. He capsulizes the history of the Christian church by saying: "Christianity did not destroy paganism; it adopted it." And again, "Christianity was the last great creation of the ancient pagan world."[29] Christianity's new God was beyond true fatherhood, which of course left his children with no true claim to being his heir. Embracing such a God required rejecting the words of his prophets and those of the Savior himself in favor of philosophical speculations. Can there be any wonder that God would be offended?

It has been the experience of virtually every missionary that has gone forth to declare the message of the Restoration to meet countless people who respond to their testimony relative to the nature of God by saying, "Yes, that is what I have always believed!" while they silently close their minds to the fact that the knowledge planted in their hearts is far from that declared by the creeds to which they are expected to give allegiance. Somehow in this combination of believing and ignoring they expect to find salvation, and yet they know that such a course is without the power to produce the kind of faith in their lives that was common to the faithful of ages past, whose faith they profess to share.

A True and Living God

The God of Joseph Smith is the same God known to the ancient prophets; he is not the God of the philosophers nor is he the God of the creeds of Christendom. Joseph Smith was not a teacher of speculative theology, he was a personal witness of the God of heaven. That God who stood face-to-face with his prophets in times past stood in like manner before Joseph Smith and spoke to him as one man speaks to another. He was and is a knowable God, not a God hidden in a shroud of mystery. He is not a spirit essence but rather an exalted, resurrected, and glorified man. Indeed, Man of Holiness is his name. He is the Father of our spirits, we are his children born in heavenly realms where we once lived with him, and thus we rightfully call him our Father in Heaven. His work and glory is to bring to pass our immortality and eternal life. Ours is a divine destiny. Our spirits and our bodies were created in his image and likeness, and in the resurrection they will be inseparably united that we might experience both a fulness of joy and the fulness of all that our Eternal Father has.

Such was the testimony and doctrine of the Prophet Joseph Smith. Such is the message that we seek to echo to the ends of the earth.

Epilogue

Were we to discover that a plot was under way to rob us of our inheritance, we would respond with some alarm. Particularly would that be the case if we knew that we were the heirs of a king who had bequeathed us all that he had. How much greater ought to be our concern to discover a conspiracy designed to hide from us our eternal inheritance, particularly given that we are heirs of the King of heaven and earth and that he has promised us the fulness of his kingdom. "I have said," the holy word reads, "Ye are gods; and all of you are children of the most High" (Psalm 82:6). "The Spirit itself beareth witness with our spirit, that we are the children of God: and if children, then heirs; heirs of God, and joint-heirs with Christ," Paul declared of all the faithful Saints (Romans 8:16–17). The repository of scripture begins with the book of Genesis, meaning the book of beginnings, and it in turn begins with the announcement that we have been created in the image and likeness of God, that we were blessed by him, and that he granted us dominion over the earth and all created things (see Genesis 1:26–28). Revelation, the concluding book of the Bible, contains a promise from the lips of the Savior. It reads: "And to him who overcometh, and keepeth my commandments unto the end, will I give power over many kingdoms; and he shall rule them with the word of God; and they shall be in his hands as the vessels of clay in the hands of a potter; and he shall govern them by faith, with equity and justice, even as I received of my Father" (JST, Revelation 2:26–27).

Well might we ask, Who dares declare such things? And who dares suppose them to be literally so? But better still ought we to ask, Who dares deny them? Who dares suppose them not to mean precisely what they say? If anything but the plain meaning of the words was intended, who but a prophet dares tell us, for surely "no prophecy of the scripture is of any private interpretation. For the prophecy came not in old time by the will of man: but holy men of God spake as they were moved by the Holy Ghost." (2 Peter 1:20–21.) And men in old time believed themselves to be the heirs of God!

What, then, happened to the divine inheritance that was once promised to us? What became of that God who walked with Adam in Eden and conversed with his holy prophets face-to-face as one man talks with another? By whose authority did he cease to be a personal being, and by what strange mishap did he lose both form and body? How was it that we ceased to be a part of his eternal family while the word *Father* ceased to mean Father, the word *Son* ceased to mean Son, the word *begotten* ceased to mean begotten, and the word *children* ceased to mean children? Who, might we ask, has taken from us our divine inheritance? And by what authority have they done it? Were prophets among their number? Was there a claim of revelation as their source? And if so, where in the library of holy books do we read it? Surely we will not be told this is the work of a council of men assembled by the authority of an emperor who in turn obtained his office by the strength of his arm and the sharpness of his sword. For were that proved to be so, would we not, as Jeremiah prophesied we would, awake and declare: "Surely our fathers have inherited lies, vanity, and things wherein there is no profit. Shall a man make gods unto himself, and they are no gods?"(Jeremiah 16:19–20.)

The Landmarks of Apostasy

The great battle of the second century, authorities tell us, was a struggle between those who asserted that "there was a single and final tradition of truth, and those who claimed that the Holy Spirit spoke to

them as truly as He had spoken to men in the days of the apostles."
Victory went to those claiming revelation had ceased. Thus was born
the doctrine of sufficiency, or the notion that what was contained in
extant records combined with the claim to apostolic traditions would
be sufficient for whatever complexities the future might bring.[1]

The battle of the third century was between those who claimed
that the scriptural records were to be taken in their literal sense, and
those who claimed that they needed a philosophical interpretation.
Victory went to the latter.[2] Interpretation, of course, belonged alone to
the church. Thus the divine voice and the voice of the majority of
bishops were announced to be one and the same. Simultaneously the
church married itself to the state. The cost to the gospel message in this
alliance was horrendous. As to the new doctrine of majority rule, it
would in later ages be supplanted by the notion of an infallible pope.[3]

So it was that the ideas of trusting in God and of converse with
him were replaced by a creed, one which represented the blending of
traditions, however far they may have wandered from their origins,
and metaphysical speculations. Indeed, the center of gravity had
changed. A faith that centered in certainty was replaced by an incomprehensible fog of mystery.

As to church membership, Edwin Hatch explains that in the beginning it had been purely voluntary, prizing above all the infinite
worth of the individual soul. "The ground of that individual worth
was a divine sonship. And the sons of God were brethren. They were
drawn together by the constraining force of love."[4] This too would
change, for when the church merged with the state, expediencies required the surrender of the notion of our infinite worth and of religious freedom.

As there is a plan of salvation, so there is a pattern to apostasy;
and in that pattern the more spiritually significant a doctrine, the
more quickly it will be discarded among those who have gone astray.[5]
The greater the truths, the greater the heresies that war against them.
The greatest body of truths are those that deal with God, his Son Jesus
Christ, and the Holy Ghost. Conversely, the greatest heresies are those
that pervert our understanding of those same doctrines. All true doctrines about God will bring us closer to him; their counterparts will always make him more abstract, distant, and mysterious. True doctrines
will always profess revelation as their source; their counterparts will
rest on the speculations of men.

The Corrupting Influence of Creeds

Both the Old and New Testaments record that as the followers of Christ gathered in congregations, they were known as Saints. The name implied holiness, and they attempted to live so as to justify the name. Their association was less intellectual than moral and spiritual. They spoke and thought of themselves in terms of sons and daughters of God, heirs of God, joint-heirs with Christ, brethren and sisters, and as fellow servants even with angels (see John 20:17; Romans 8:15–17; Revelation 19:10).

After the death of the Apostles, scholarly sources tell us, this community of Saints was transformed into a church whose moral ideal and practice differed little from those of their Gentile neighbors.[6] No longer did fellowship center in the quest for the godly life, rather it centered in assent to the creed.[7] Where the gate to Church membership had once been associated with the ordinance of baptism—which was viewed as a washing away of sins, a birth into a newness of life, and an adoption into a divine sonship—the gate now became conformity to the resolutions of the councils. "One who accepted them received immunity and privileges," writes Hatch. "One who did not was liable to confiscation, to banishment, to death."[8] The creed, according to the pattern of apostasy, so defined God that any meaningful doctrine of divine sonship was negated.

In the conclusion of his remarkably insightful work on the way Greek ideas influenced Christianity, Hatch observes that the victories Christianity has won have come from "preaching, not Greek metaphysics, but the love of God and the love of man. Its darkest pages are those which record the story of its endeavouring to force its transformed Greek metaphysics upon men or upon races to whom they were alien."[9]

Hatch goes on to say that he sees on the horizon "a Christianity which is not new but old, which is not old but new, a Christianity in which the moral and spiritual elements will again hold their place, in which men will be bound together by the bond of mutual service, which is the bond of the sons of God, a Christianity which will actually realize the brotherhood of men, the ideal of its first communities."[10]

Ours is that day of restoration. The heavens have been opened and the God of our ancient fathers has manifested himself once again. Our divine inheritance has been restored. "Let all the saints rejoice, therefore, and be exceedingly glad; for Israel's God is their God" (D&C 127:3), and we are in very truth his sons and his daughters.

Notes

Publication details for sources cited in the notes that follow are listed in the Bibliography.

Introduction

1. Baker, *The Foolishness of God*, p. 152.
2. See Eiselen, Lewis, and Downey, eds., *The Abingdon Bible Commentary*, p. 223.

Prologue

1. Tertullian, quoted in Chadwick, *Early Christian Thought*, p. 1.
2. Mosheim, *An Ecclesiastical History* 1:53–54.
3. For instance, *The Oxford Dictionary of the Christian Church* calls it Christological "speculation" (p. 281). See also Bokenkotter, *A Concise History*, p. 46; Paterson, *Rule of Faith*, p. 5; and Durant, *Caesar and Christ*, p. 595.
4. Hatch, *The Influence of Greek Ideas*, p. 1.

5. Mosheim, *An Ecclesiastical History* 1:47.
6. Ibid.

Chapter 1. What Think Ye of Christ? Whose Son Is He?

1. See Bruce R. McConkie, *The Mortal Messiah* 1:205–8.
2. See Edersheim, *The Life and Times of Jesus the Messiah* 2:777–87. Also see *The Mishnah*, pp. 100–121.
3. Benson, *Come unto Christ*, p. 4.
4. See *The Koran Interpreted*, pp. 309–10.
5. F. LaGard Smith, *Blasphemy and the Battle for Faith*, p. 67.
6. Spong, *Born of a Woman*, p. 33.
7. Ibid.
8. See ibid., p. 34.
9. Ibid., pp. 44–45.
10. See Young, *Our God Is Still Too Small*, p. 131.
11. For instance, in his work *Scripture Twisting: 20 Ways the Cults Misread the Bible*, James W. Sire states: "A cult is simply any religious movement that is organizationally distinct and has doctrines and/or practices that contradict those of the Scriptures as interpreted by traditional Christianity as represented by the major Catholic and Protestant denominations, and as expressed in such statements as the Apostles' Creed" (p. 20). It might be observed that those attacked by Sire in this book would be hard pressed to twist the scriptures into tighter knots than he does to sustain his arguments against them.

Chapter 2. In the Image of God

1. Poulson, *God—the Power Who Rules*.
2. The Westminster Confession of Faith states the matter thus: "The whole counsel of God, concerning all things necessary for his own glory, man's salvation, faith and life, is either expressly set down in scripture, or by good and necessary consequence may be deduced from scripture: unto which nothing at any time is to be added, whether by new revelations of the Spirit, or traditions of men." And further, "The supreme Judge, by which all controversies of religion are to be determined, and all decrees of councils, opinions of ancient

writers, doctrines of men, and private spirits, are to be examined, and in whose sentence we are to rest, can be no other but the Holy Spirit speaking in the scripture." (Chapter I, sections VI and X, *The Confession of Faith,* pp. 22, 24.)

3. *The Shorter Oxford English Dictionary on Historical Principles* 1:866.

4. See Girdlestone, *Synonyms of the Old Testament,* p. 27.

5. Joseph Smith, *Teachings of the Prophet Joseph Smith,* pp. 371, 372.

6. Friedman, *Who Wrote the Bible?* p. 235.

7. Segal, "El, Elohim, and YHWH in the Bible," p. 92.

8. Adam Clarke, *Clarke's Commentary* 1:38, italics in original.

9. See Keil and Delitzsch, *Biblical Commentary* 1:62. See also Dummelow, ed., *A Commentary on the Holy Bible,* p. 5.

10. *The International Standard Bible Encyclopaedia* 2:1254.

11. Eiselen, Lewis, and Downey, eds., *The Abingdon Bible Commentary,* pp. 220–21.

12. See Joseph Smith, *History of the Church* 1:226.

13. See Allis, *The Five Books of Moses,* p. 23.

14. See Friedman, *Who Wrote the Bible?* pp. 22–25.

15. Beltz, *God and the Gods,* p. 44.

16. Ibid., p. 36.

17. All of the documents—J, E, P, and D—are assumed to have been written long after Moses. The ninth century B.C. is the time accorded to the E document. The LDS Bible chronology gives Abraham's birth as 1996 B.C. We have a record "written by his own hand" in the book of Abraham. The Abraham papyrus doesn't accord well with the documentary hypothesis.

18. Beltz, *God and the Gods,* p. 42.

19. Ibid., p. 43.

20. Blenkinsopp, *The Pentateuch,* p. 28.

21. In his book *The American Religion,* Harold Bloom, an intellectual Jew, attributes to Joseph Smith an uncanny genius for seeing past the deliberate expunging of biblical texts to uncover the faith and beliefs of ancient Israel. He notes: "The Yahwist [writer of the J document, believed by scholars to be the earlier] clearly uses Elohim to refer to a variety of divine beings, and Joseph Smith . . . had an impulse of genius in finding his own way back to the J writer, whose Yahweh was one of the Elohim, surrounded by others. Joseph Smith's gods, it will

be remembered, were not only plural, but of flesh and bone, like the Yahwist's quite substantial Yahweh and his attendant Elohim." (Pp. 113–14.) "Researchers," Bloom notes elsewhere in his book, "have not yet established, to my satisfaction, precisely how much the Prophet Joseph knew about Jewish esoteric tradition or Kabbalah, or about the Christian Gnostic heresies" (p. 98).

The real issue here is that the full religion of the peoples of the Bible is not contained in that book. The peoples of the Bible had their mysteries, their sacred rites, knowledge, and truth, things known only to the initiate, and somehow Joseph Smith, the unlearned frontier prophet, got ahold of them. No scholarly explanation can account for it. Bloom acknowledges that Brigham Young had knowledge from these same sources, sources that Brigham, like Joseph, had no access to.

"What is clear," Bloom writes, "is that Smith and his apostles re-stated what Moshe Idel, our great living scholar of Kabbalah [the mystical interpretation of Hebrew scripture], persuades me was the archaic or original Jewish religion, a Judaism that preceded even the Yahwist, the author of the earliest stories in what we now call the Five Books of Moses." (So the question is, how was Joseph Smith able to find what the ancients were laboring so hard to hide? The initiated weren't telling what they knew, and the uninitiated disbelievers were erasing all hints and clues that such ideas existed.) "To make such an assertion," Bloom continues, "is to express no judgment, one way or the other, upon the authenticity of the Book of Mormon or of the Pearl of Great Price. But my observation certainly does find enormous validity in Smith's imaginative recapture of crucial elements in the archaic Jewish religion, elements evaded by normative Judaism and by the [Christian] Church after it. The God of Joseph Smith is a daring revival of the God of some of the Kabbalists and Gnostics, prophetic sages who, like Smith himself, asserted that they had returned to the true religion of Yahweh or Jehovah. If Smith was mistaken, then so were they, but I hardly know just what it could mean to say that the Kabbalists or Joseph Smith were mistaken. The God of normative Judaism and of the mainline churches, at this time, is rather more remote from the God of the earliest or Yahwist portions of the Bible than is the initially surprising God of Joseph Smith." (P. 99.)

Chapter 3. Key of the Knowledge of God

1. Baker, *The Foolishness of God,* p. 404.
2. Ibid., p. 33, emphasis added.
3. See Hatch, *The Influence of Greek Ideas,* p. 1.
4. See Bruce R. McConkie, in Conference Report, October 1969, pp. 81–84.
5. Nowhere in the scriptures is there the suggestion that revelation will ever cease. Those attempting to argue otherwise usually quote Hebrews 1:1–2 to that end. It reads: "God, who at sundry times and in divers manners spake in time past unto the fathers by the prophets, hath in these last days spoken unto us by his Son, whom he hath appointed heir of all things, by whom also he made the worlds." The text clearly affirms revelation in Old Testament times through prophets and announces Christ as a source of revelation in New Testament times. The argument is that thereafter revelation is to cease. The text does not say it, nor could it possibly be true. If that were the case, we would not have the New Testament, for all of its twenty-seven books were written after the death of Christ. Further, Christ himself promised ongoing revelation to his disciples (see Matthew 7:7–8; John 16:12–14).
6. Talmage, *The Articles of Faith,* p. 3.
7. Beltz, *God and the Gods,* p. 36.
8. See Joseph Fielding Smith, *Doctrines of Salvation* 1:74–75.
9. Bruce R. McConkie, *A New Witness,* p. 63.
10. In Clark, ed., *Messages of the First Presidency* 4:201–3, 205.
11. Joseph Smith, "A Vision," pp. 82–83.
12. See Joseph Smith, *History of the Church* 4:536.
13. See Porter, "Dating the Restoration of the Melchizedek Priesthood."

Chapter 4. Textual Tampering

1. See Joseph Smith, *History of the Church* 4:536.
2. See ibid., 3:28.
3. Clines, "Yahweh and the God of Christian Theology," p. 323.
4. MacKenzie, "The Divine Soliloquies in Genesis," p. 277.

5. See *The International Standard Bible Encyclopaedia* 4:2722–31. "Philo, as well as later writers such as Pseudo-Justin, Irenaeus, and Clement of Alexandria, insist that the translators worked independently" (*The Interpreter's Dictionary of the Bible* 4:274).

6. See Bruce, *The Books and the Parchments*, pp. 146–47.

7. See Brenton, *The Septuagint*, pp. 74, 75, 89, 94–95, 102, 191, 284.

8. See Gehman, ed., *The New Westminster Dictionary of the Bible*, p. 972.

9. *The Interpreter's Dictionary of the Bible* 4:275.

10. Bruce R. McConkie, *A New Witness*, p. 403.

11. See Kittel and Friedrich, eds., *Theological Dictionary of the New Testament*, p. 329.

12. Peters, *The Harvest of Hellenism*, p. 229.

13. *Encyclopaedia Judaica* 3:56.

14. While strict Jews would not use the LXX, Jesus and his disciples did. Thus the LXX is frequently quoted in the New Testament. It was the Bible of Stephen and Paul (see Acts 6:9; 2 Timothy 3:15). "Thirty-three out of thirty-seven quotations from the Old Testament in the New Testament accredited to Jesus, and three hundred out of the entire three hundred and fifty quotations from the Old Testament in the New Testament are from this Greek-Hebrew Bible." (Heysham, *The Birth of the Bible*, pp. 24, 26.)

15. Hastings, ed., *A Dictionary of Christ and the Gospels* 1:582.

16. Ibid.

17. The Living Bible renders this verse, in part, "For ye hide the truth from the people."

18. Justin Martyr, *Dialogue with Trypho*, in *The Ante-Nicene Fathers* 1:234–35.

19. Quoted in Nibley, *The World and the Prophets*, p. 28.

20. Fishbane, *Biblical Interpretation in Ancient Israel*, p. 66.

21. Harrison et al., *Biblical Criticism*, pp. 51–52.

22. Ibid., pp. 53–54.

23. Fishbane, *Biblical Interpretation in Ancient Israel*, p. 67.

24. Ibid., p. 70.

25. See ibid., p. 70; and Exodus 32:4, 23, in *The Holy Scriptures, According to the Masoretic Text*, pp. 116, 117.

26. See Fishbane, *Biblical Interpretation in Ancient Israel*, pp. 70–71.

27. *Encyclopaedia Judaica* 3:53.

28. Fishbane, *Biblical Interpretation in Ancient Israel*, p. 71.

29. Eusebius, *The History of the Church*, p. 96.

30. Backhouse, *Early Church History*, pp. 142–43.

31. Romer, *Testament*, p. 195.

32. Backhouse, *Early Church History*, p. 143. The original source for the quotation from Dionysius is Eusebius (see Eusebius, *The History of the Church*, p. 132).

33. Schonfield, ed. and trans., *The Original New Testament*, p. 286 n. 9.

34. See Eusebius, *The Ecclesiastical History*, pp. 215, 216.

35. Scrivener, *A Plain Introduction*, p. 511.

36. Celsus, *On the True Doctrine*, p. 64.

37. See Fisher, *The History of the Church*, pp. 78–79.

38. See Eusebius, *The History of the Church*, pp. 88–89.

39. Joseph Smith, *Teachings*, pp. 9–10.

40. Ibid., p. 327.

41. See Ostling, "The Second Reformation," p. 55.

42. See ibid., p. 54.

43. See Funk, Hoover, and the Jesus Seminar, *The Five Gospels*.

44. Bruce R. McConkie, *A New Witness*, p. 403.

Chapter 5. Traditions of the Fathers

1. Neander, *General History of the Christian Religion* 1:53.

2. See Durant, *Caesar and Christ*, p. 501.

3. See ibid., pp. 501–2.

4. See ibid., p. 502.

5. See Schaff, *History of the Christian Church* 2:113–14.

6. See Fredriksen, *From Jesus to Christ*, p. 13.

7. Mosheim, *An Ecclesiastical History* 1:61.

8. Hatch, *The Influence of Greek Ideas*, p. 49.

9. Ibid., p. 350.

10. Ibid., pp. 238–39.

11. See ibid., pp. 239–41.

12. Philo, quoted in Hatch, *The Influence of Greek Ideas*, pp. 244–45.

13. See Hatch, *The Influence of Greek Ideas*, pp. 245–47.

14. See ibid., pp. 247–50.

15. Justin Martyr, quoted in Hatch, *The Influence of Greek Ideas,* p. 253.

16. Athenagoras, quoted in Hatch, *The Influence of Greek Ideas,* p. 253.

17. Theophilus, quoted in Hatch, *The Influence of Greek Ideas,* pp. 253–54.

18. Bavinck, *The Doctrine of God,* p. 23.

19. See Farrar, *History of Interpretation,* p. 172.

20. Justin Martyr, quoted in Hatch, *The Influence of Greek Ideas,* pp. 265–66.

21. See Stone, ed., *Jewish Writings,* p. 273.

22. Hastings, ed., *A Dictionary of Christ and the Gospels* 2:50.

23. Harnack, *History of Dogma* 1:113–14.

24. Ibid., 3:2, italics in original.

25. See ibid., 3:2–3.

26. See Hastings, ed., *A Dictionary of Christ and the Gospels* 2:52.

27. Hatch, *The Influence of Greek Ideas,* p. 251.

28. See Neander, *General History of the Christian Religion* 1:656–57.

29. Mosheim, quoted in Roberts, *The "Falling Away,"* p. 29.

30. Eusebius, *The Ecclesiastical History,* p. 118.

31. See Drake, *In Praise of Constantine,* p. 54.

32. Origen, quoted in McLintock and Strong, eds., *Cyclopedia* 7:430.

33. Ackroyd and Evans, eds., *The Cambridge History of the Bible* 1:452.

34. Novotný, *The Posthumous Life of Plato,* p. 125.

35. Ehrman, *The Orthodox Corruption of Scripture,* p. 4.

36. Newman, *An Essay on the Development of Christian Doctrine,* pp. 342, 343, 344.

Chapter 6. How God Became Invisible

1. Joseph Smith corrected this text to read: "And they heard the voice of the Lord God, as they were walking in the garden" (Moses 4:14). Thus it is Adam and Eve who are walking in the garden instead of God's voice.

2. See Dummelow, ed., *A Commentary on the Holy Bible,* p. 6.

3. Adam Clarke, *Clarke's Commentary* 1:52.

4. W. K. Lowther Clarke, *Concise Bible Commentary,* p. 343.

5. *The Interpreter's Bible* 1:507.

6. Eiselen, Lewis, and Downey, eds., *The Abingdon Bible Commentary*, p. 223.

7. Haley, *Alleged Discrepancies*, p. 74.

8. *Webster's Third*, p. 2371.

9. Haley, *Alleged Discrepancies*, p. 74.

10. The Samaritan texts are the most obvious illustration of how manuscripts were changed to sustain the interests of those changing them. In his *Textual Criticism of the Old Testament*, Ralph W. Klein gives the following brief illustration: "One of the principal tenets of the Samaritan sect was its belief that Schechem rather than Jerusalem was the only proper worship site. Through several devices the theological justification for this belief was inserted into their Pentateuch. Abraham's sacrifice of Isaac is transferred to Moreh (instead of MT's Moriah) near Shechem while the standard Deuteronomic cliché 'the place which Yahweh will choose' is systematically emended to read 'the place which Yahweh has chosen.' This tense change transfers the Pentateuch's reference from God's choice of Jerusalem to his choice in patriarchal times of the city of Shechem. After Exod. 20:17 SP adds a command to build a sanctuary on Mt. Gerizim (cf. Deut. 11:29–30; 27:2–7). Likewise it makes Gerizim instead of Ebal the mount of blessing in Deut. 27:4. In recent years the Samaritan temple on Mt. Gerizim has been identified by archaeologists." (P. 16.)

11. Haley, *Alleged Discrepancies*, p. 75, emphasis added.

12. Ginzberg, *The Legends of the Jews* 3:88–89, 97–98.

13. Gleerup, *The Dethronement of Sabaoth*, p. 48.

14. Ibid., pp. 49–50.

15. Ibid., p. 124.

16. Clines, "Yahweh and the God of Christian Theology," p. 323.

17. A brief discussion of this problem is found in the LDS Bible Dictionary, pp. 710–11. Other sources include Jukes, *The Names of God in Holy Scripture*, p. 35 n; Loewen, "The Names of God in the Old Testament," pp. 201–7; Girdlestone, *Synonyms of the Old Testament*, pp. 1–17.

18. See Thomas, "The Influence of Asceticism," pp. 22–23.

19. Thomas, "The Influence of Asceticism," p. 4.

20. See *The Nag Hammadi Library*, pp. 100–109.

21. See 1 Hermas 2:10, in *The Lost Books of the Bible*, p. 200; see also 2 Hermas 4:26 and 3 Hermas 9:108, in *The Lost Books of the Bible*, pp. 216, 255.

22. See Thomas, "The Influence of Aesceticism," p. 107; see also chapter 3 of Thomas's dissertation.

23. Ibid., pp. 111–12.

24. See *Encyclopaedia Judaica* 3:53.

25. See Thomas, "The Influence of Asceticism," p. 116.

26. See ibid., p. 161.

27. Cherbonnier, "The Logic of Biblical Anthropomorphism," p. 200.

28. See Paulsen, "Must God Be Incorporeal?" p. 82.

29. Parley P. Pratt, *Writings*, p. 29.

30. Joseph Smith, *Teachings*, p. 350.

31. Parley P. Pratt, *Writings*, p. 28.

32. Ibid., p. 32.

33. See Schaff and Wace, eds., *A Select Library of Nicene and Post-Nicene Fathers*, p. 320; see also *New Catholic Encyclopedia* 8:96–101; 10:771–73; 14:145.

34. See Joseph F. McConkie, "Premortal Existence, Foreordinations, and Heavenly Councils," pp. 173–98.

35. Orson Pratt, *Masterful Discourses*, p. 61.

36. See ibid., pp. 61–62.

37. *Spiritual* as used by Orson Pratt does not mean "spirit" but rather that which is not subject to death or corruption (see Alma 11:45; D&C 88:27–28; and 1 Corinthians 15:44).

38. Orson Pratt, *Masterful Discourses*, pp. 62–63.

39. Ibid., p. 64.

Chapter 7. How God Lost His Body

1. Clines, "Yahweh and the God of Christian Theology," p. 328.

2. C. Van Der Donckt, in Roberts, *The Mormon Doctrine of Deity*, p. 48, italics in original.

3. Roberts, *The Mormon Doctrine of Deity*, pp. 84–85, italics in original.

4. Celsus, *On the True Doctrine*, p. 103.

5. Ibid., pp. 103–4.

6. See Harnack, *History of Dogma* 1:180 n. 1.

7. Paulsen, "Early Christian Belief," p. 107.

8. Origen, quoted in Paulsen, "Early Christian Belief," p. 109.

9. See Paulsen, "Early Christian Belief," p. 109.

10. Origen, quoted in McLintock and Strong, eds., *Cyclopedia* 7:430.

11. See Paulsen, "Early Christian Belief," p. 113.

12. Ibid., p. 114.

13. Augustine, quoted in Paulsen, "Early Christian Belief," p. 115.

14. Xenophanes, quoted in Caird, *The Language and Imagery of the Bible*, p. 172.

15. Cicero, *The Nature of the Gods*, pp. 100–101.

16. Cherbonnier, "The Logic of Biblical Anthropomorphism," p. 187.

17. Ibid., p. 188.

18. Reade, *The Christian Challenge to Philosophy*, p. 67.

19. Stendahl, "To Think and to Pray," p. 16.

20. See Paulsen, "Must God Be Incorporeal?" pp. 76–78.

21. See Cherbonnier, "The Logic of Biblical Anthropomorphism," p. 191.

22. Ibid., pp. 191–92.

23. Ibid., p. 194.

24. See ibid., pp. 194–95.

25. Philo, quoted in Clines, "Yahweh and the God of Christian Theology," p. 325.

26. *Encyclopaedia Judaica* 3:55–56.

27. Ibid., p. 51.

28. *The Oxford Dictionary of the Christian Church*, p. 63.

29. Cherbonnier, "In Defense of Anthropomorphism," p. 157.

Chapter 8. A Fight in the Dark

1. See Durant, *Caesar and Christ*, p. 654.

2. Wilson, *Jesus: The Evidence*, p. 134.

3. See Cutts, *Constantine the Great*, p. 107.

4. See Wilson, *Jesus: The Evidence*, p. 136, and Romer, *Testament*, p. 212.

5. Durant, *Caesar and Christ*, p. 657.

6. Ibid., pp. 657–58.

7. Some scholars are skeptical of the number 318, it being the same as the number who followed Abram to rescue Lot (see Genesis 14:14). Henry Chadwick places the number of bishops present at 220,

with four or five coming from the West (see *The Early Church,* p. 130). Robert Rainy notes that the number has been variously reckoned from 218 to 318 (see *The Ancient Catholic Church,* p. 330). Constantine uses the number 300 in his correspondence (see Stevenson, ed., *A New Eusebius,* p. 350). Eusebius of Caesarea placed the number at 250 (see Boyle, "Historical View," p. 9 n).

8. See Cutts, *Constantine the Great,* p. 307; Backhouse, *Early Church History,* p. 386.

9. See Cutts, *Constantine the Great,* pp. 301–3.

10. See Backhouse, *Early Church History,* p. 387.

11. See Cutts, *Constantine the Great,* p. 303.

12. See Stevenson, ed., *A New Eusebius,* p. 326; see also Cutts, *Constantine the Great,* p. 300.

13. Rosa, *Vicars of Christ,* p. 48.

14. Other sources suggest that Constantine was present to open the council on 20 May (see Chadwick, *The Early Church,* p. 130).

15. Backhouse, *Early Church History,* p. 389.

16. Cutts, *Constantine the Great,* pp. 313–14.

17. Boyle, "Historical View," p. 17.

18. Stuart G. Hall states: "The true nature of the original issue is clouded. Modern theologians have read into Arianism whatever views they themselves particularly abominate. Our ancient sources reveal other problems. First, what we have of Arius' own writing is meagre, and even these documents are preserved by his critics, and selected to be damaging, if not actually misquoted or misconstrued. Secondly, his critics often attribute to him views which he never stated." (*Doctrine and Practice in the Early Church,* pp. 121–22.)

19. See Romer, *Testament,* pp. 213–15.

20. Socrates, quoted in Foakes-Jackson, *The History of the Christian Church,* p. 307.

21. Foakes-Jackson, *The History of the Christian Church,* p. 300.

22. González, *The Story of Christianity* 1:160–61.

23. See Walker, Norris, Lotz, and Handy, *A History of the Christian Church,* p. 132.

24. Cutts, *Constantine the Great,* pp. 317–18.

25. Durant, *Caesar and Christ,* p. 660.

26. González, *The Story of Christianity* 1:164.

27. Cutts, *Constantine the Great,* p. 296.

28. Quoted in ibid., pp. 321–22.

29. Romer, *Testament*, p. 215.

30. See Cutts, *Constantine the Great*, p. 335.

31. See ibid., pp. 333, 335.

32. See Durant, *Caesar and Christ*, p. 660.

33. See Chadwick, *The Early Church*, p. 130.

34. Neander, *General History of the Christian Religion* 2:164.

35. Mosheim, *An Ecclesiastical History* 1:126.

36. See Backhouse, *Early Church History*, pp. 408–9, including n. 1.

37. Gibbon, *The Decline and Fall*, p. 402.

38. Archibald MacLaine, footnote in Mosheim, *An Ecclesiastical History* 1:126.

39. See Mosheim, *An Ecclesiastical History* 1:99–100; Rainy, *The Ancient Catholic Church*, p. 342.

40. See Backhouse, *Early Church History*, p. 411.

41. These issues included the time of celebrating Easter and the matter of celibacy.

42. Paine, *The Age of Reason*, p. 6.

43. See Barnes, *Constantine and Eusebius*, p. 220.

44. Gibbon, *The Decline and Fall*, p. 392.

45. Talmage, *The Articles of Faith*, p. 48.

46. Guthrie, *Christian Doctrine*, p. 92.

47. Hall, *Doctrine and Practice in the Early Church*, p. 36.

48. See Romer, *Testament*, p. 215.

49. Thomas Jefferson, quoted in McGrath, *Understanding the Trinity*, p. 110.

Chapter 9. A House Built upon the Sand

1. Baker, *The Foolishness of God*, p. 137.

2. Christie-Murray, *A History of Heresy*, p. 4.

3. See Isaac Kramnick, editor's introduction, in Paine, *Common Sense*, pp. 7–8.

4. Paine, *Common Sense*, p. 63.

5. Paine, *The Age of Reason*, pp. 6–7.

6. Thomas Jefferson, quoted in Gaustad, *Faith of Our Fathers*, p. 43.

7. Thomas Jefferson, quoted in ibid., p. 41.

8. Paine, *The Age of Reason*, p. 6.

9. Ibid., p. 7.

10. Backman, *American Religions,* pp. 177–78.

11. See ibid., p. 185.

12. Joseph Smith, *History of the Church* 5:215.

13. Paine, *The Age of Reason,* p. 58, italics in original.

14. See ibid., pp. 58–59.

15. Thomas Jefferson, quoted in Richard, "The Founding Fathers," p. 97.

16. See Léon-Dufour, *Dictionary of the New Testament,* p. 298; Vine, *An Expository Dictionary* 3:97.

17. Priestley, *History of the Corruptions of Christianity,* p. 13, italics in original.

18. Harnack, *History of Dogma* 3:2–3, italics in original.

19. Jefferson, *Writings,* p. 1342.

20. Thomas Jefferson, quoted in Gaustad, *Faith of Our Fathers,* p. 104.

21. Priestley, *History of the Corruptions of Christianity,* p. 2.

22. Quoted in Martineau, *The Seat of Authority,* p. 177.

23. Thomas Jefferson, quoted in Gaustad, *Faith of Our Fathers,* p. 105.

24. See Harris, Archer, and Waltke, eds., *Theological Wordbook of the Old Testament* 1:51–52.

25. See Hatch, *The Influence of Greek Ideas,* pp. 310–13.

26. Hatch, *The Influence of Greek Ideas,* p. 328.

27. At Constantinople in A.D. 381 and again at Chalcedon in 452, the debate over the nature of God begun in the Council of Nicaea was continued.

28. Hatch, *The Influence of Greek Ideas,* pp. 328–29.

29. Ibid., p. 2.

30. Ibid., p. 320.

31. Ibid., pp. 329–30.

32. Ibid., p. 331.

33. Ibid., p. 332.

34. Ibid., p. 333.

Chapter 10. The Fatherhood of God

1. See Joseph Smith, *Teachings,* p. 191.

2. Taylor, "The Living God," p. 808.

3. "In traditional exegesis of the Gospels the term 'Son of Man' is held to signify esp. the humility of Christ's incarnate manhood as contrasted with the majesty of His Divinity denoted by 'Son of God' " (*The Oxford Dictionary of the Christian Church,* p. 1290). "The two titles 'Son of God' and 'Son of Man,' declaring that in the one Person of Christ there are two natures, the nature of God and the nature of man, joined together, but not confused, are presented to us in two memorable passages of the Gospel, which declare the will of Christ that all men should confess Him to be God and man, and which proclaim the blessedness of this confession" (William Smith, *Dictionary of the Bible* 4:3092).

4. Vine, *An Expository Dictionary* 4:48.

5. See ibid., p. 49.

6. For a discussion on Christ and the law of witnesses, see Joseph Fielding Smith, *Doctrines of Salvation* 1:206–8.

7. See Orson Pratt, in *Journal of Discourses* 2:342.

8. See Bruce R. McConkie, *Mormon Doctrine,* p. 29.

9. See *The International Standard Bible Encyclopaedia* 4:2826–27. See also Vine, *An Expository Dictionary* 4:48–49, and Hastings, ed., *A Dictionary of Christ and the Gospels* 2:654.

10. Bruce R. McConkie, *Doctrinal New Testament Commentary* 1:95.

11. Taylor, "The Living God," p. 809.

12. See Léon-Dufour, *Dictionary of the New Testament,* p. 81.

13. See Vine, *An Expository Dictionary* 1:9.

14. Hastings, ed., *A Dictionary of Christ and the Gospels* 1:582.

15. See ibid., p. 580.

16. Lidgett, *The Fatherhood of God,* p. 142.

17. Ibid., p. 143.

18. One source relates that "the first of these movements occurred under Pontius Pilate, not among the Jews proper, but among the Samaritans." Pilate attacked and killed the would-be Messiah along with many of his followers. About ten years later, when Fadus was governor of Judea, a man by the name of Theudas persuaded many of the common people to take their possessions and follow him to the Jordan River. Fadus attacked and killed many of Theudas's followers and captured and beheaded Theudas. A third movement was led by an Egyptian prophet for whom the Apostle Paul was mistaken in the temple precincts on his last journey to Jerusalem (see Acts 21:38), during the administration of Felix. (See Horsley, with Hanson, *Bandits,*

Prophets, and Messiahs, pp. 161–67.) Earlier, Judas of Galilee raised a revolt in opposition to the census ordered by Augustus. This uprising was also cruelly suppressed. Judas was killed, and two thousand of his followers were crucified. The momentum survived underground in the form of a guerrilla movement, the members of which were known as Zealots. (See Comay and Brownrigg, *Who's Who in the Bible* 2:250.)

19. The verse that follows has been the conscripted servant of spiritual pirates. As it begins, the verse is rendered, "God is a Spirit" (John 4:24). Obviously much has been made of this by those who have sought to rob Deity of his body. Many modern translations correct the misimpression thus given, rendering the verse, "God is spirit" (see, for example, the Revised Standard Version and the New International Version). The theology of the verse is similar to such statements as "God is light" (1 John 1:5) or "God is love" (1 John 4:8). It is not intended that we conclude he is nothing more than that which is being immediately stated, or the other verses would be contradictory. Rather, this is simply a dramatic way of describing a particular attribute in a particular setting.

Chapter 11. The Doctrine of Divine Sonship

1. Brown, *The Virginal Conception and Bodily Resurrection of Jesus,* p. 21.

2. In addition to being taught to those who did not have the opportunity to hear it in mortality, the gospel is taught a second time to those who rejected it while in the flesh. Such will be blessed by accepting it in the spirit world and conforming their lives to it. We are told in the revelation on the degrees of glory that they can attain the terrestrial but not the celestial kingdom (see D&C 76:73–74).

Chapter 12. The God of Joseph Smith

1. See Joseph Smith, *Lectures on Faith* 3:2–5 (p. 38).
2. Joseph Smith, *History of the Church* 6:50.
3. Ibid., 6:252.
4. Ibid., 5:402.
5. Joseph Smith, *Teachings,* p. 191.
6. Hastings, ed., *A Dictionary of Christ and the Gospels* 2:520.

7. *The Evening and the Morning Star* 1:22.

8. Joseph Smith, *Teachings*, p. 61.

9. Oliver Cowdery, quoted in the Pearl of Great Price, p. 59 n; the original source is *Messenger and Advocate* 1 (October 1834): 14–16.

10. See Joseph Smith, *Teachings*, p. 349.

11. See ibid., p. 180.

12. Ibid., p. 149.

13. See Joseph Smith, *Lectures on Faith* 7:20 (pp. 82–83).

14. Lucy Mack Smith, *History of Joseph Smith*, p. 161.

15. Joseph Smith, *Teachings*, p. 181.

16. Ibid.

17. Ibid., p. 207; see also D&C 131:7–8.

18. See Joseph Smith, *Teachings*, p. 297.

19. There are some who are quite anxious that we be advised that the *Lectures on Faith* were not written by the Prophet himself but rather by others acting under his direction. If the lectures presented represent the revelations of heaven to the Prophet, the concern is unfounded. That is the same way we perform baptisms and all the ordinances of salvation. Someone commissioned by Jesus Christ acts in the first person for the Father, the Son, and the Holy Ghost and does the actual baptizing. Yet the baptism represents the mind and will of the Godhead. The whole system of salvation centers in and around this system; we call it "divine investiture of authority." Without this principle, God would be required to do everything personally that is done for the salvation of his children. Every baptism would have to be performed by him. Because of this principle, all who are part of the household of faith are called upon to do things in his name. If done under the direction of the Spirit, such actions are approved by him and are binding on us. The point here is simply that if a sixteen-year-old priest in the Aaronic Priesthood can stand in the stead of the Father, the Son, and the Holy Ghost in the performance of an ordinance of salvation, surely elders of Israel, men holding the holy Melchizedek Priesthood, can prepare lectures under the direction of the Prophet and enjoy the sanction and direction of the Spirit in so doing. To make the argument that because they may have done so, the validity of the *Lectures on Faith* is to be questioned is no more sound than to argue that a baptism is not valid unless God himself performed it or a sermon uninspired unless he gave it.

20. Joseph Smith, *Lectures on Faith* 5:2–3 (pp. 60–61).

21. See Joseph Smith, *Teachings*, pp. 346–48.

22. Ibid., p. 345.
23. Ibid., pp. 345–46.
24. See ibid., pp. 346–49.
25. Ibid., p. 372.
26. Ibid., p. 312.
27. Ibid., p. 190.
28. Ibid., p. 370.
29. Durant, *Caesar and Christ*, p. 595.

Epilogue

1. See Hatch, *The Influence of Greek Ideas*, pp. 324–25.
2. See ibid., p. 325.
3. See Bokenkotter, *A Concise History of the Catholic Church*, pp. 109–19.
4. Hatch, *The Influence of Greek Ideas*, p. 334.
5. See Maxwell, *A Wonderful Flood of Light*, p. 40.
6. See Hatch, *The Influence of Greek Ideas*, p. 339.
7. See ibid., p. 341.
8. Ibid., pp. 342, 347.
9. Ibid., p. 349.
10. Ibid., p. 353.

Glossary

Alexander. d. 328. Bishop of Alexandria from 313, he stirred up the Arian controversy by excommunicating Arius. He took a leading part in the Council of Nicaea.

Anathema. (Gr. lit. "suspended"); to be cut off from the body of the church. It is distinguished from excommunication, which is a barring from the sacraments and worship. Anathema is a complete separation from the body.

Anthropomorphic. That which is described or conceived as having human form or attributes. In the context of theology, it is the ascription to God of physical or psychological characteristics in common with man. For instance, it is to say that God sees, hears, knows, or loves. Mormonism is anthropomorphic; traditional Christianity is not, though most of its adherents are.

The word combines two Greek roots, *anthropos,* meaning a human being, and *morphic,* meaning shape or form. (See also *Theomorphic.*)

Anthropopathism. Ascribing human passions, feelings, or attitudes to that which is not human. It combines the Greek *anthropos* (human being) with *pathos,* which means susceptible to pain or suffering. Thus it would refer to a God who loved his creations or who suffered for them. The Greek view, which was adopted by traditional Christianity, holds that God must be above all such limitations. For him to have passions would make him subject to his emotions. Thus the God of the creeds is without body, parts, or passions, for these are held to be limitations. He feels nothing. It is held that it was the human nature of Christ that suffered on the cross, not the divine part of his nature.

The God of the prophets is anthropopathic. He can weep over his children (see Moses 7:28–31), and he can suffer for them in an infinite atonement (see D&C 19:16–18).

Apologists. Christian writers, mainly of the second century, who wrote to the emperor in defense of their religion. The writings answered suspicions which arose against early Christians, and pleaded for release from persecution. Often these writers used Greek philosophy to explain Christianity to their pagan fellows. Christians were commonly accused of atheism (denial of the existence of the gods) and immorality. The first charge was met by the explanation that they were monotheists, the second with explanations of the fraternal love found in the Christian community.

Apostles. The most important leaders of first-generation Christianity; usually meaning the original twelve Apostles and Matthias (who filled the vacant place left by Judas Iscariot). Paul also defends his right to this title.

Apostolic Fathers. The title given (since the late seventeenth century) to the Christian writers whose works immediately followed that of the New Testament period. They are said either to have known an Apostle or to have known someone who knew an Apostle. Also known as ante-Nicene Fathers.

Arius. d. 336; presbyter of Alexandria; regarded by Christian writers as the great heresiarch for advocating the doctrine that Christ was created by the Father and was subordinate to him. Apparently he was poisoned when Constantine ordered that he be received back into communion.

Asceticism. The act of practicing self-denial for religious reasons. In the first three centuries A.D., Christian asceticism found expression especially in the preparation of Christians for martyrdom and in the ideal of virginity. The third century saw a movement into the desert, and the beginnings of monasticism were seen in the fourth century.

Athanasius. d. 373; succeeded Alexander as bishop of Alexandria in

328. He was the great apostle of the doctrine of Nicaea, which held that in some mysterious way Christ became his own Father. Because of his refusal to compromise with Arianism, he incurred the enmity of the powerful Arianizing party in the reigns of Constantine and Constantius, being forced into exile five times. He is now considered to be a saint and is applauded as a great hero by trinitarians.

Athenagoras. Second century; known as the Christian philosopher of Athens. He was the first to elaborate a philosophical defense of the doctrine of God as three in one.

Augustine. d. 430; is held to be the greatest Christian theologian since the Apostle Paul. He is the father of the Western church. His thought dominated the Middle Ages. In his student days he re-solved to devote himself to a life of philosophy. As a candidate for Christian baptism he discovered the Old Testament, which, filtered through his philosophical background, appeared crude and unspir-itual. He turned his interest elsewhere and found more satisfying answers to the mysteries of life in Neoplatonist works; these, coupled with the idea that the Old Testament was really an allegory, enabled him to reconcile himself to the Christian faith. After his conversion he sought to devote himself to an ascetic life of study and writing. He went to Africa for that purpose, where he was or-dained a bishop against his will. In his responsibilities as a cleric he was confronted with the Donatist schism. He wrote and preached against their theology and also embraced state power to coerce them. At first he opposed the use of force, but eventually came to accept it as a necessary response to Donatist violence and as a valid educational tool. In his writings he provided the church with a the-ological justification for the medieval inquisition.

Bibliolater. One who worships the Bible.

Canon. A list of books of scripture accepted as genuine by a church. Which books were to constitute what we know as the New Testament was not agreed upon until the latter part of the fourth century. Eusebius lists the writings of the New Testament in three categories: (1) those generally acknowledged—the four Gospels, the Acts of the Apostles, the Epistles of Paul (the Roman church de-nied that Hebrews was written by Paul), 1 John, and 1 Peter; (2) those which were disputed—James, Jude, 2 Peter, 2 and 3 John; (3) the spurious books—the Acts of Paul, the Shepherd of Hermas, the

Revelation of Peter, the Epistle of Barnabas, the Teachings of the Apostles (the *Didache*), and the book of Revelation. He also lists other works attributed to the Apostles which he discarded as heretical.

Celsus. Second century; pagan philosopher. He is the author of the oldest surviving literary attack on Christianity (ca. 178). He criticized the Christians for failure to study Plato and for their belief in God as an anthropomorphic being.

Cicero. d. 43; Roman orator and philosopher. He was a disciple of Philo, whom he judged to be the most cultivated and shrewdest of all the philosophers. His work *The Nature of the Gods* became an important document in the great struggle of religions for supremacy in the Roman Empire. The Christians found it a very useful weapon against the old pagan religion.

Clement of Alexandria. d. 214; early Christian philosopher-theologian who taught in Alexandria at the end of the second century. He regarded both the original revelations of the Bible and Greek philosophy as threads of the divine which he wove together. He saw ignorance as a greater evil than sin, and labored to show that Christ, as the Logos, represented the reason of God.

Clement of Rome. Believed to be the third bishop of Rome and author of *The First Epistle of Clement*, addressed to the church at Corinth; thought to be a friend and disciple of Peter.

Constantine the Great. d. 337; Roman emperor. He became senior ruler of the empire in 312 after defeating his rival, Maxentius, at the Milvian Bridge. His troops marched under the symbol X and P superimposed over each other, these being the first two letters of the name of Christ in Greek. He put an end to the persecution of Christians by the state, summoned the Council of Nicaea to settle the Arian dispute, presided over that council, and banished those who would not consent to its decisions. Thus he formed the union of church and state. Twelve years later he was baptized on his deathbed.

Dialectician. A person skilled in critical inquiry by discussion or logical disputation.

Diaspora. The scattering of Israel. It had its beginnings in the Assyrian and Babylonian deportations (722 and 597 B.C.).

Diocletian. Emperor from 284 to 305. In 303 he began what is called the "Great Persecution" against the Christians. There were four edicts: (1) the closing of churches, the handing over of the scriptures, and the loss of civil rights; (2) imprisonment of the clergy; (3) torture and death for the clergy; and (4) the requirement that everyone sacrifice to the gods. Many were tortured and martyred. Its severity varied in different parts of the empire according to the changing fortunes of the imperial rulers in the next decades. Its final collapse was due to Constantine's defeat of Maxentius in 312.

Docetism. The various attempts to explain Christ's incarnation and suffering in a dualistic and spiritualistic way—that is, by excluding from them everything that philosophers deemed unworthy of God. It holds that all of Christ's suffering was apparent rather than real. It opposes such corporeal values as sexuality and marriage.

Donatists. Donatus was a bishop of Carthage who played a leading role in a schism linked with events in North Africa during the Great Persecution of 303 to 305. Many of the clergy obeyed the authorities and surrendered their copies of the scriptures. In the eyes of those who had resisted, they were considered traitors and apostates, as were those who received the sacraments from them. The Donatists refused to recognize their ordinations and authority. They liked to call themselves a church of martyrs. Their desire for martyrdom went so far as to include suicide.

Eusebius of Caesarea in Palestine. d. 339. He is best known as the father of church history but also wrote extensively as an apologist and theologian. His *Ecclesiastical History* is our chief primary source for the history of the church up to about 300. He was one of the chief actors in the Nicene Council. After the death of Constantine in 337, Eusebius wrote the *Life of Constantine,* which, despite having been written to glorify the emperor, has some historical value.

Eusebius of Nicomedia. d. 341. He was a leading adviser of Constantine, and leader of the Arian party in the first half of the fourth century. He found it within his conscience to sign the Nicene Creed but continued to work against it. It was he who baptized Constantine shortly before the emperor died.

Fathers of the Church. See *Apostolic Fathers.*

Gibbon, Edward. d. 1794; historian of the later Roman Empire; author of *The Decline and Fall of the Roman Empire.* A convert to Catholicism as a young man, he reconverted to Protestantism after wide reading. The overwhelming evidence of the Great Apostasy

left him hostile toward the Christian faith and unbelieving of claims
to the supernatural.

Gloss. A brief explanation or definition appearing in the margin or
between the lines of a text. In the course of repeated copying of
biblical texts, some clearly uninspired marginal notes have been incorporated into the text and are represented as scripture today.

Gnostics. The name is derived from a Greek word meaning knowledge. It was given to a complex religious movement which in its
Christian form came into prominence in the second century. It is
rooted in pagan religious practices. The central idea was the possession of a special "gnosis" which brought redemption. The source of
this "gnosis" was said to be either the Apostles, from whom it was
claimed in a secret tradition, or a direct revelation given to the
founder of the sect. Beliefs varied widely, but almost all agreed that
the creator of the world was not the true God. They chose to worship a supreme, remote, and unknowable being.

Great Persecution. See *Diocletian.*

Harnack, Adolf von. d. 1930; a German church historian and theologian. He is regarded as the most outstanding patristic scholar of his
generation. His expertise was early Christian literature, especially
the pre-Nicene period. His criticism of the Hellenization of the
Church evoked strong opposition from conservative theologians.

Hastings, James. d. 1922; a Presbyterian divine. He is famous as the
editor of the *Dictionary of the Bible* (1898–1904) and his *Dictionary
of Christ and the Gospels* (1906–7).

Hatch, Edwin. d. 1889; an Anglican divine. Educated at Pembroke
College, Oxford, he eventually became a reader in ecclesiastical history at Oxford.

Hellenic. From Hellen, the legendary ancestor after whom the
Hellenes, or Greeks, were named. Hellenism is the adoption of
Greek language and culture.

Ignatius. A bishop of Antioch who was taken to Rome and martyred.
During his journey to Rome, Ignatius wrote letters to various
churches encouraging the members to stay faithful, and to the
church of Rome begging them not to deprive him of martyrdom by
intervening with the authorities.

Impassible. That which has no passions or emotions. (See
Anthropopathism.)

Justin Martyr. d. 165; converted to Christianity in adult life after a pilgrimage that led him through various schools of philosophy, especially Platonism. As a Christian he continued to wear the robe of a philosopher and taught Christianity as the true philosophy. He set up a school of Christian instruction in Rome. He is regarded as the most important apologist of the second century. He died a martyr.

Logos. (Gr. "Word" or "Reason"); used in Christian theology with reference to the second person of the Trinity. The term was rooted in pagan and Jewish antiquity. The Apologists of the second century found in the concept of Logos the means for making Christian teachings compatible with Hellenistic philosophy. It enabled them to have a monotheistic God who was represented on earth by Logos, meaning his Mind or Reason, which they referred to as the Son of God.

Marcion. Second-century founder of a sect which taught that the Christian gospel was new and so different from Judaism that the Old Testament must be disregarded. Marcion and his followers taught that the creator God of the Old Testament was a totally different God from the one that Christ proclaimed.

Martyrs. The name (meaning "witness") given to those who died rather than deny their faith in Christ. In its apostate form, it was adopted as the ideal goal of Christian life. Many unnecessarily sought martyrdom.

Masoretic Text. (Heb. *masora,* meaning traditional); a Hebrew translation of the Old Testament which is the work of Jewish grammarians between the sixth and tenth centuries A.D. They sought a biblical text free from alteration or corruption by providing marginal notes and commentaries. They also introduced vowel points and accents to show how the words should be pronounced.

Metaphysics. The branch of philosophy concerned with the ultimate nature of existence. The term comes from the metaphysical treatises of Aristotle, who presented the First Philosophy. The title was merely intended to indicate the position of the books on this subject in the Aristotelian corpus—they were those books that succeed the Physics.

Mortification. An ecclesiastical term used to describe the act of "killing" or "deadening" the flesh and its lusts through ascetic practices (for example, the infliction of bodily discomfort or fasting).

Mosheim, Johann Lorenz von. d. 1755; an ecclesiastical historian and divine educated at the university of Kiel, he became a professor of theology at Hellmstedt and at Göttingen, which he helped found. His historical work was acclaimed for its unprecedented objectivity.

Mystic. An initiate in the mystery religions; one indoctrinated in occult or esoteric rites.

Mystical. Symbolical or allegorical.

Mysticism. An immediate knowledge of God attained through personal religious experience.

Neander, Johann August Wilhelm. d. 1850; an ecclesiastical historian. He differed from Mosheim, whose interest was in institutions while Neander's was in persons.

Neoplatonism. The philosophical system of Plotinus (ca. 205–70) and his successors. It drew its inspiration from Plato and sought to provide a satisfying intellectual basis for a religious and moral life. A scholarly source explains: "In the ultimate One which lies behind all experience, the dualism between Thought and Reality was to be overcome. This One can be known by man only by the method of abstraction. He must gradually divest his experience of all that is specifically human, so that in the end, when all attributes have been removed, only God is left. Yet the Neoplatonists were too serious to rest in a merely negative agnosticism, and maintained that the Absolute, which, as Plotinus said, 'has its centre everywhere but its circumference nowhere,' could be reached by mystical experience." (*The Oxford Dictionary of the Christian Church*, ed. F. L. Cross and E. A. Livingstone, 2d ed. [New York: Oxford University Press, 1983], p. 960.)

Though hostile to the testimony of New Testament theology, particularly the idea of a God being born in the flesh, its influence is now claimed to represent traditional Christianity.

Origen. d. 254; an ascetic who followed literally Matthew 19:12 and emasculated himself. Ironically, he did much to persuade the church toward a metaphorical interpretation of scripture. He was a scholar, teacher, writer, and preacher without equal in the early church. He was well versed in the works of the Middle Platonists and was a student of pagan philosophy. He was originally thought of as a saint, but as doctrines changed he lost his place in heaven and has been labeled a heretic from the sixth century onward.

Patripassians. See *Sabellians*.

Pentateuch. The five books of Moses.

Philo. d. 50; Jewish thinker and exegete. He is the most important figure among the Hellenistic Jews of his age. He reproduced a variety of doctrines, gathered from contemporary philosophical systems as well as from Jewish sources. His most influential achievement was his development of the allegorical interpretation of scripture, which enabled him to find Greek philosophy in the Old Testament. He also gave a central place to the concept of Logos as the intermediary for God. Philo's influence was especially strong in the Alexandrine school of theology. He had greater influence on Christian writers than Jewish, two of his great disciples being Clement and Origen.

Plato. d. 347 B.C. "Of all the Greek philosophers, Plato was undoubtedly the one most venerated by the Fathers" (Angelo Di Berardino, ed., *Encyclopedia of the Early Church*, trans. Adrian Walford, 2 vols. [Cambridge: James Clarke and Co., 1992], 2:689). It may well be said of him that he had a greater influence in forming the traditional Christian concept of God than Christ himself. Clement of Alexandria and Origen were two of his disciples who had leading roles in the Hellenization of Christianity. "Of perhaps even greater moment for the history of Christian theology was the fact that the thought of St. Augustine was radically influenced . . . by Platonic doctrines. The authority accorded to his teaching throughout the Middle Ages did much to secure for many Platonic notions a permanent place in Latin Christianity." (*The Oxford Dictionary of the Christian Church*, ed. F. L. Cross and E. A. Livingstone, 2d ed. [New York: Oxford University Press, 1983], p. 1102.) (See *Clement of Alexandria; Origen*.)

Pontifex Maximus. As the head of the religious cults of Rome, he presided over festivals and sacrifices.

Priestley, Joseph. d. 1804; an unorthodox Presbyterian minister who came to hold Arian views on the person of Christ, and rejected the doctrine of the Atonement and the inspiration of the Bible. He became a founder of the Unitarian Society.

Sabellians. The name given to those Christians who argued that the unity of God entailed that Father, Son, and Holy Spirit were different manifestations of the same Person. They were also called Patripassians.

Septuagint ("LXX"). The earliest Greek translation of the Hebrew Bible (Old Testament), which was used by Greek-speaking Christians. First acclaimed and then condemned, it contains classic examples of scriptural tampering as its translators attempted to remove references to the anthropomorphic nature of Deity from the text. Though an imperfect text, it was used by Christ and his disciples.

Socrates Scholasticus. d. 450; a Greek lawyer and church historian. He is one of our closest sources to the events of the Council of Nicaea.

Syncretism. The uncritical acceptance of conflicting or divergent beliefs or principles; the union of conflicting religions.

Targum. An interpretation or paraphrase of the Old Testament made when Hebrew had ceased to be the normal medium of speech among the Jews.

Tertullian. d. 225. Born a heathen and converted in adult life, Tertullian was well trained in the Roman rhetorical system of education and was a man of great erudition. After his conversion he wrote apologetic works defending Christianity and polemical works attacking heretics, Jews, and pagans. He is known as the father of Latin theology. In about 207 he became a Montanist in search for a church that styled itself after the faith of the New Testament, and thereafter used the same vigor in attacking the Catholic church that he had once used to defend it.

Theo. God.

Theology. The science of things divine.

Theomorphic. (God-form); formed in the image of Deity as contrasted with man's forming God in his likeness.

Theophany. A personal manifestation of Deity.

Transcendent. As applied to Deity, a term describing a being who in all things is beyond the comprehension of man.

Trinity. The doctrine that one God exists in three persons of one substance. The doctrine is held to be a mystery, meaning that it does not accord with reason and cannot therefore be rationally defended. The word *trinity* is not found in the scriptures, nor does it give description of a God known to those in Bible times.

Yahweh. The Hebrew proper name for Deity. It may represent the correct original pronunciation of the tetragrammaton (YHWH or JHVH). Because of its sacred character, from 300 B.C. the Jews tended to avoid uttering it when reading scripture and substituted "Adonai" (i.e., the Hebrew word for "Lord"). Latter-day Saint scripture uses the traditional English equivalent, Jehovah (see Moroni 10:34; D&C 110:3; 128:9; Abraham 1:16). Spelling and pronunciation of names will virtually always change as they are taken from one language to another.

Bibliography

Ackroyd, P. R., and C. F. Evans, eds. *The Cambridge History of the Bible.* 3 vols. Cambridge: Cambridge University Press, 1970.

Allis, Oswald T. *The Five Books of Moses.* Grand Rapids, Mich.: Baker Book House, 1943.

The Ante-Nice Fathers. Edited by Alexander Roberts and James Donaldson. Grand Rapids, Mich.: Wm. B. Eerdmans, 1979.

Backhouse, Edward. *Early Church History.* London: Hamilton, Adams and Co., 1884.

Backman, Milton V. Jr. *American Religions and the Rise of Mormonism.* Salt Lake City: Deseret Book Co., 1970.

Baker, John Austin. *The Foolishness of God.* London: Darton, Longman and Todd, 1970.

Barnes, Timothy D. *Constantine and Eusebius.* Cambridge, Mass.: Harvard University Press, 1981.

Bavinck, Herman. *The Doctrine of God.* Translated by William Hendriksen. Edinburgh: The Banner of Truth Trust, 1977.

Beltz, Walter. *God and the Gods: Myths of the Bible.* Translated by Peter Heinegg. Middlesex, England: Penguin Books, 1983.

Benson, Ezra Taft. *Come unto Christ.* Salt Lake City: Deseret Book Co., 1983.

Berardino, Angelo Di, ed. *Encyclopedia of the Early Church*. Translated by Adrian Walford. 2 vols. Cambridge: James Clarke and Co., 1992.

Blenkinsopp, Joseph. *The Pentateuch: An Introduction to the First Five Books of the Bible*. New York: Doubleday, 1992.

Bloom, Harold. *The American Religion: The Emergence of the Post-Christian Nation*. New York: Simon and Schuster, 1992.

Bokenkotter, Thomas. *A Concise History of the Catholic Church*. Rev. and expanded ed. New York: Doubleday, 1990.

Bowden, John. *Jesus: The Unanswered Questions*. SCM Press, 1988.

Boyle, Isaac. "Historical View of the Council of Nice." Published as an addendum to Eusebius, *The Ecclesiastical History of Eusebius Pamphilus* (see entry herein).

Brenton, Sir Lancelot C. L. *The Septuagint with Apocrypha: Greek and English*. 1851. Reprint, Grand Rapids, Mich.: Zondervan, 1982.

Brown, Raymond E. *The Virginal Conception and Bodily Resurrection of Jesus*. New York: Paulist Press, 1973.

Bruce, F. F. *The Books and the Parchments*. Rev. Old Tappan, N. J.: Fleming H. Revell Co., 1963.

Caird, G. B. *The Language and Imagery of the Bible*. London: Duckworth, 1980.

Celsus. *On the True Doctrine: A Discourse Against the Christians*. Translated by R. Joseph Hoffmann. New York: Oxford University Press, 1987.

Chadwick, Henry. *Early Christian Thought and the Classical Tradition*. Oxford: Clarendon Press, 1984.

———. *The Early Church*. London: Penguin Books, 1967.

Cherbonnier, Edmond LaB. "In Defense of Anthropomorphism." In *Reflections on Mormonism: Judaeo-Christian Parallels*, edited by Truman G. Madsen, pp. 155–73. Provo, Utah: Religious Studies Center, Brigham Young University, 1978.

———. "The Logic of Biblical Anthropomorphism," *Harvard Theological Review* 55 (July 1962): 187–209.

Christie-Murray, David. *A History of Heresy*. Oxford: Oxford University Press, 1989.

Cicero. *The Nature of the Gods*. Translated by Horace C. P. McGregor. London: Penguin Books, 1972.

Clark, James R., ed. *Messages of the First Presidency of The Church of Jesus Christ of Latter-day Saints*. 6 vols. Salt Lake City: Bookcraft, 1965–75.

Clarke, Adam. *Clarke's Commentary.* 3 vols. Nashville: Abingdon, n.d.

Clarke, W. K. Lowther. *Concise Bible Commentary.* New York: Macmillan, 1953.

Clines, David. "Yahweh and the God of Christian Theology." *Theology* 83 (September 1980): 323–30.

Comay, Joan, and Ronald Brownrigg. *Who's Who in the Bible.* 2 vols. in 1. New York: Bonanza Books, 1980.

Conference Reports. Salt Lake City: The Church of Jesus Christ of Latter-day Saints.

The Confession of Faith. Inverness, Scotland: John G. Eccles Printers, 1983.

Cutts, Edward L. *Constantine the Great: The Union of the State and the Church.* London: Society for Promoting Christian Knowledge, 1881.

Dockery, David S. *Biblical Interpretation.* Grand Rapids, Mich.: Baker Book House, 1992.

Drake, H. A. *In Praise of Constantine: A Historical Study and New Translation of Eusebius' Tricennial Orations.* University of California Press, 1975.

Dummelow, J. R., ed. *A Commentary on the Holy Bible.* New York: Macmillan, 1908.

Durant, Will. *Caesar and Christ.* New York: Simon and Schuster, 1944.

Edersheim, Alfred. *The Life and Times of Jesus the Messiah.* 8th ed. 2 vols. New York: Longmans, Green, and Co., 1897.

Ehrman, Bart D. *The Orthodox Corruption of Scripture: The Effect of Early Christological Controversies on the Text of the New Testament.* New York: Oxford University Press, 1993.

Eiselen, Frederick Carl, Edwin Lewis, and David G. Downey, eds. *The Abingdon Bible Commentary.* New York: Abingdon-Cokesbury Press, 1929.

Encyclopaedia Judaica. Jerusalem: Keter Publishing House, n.d.

Eusebius. *The Ecclesiastical History of Eusebius Pamphilus.* Translated by Christian Frederick Cruse. Grand Rapids, Mich.: Baker Book House, 1991.

———. *The History of the Church from Christ to Constantine.* Translated by G. A. Williamson. Revised and edited with a new introduction by Andrew Louth. London: Penguin Books, 1989.

Farrar, Frederic W. *History of Interpretation.* 1886. Reprint, Grand Rapids, Mich.: Baker Book House, 1961.

Fishbane, Michael. *Biblical Interpretation in Ancient Israel*. Oxford: Clarendon Press, 1988.

Fisher, G. P. *The History of the Church*. London: Hodder and Stoughton, 1887.

Foakes-Jackson, F. J. *The History of the Christian Church*. New York: George H. Doran Co., 1927.

Fredriksen, Paula. *From Jesus to Christ: The Origins of the New Testament Images of Jesus*. New Haven: Yale University Press, 1988.

Friedman, Richard Elliott. *Who Wrote the Bible?* New York: Summit Books, 1987.

Fuller, David Otis. *Which Bible?* Grand Rapids, Mich.: Grand Rapids International Publications, 1975.

Funk, Robert W., Roy Hoover, and the Jesus Seminar. *The Five Gospels: The Search for the Authentic Jesus*. New York: Macmillan, 1994.

Gaustad, Edwin S. *Faith of Our Fathers: Religion and the New Nation*. San Francisco: Harper and Row, 1987.

Gehman, Henry Snyder, ed. *The New Westminster Dictionary of the Bible*. Philadelphia: The Westminster Press, 1970.

Gersh, Stephen, and Charles Kannengiesser, eds. *Platonism in Late Antiquity*. Notre Dame, Ind.: University of Notre Dame Press, 1992.

Gibbon, Edward. *The Decline and Fall of the Roman Empire*. Abridged version. Edited by Dero A. Saunders. London: Penguin Books, 1985.

Ginzberg, Louis. *The Legends of the Jews*. Translated by Paul Radin. Philadelphia: Jewish Publication Society of America, 1911.

Girdlestone, Robert Baker. *Synonyms of the Old Testament: Their Bearing on Christian Doctrine*. 2d ed. London: James Nisbet and Co., 1897.

Gleerup, CWK. *The Dethronement of Sabaoth: Studies in the Shem and Kabod Theologies*. 1982.

Gnuse, Robert. *The Authority of the Bible*. New York: Paulist Press, 1985.

González, Justo L. *The Story of Christianity*. San Francisco: Harper and Row, 1984.

Guthrie, Shirley C. Jr. *Christian Doctrine: Teachings of the Christian Church*. Atlanta: John Knox Press, 1968.

Haley, John W. *Alleged Discrepancies of the Bible*. Springdale, Pa.: Whitaker House, n.d.

Hall, Stuart G. *Doctrine and Practice in the Early Church*. London: SPCK, 1991.

Harnack, Adolph. *History of Dogma*. Translated by Neil Buchanan. 7 vols. New York: Dover, 1961.

Harris, R. Laird, Gleason L. Archer Jr., and Bruce K. Waltke, eds. *Theological Wordbook of the Old Testament.* 2 vols. Chicago: Moody Press, 1980.

Harrison, R. K., B. K. Waltke, D. Guthrie, and G. D. Fee. *Biblical Criticism: Historical, Literary and Textual.* Grand Rapids, Mich.: Zondervan, 1978.

Hastings, James, ed. *A Dictionary of Christ and the Gospels.* 2 vols. Edinburgh: T. and T. Clark, 1906–7.

Hatch, Edwin. *The Influence of Greek Ideas on Christianity.* 1890. Reprint, Gloucester, Mass.: Peter Smith, 1970.

Heysham, Theodore. *The Birth of the Bible.* Philadelphia: The Judson Press, 1923.

Horsley, Richard A., with John S. Hanson. *Bandits, Prophets, and Messiahs: Popular Movements in the Time of Jesus.* San Francisco: Harper and Row, 1988.

The International Standard Bible Encyclopaedia. Edited by James Orr. 4 vols. Grand Rapids, Mich.: Wm. B. Eerdmans, 1939.

The Interpreter's Bible. 12 vols. New York: Abingdon Press, 1952.

The Interpreter's Dictionary of the Bible. 4 vols. Nashville: Abingdon Press, 1962.

Jefferson, Thomas. *Writings.* Edited by Merrill D. Peterson. The Library of America, 1984.

Journal of Discourses. 26 vols. London: Latter-day Saints' Book Depot, 1854–86.

Jukes, Andrew. *The Names of God in Holy Scripture.* Grand Rapids, Mich.: Kregel, 1984.

Keil, C. F., and F. Delitzsch. *Biblical Commentary on the Old Testament.* Translated by James Martin. 10 vols. Grand Rapids, Mich.: Wm. B. Eerdmans, 1949.

Kelly, J.N.D. *Early Christian Doctrines.* San Francisco: Harper and Row. 1978.

Kittel, Gerhard, and Gerhard Friedrich, eds. *Theological Dictionary of the New Testament.* Translated by Geoffrey W. Bromiley. Abridged in 1 vol. Grand Rapids, Mich.: Wm. B. Eerdmans, 1985.

Klein, Ralph W. *Textual Criticism of the Old Testament: The Septuagint after Qumran.* Philadelphia: Fortress Press, 1974.

The Koran Interpreted. Translated by Arthur J. Arberry. Oxford: Oxford University Press, 1983.

Léon-Dufour, Xavier. *Dictionary of the New Testament.* Translated by Terrence Prendergast. London: Geoffrey Chapman, 1980.

Lidgett, J. Scott. *The Fatherhood of God.* Edinburgh: T. and T. Clark, 1902.

Loewen, Jacob A. "The Names of God in the Old Testament." *The Bible Translator* 35 (April 1984): 201–7.

The Lost Books of the Bible and The Forgotten Books of Eden. Cleveland: World Publishing Co., 1927.

MacKenzie, Roderick A. F. "The Divine Soliloquies in Genesis." *Catholic Biblical Quarterly* 17 (April 1955): 277–86.

Martineau, James. *The Seat of Authority in Religion.* 4th ed. London: Longmans, Green, and Co., 1898.

Maxwell, Neal A. *A Wonderful Flood of Light.* Salt Lake City: Bookcraft, 1990.

McConkie, Bruce R. *Doctrinal New Testament Commentary.* 3 vols. Salt Lake City: Bookcraft, 1965–73.

———. *Mormon Doctrine.* 2d ed. Salt Lake City: Bookcraft, 1966.

———. *The Mortal Messiah.* 4 vols. Salt Lake City: Deseret Book Co., 1979–81.

———. *A New Witness for the Articles of Faith.* Salt Lake City: Deseret Book Co., 1985.

McConkie, Joseph F. "Premortal Existence, Foreordinations, and Heavenly Councils." In *Apocryphal Writings and the Latter-day Saints,* edited by C. Wilfred Griggs, pp. 173–98. Provo, Utah: Religious Studies Center, Brigham Young University, 1986.

McGrath, Alister. *Understanding the Trinity.* Eastbourne, Great Britain: Kingsway Publications, 1987.

McLintock, John, and James Strong, eds. *Cyclopedia of Biblical, Theological, and Ecclesiastical Literature.* New York: Harper and Brothers, 1877.

The Mishnah. Translated by Herbert Danby. London: Oxford University Press, 1933.

Mosheim, John Laurence. *An Ecclesiastical History, Ancient and Modern.* Translated by Archibald MacLaine. 2 vols. New York: Harper and Brothers, 1860.

The Nag Hammadi Library: In English. San Francisco: Harper and Row, 1977.

Neander, Augustus. *General History of the Christian Religion and Church.* Translated by Joseph Torrey. New York: Hurd and Houghton, 1871.

New Catholic Encyclopedia. 17 vols. New York: McGraw-Hill, 1967.

Newman, John Henry Cardinal. *An Essay on the Development of Christian Doctrine.* 6th ed. Notre Dame, Indiana: University of Notre Dame Press, 1989.

Nibley, Hugh. *The World and the Prophets.* Vol. 3 of *The Collected Works of Hugh Nibley.* Salt Lake City and Provo, Utah: Deseret Book Co., and Foundation for Ancient Research and Mormon Studies, 1987.

Novotný, František. *The Posthumous Life of Plato.* The Hague: Martinus Nijhoff, 1977.

Ostling, Richard N. "The Second Reformation." *Time,* November 23, 1992.

The Oxford Dictionary of the Christian Church. Edited by F. L. Cross and E. A. Livingstone. 2d ed. New York: Oxford University Press, 1983.

Paine, Thomas. *The Age of Reason.* Library of Freedom. New York: Gramercy Books, 1993.

———. *Common Sense.* Edited by Isaac Kramnick. Middlesex, England: Penguin Books, 1982.

Paterson, W. P. *The Rule of Faith.* London: Hodder and Stoughton, 1912.

Paulsen, David L., "Early Christian Belief in a Corporeal Deity: Origen and Augustine as Reluctant Witnesses." *Harvard Theological Review* 83 (1990): 105–16.

———. "Must God Be Incorporeal?" *Faith and Philosophy* 6 (January 1989): 76–87.

Peters F. E. *The Harvest of Hellenism.* New York: Simon and Schuster, 1970.

Philo. Translated by F. H. Colson and G. H. Whitaker. 10 vols. Cambridge, Mass.: Harvard University Press, 1981.

Porter, Larry C. "Dating the Restoration of the Melchizedek Priesthood." *Ensign* 9 (June 1979): 5–10.

Poulson, Tom. *God—the Power Who Rules.* South Molton, Devon, England: Gospel Press, 1981.

Pratt, Orson. *Masterful Discourses and Writings of Orson Pratt.* Compiled by N. B. Lundwall. Salt Lake City: Bookcraft, 1962.

Pratt, Parley P. *Writings of Parley Parker Pratt.* Edited by Parker Pratt Robison. Salt Lake City: Deseret News Press, 1952.

Priestley, Joseph. *History of the Corruptions of Christianity.* 1793.

Rainy, Robert. *The Ancient Catholic Church.* Edinburgh: T. and T. Clark, 1902.

Reade, W.H.V. *The Christian Challenge to Philosophy.* London: S.P.C.K., 1951.

Richard, Carl J. "The Founding Fathers and the Classics." Ph.D. diss., Vanderbilt University, 1988.

Richards, Franklin D., and James A. Little. *A Compendium of the Doctrines of the Gospel*. Salt Lake City: Deseret Book, 1925.

Roberts, B. H. *The "Falling Away," or The World's Loss of the Christian Religion and Church*. Salt Lake City: Deseret News Press, 1931.

———. *The Mormon Doctrine of Deity*. Salt Lake City: Deseret News Press, 1903.

Romer, John. *Testament: The Bible and History*. London: Michael O'Mara Books, 1988.

Rosa, Peter de. *Vicars of Christ: The Dark Side of the Papacy*. London: Corgi Books, 1989.

Schaff, Philip. *History of the Christian Church*. 7 vols. New York: Charles Scribner's Sons, 1910.

Schaff, Philip, and Henry Wace, eds. *A Select Library of Nicene and Post-Nicene Fathers of the Christian Church*. Second Series, vol. 14. Grand Rapids, Mich.: Wm. B. Eerdmans, 1979.

Schonfield, Hugh J., ed. and trans. *The Original New Testament*. London: Waterstone and Co., 1985.

Scrivener, Frederick Henry Ambrose. *A Plain Introduction to the Criticism of the New Testament*. 3d ed. Cambridge: Deighton, Bell and Co., 1883.

Segal, M. H. "El, Elohim, and YHWH in the Bible." *Jewish Quarterly Review* 46 (October 1955): 89–115.

The Shorter Oxford English Dictionary on Historical Principles. 3d ed. 2 vols. Oxford: Oxford University Press, 1973.

Sire, James W. *Scripture Twisting: 20 Ways the Cults Misread the Bible*. Downers Grove, Ill.: Inter Varsity Press, 1980.

Smith, F. LaGard. *Blasphemy and the Battle for Faith*. London: Hodder and Stoughton, 1990.

Smith, Joseph. *History of The Church of Jesus Christ of Latter-day Saints*. Edited by B. H. Roberts. 7 vols. Salt Lake City: The Church of Jesus Christ of Latter-day Saints, 1932–51.

———. *Lectures on Faith*. Salt Lake City: Deseret Book Co., 1985.

———. *Teachings of the Prophet Joseph Smith*. Selected by Joseph Fielding Smith. Salt Lake City: Deseret Book Co., 1938.

———. "A Vision." *Times and Seasons* 4 (1 February 1843): 82–85.

Smith, Joseph Fielding. *Doctrines of Salvation*. Compiled by Bruce R. McConkie. 3 vols. Salt Lake City: Bookcraft, 1954–56.

Smith, Lucy Mack. *History of Joseph Smith by His Mother.* Edited by Preston Nibley. Salt Lake City: Bookcraft, 1954.

Smith, William. *Dictionary of the Bible.* 4 vols. New York: Hurd and Houghton, 1870.

Spong, John Shelby. *Born of a Woman: A Bishop Rethinks the Birth of Jesus.* San Francisco: HarperSanFrancisco 1992.

Stendahl, Krister. "To Think and to Pray." *Harvard Divinity Bulletin* 15 (December 1984–January 1985): 16, 12.

Stevenson, J., ed. *A New Eusebius: Documents Illustrating the History of the Church to AD 337.* 2d rev. ed. London: SPCK, 1987.

Stone, Michael E., ed. *Jewish Writings of the Second Temple Period.* Assen: Van Gorcum, 1984.

Talmage, James E. *The Articles of Faith.* Salt Lake City: The Church of Jesus Christ of Latter-day Saints, 1950.

Taylor, John. "The Living God." *Times and Seasons* 6 (15 February 1845): 808–9.

Thomas, M. Catherine. "The Influence of Asceticism on the Rise of Christian Text, Doctrine, and Practice in the First Two Centuries." Ph.D. diss., Brigham Young University, 1989.

Vine, W. E. *An Expository Dictionary of New Testament Words.* 4 vols. Old Tappan, N.J.: Fleming H. Revell Co., 1940.

Walker, Williston, Richard A. Norris, David W. Lotz, and Robert T. Handy. *A History of the Christian Church.* 4th ed. New York: Charles Scribner's Sons, 1985.

Webster's Third New International Dictionary. Springfield, Mass.: Merriam-Webster, 1981.

Westcott, Brooke Foss. *The Bible in the Church.* Grand Rapids, Mich.: Baker Book House, 1979.

Wilson, Ian. *Jesus: The Evidence.* London: Pan Books, 1984.

Young, John. *Our God Is Still Too Small.* London: Hodder and Stoughton, 1988.

Index

Solomon, 119
Spirit matter, 200
Spirit world, 193
Spirits, 44–45
Spiritual death, 15
Spiritual rebirth, 164
Spong, John Shelby, on myths in the
    Bible, 17–18
Stendahl, Krister, on God, 114
Stephen, 23, 216 n. 14
Syncretism, 238

— T —

Talmage, James E., on the Athanasian
    Creed, 136–37
  on theology, 37–38
Targum, 238
Taylor, John, on Father of Christ, 158
  on Gods, 163–64
Temple, 89–91
Terrestrial kingdom, 226 n. 2
Tertullian, 5, 238
Theology, 37–38
  speculative, 35–36
Theophanies, 87
Theophilus, on God, 76
Theudas, 225 n. 18
Thomas, M. Catherine, on asceticism
    and dematerialization of God, 95
  on penance, 93
Tolerance, religious, 143–44
Torah, 88–89
Tradition, 13–14, 59–60, 62, 68–83,
    88–89, 141–42, 151
Tree of life, 178–81
Trinity. *See* Doctrine of the Holy Trinity
Truth, 11, 43, 54
Tyndale, William, 141–42

— U —

United States Constitution, 142

— V —

Van Der Donckt, D., on literal interpre-
    tation of the scriptures, 107
Vision of the degrees of glory, 195, 196,
    226 n. 2
Vision of the Redemption of the Dead,
    177–78, 185
Voltaire, 112

— W —

War in Heaven, 22
Whitmer, David, 194
Wycliffe, John, 142

— X —

Xenophanes, on gods, 111, 119

— Y —

Yahweh, 30–31, 62, 85, 91–92, 116,
    214, 238
  See also Jehovah
Young, Brigham, 214

— Z —

Zealots, 226 n. 18
Zenock, 183
Zenos, 183